T0281383

# Advanced Digital Image Processing and Its Applications in Big Data

# Advanced Digital Image Processing and Its Applications in Big Data

Authored by

Ankur Dumka
Alaknanda Ashok
Parag Verma
Poonam Verma

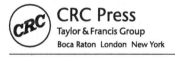

CRC Press
Taylor & Francis Group
Boca Raton London New York

CRC Press is an imprint of the
Taylor & Francis Group, an **informa** business

First edition published 2020
by CRC Press
6000 Broken Sound Parkway NW, Suite 300, Boca Raton, FL 33487-2742

and by CRC Press
2 Park Square, Milton Park, Abingdon, Oxon, OX14 4RN

*Library of Congress Cataloging-in-Publication Data*

ISBN: 978-0-367-36768-8 (hbk)
ISBN: 978-0-429-35131-0 (ebk)

Typeset in Times
by SPi Global, India

# Content

## PART I  *Concept and Background of Image Processing, Techniques, and Big Data*

## PART II  *Advanced Image Processing Technical Phases for Big Data Analysis*

## PART III  *Various Application of Image Processing*

# Preface

The authors of this book would like to thank Taylor & Francis Group (CRC press) for agreeing to publish this book and the cooperation extended during the development of this book. The final version of this book contains 11 chapters which are related to emerging technology of image processing and its application in various domains. The entire content of this book is divided into three parts to increase the readability of the authors as follows: Concept and Background of Image processing, Techniques, and Big Data, Advanced Image Processing Technical Phases for Big Data Analysis and Various Applications of Image Processing.

This book will be a valuable resource for undergraduates, graduates, and post-graduates doing research in the field of image processing and its advanced concepts related to Big Data technology. This book will also be valuable to the researchers and developers of advanced image processing techniques and their applications in different fields.

The entire book is divided into three segments to increase the readability of the book. The first section, "Concept and Background of Image Processing," discusses the concepts of advanced digital image processing. In Chapter 2, the authors describe different techniques involved for processing of images, and finally Chapter 3 discusses about the role and support of image processing in big data. This first section includes details about image processing concepts and the background associated with image processing and big data.

The second section, "Advanced Image Processing Technical Phases for Big Data Analysis," discusses different advanced techniques involved in image processing with big data. Chapter 4 covers various advanced object detection and clustering techniques used for big data, whereas Chapter 5 discusses advanced image segmentation techniques used for big data, and Chapter 6 discusses various advanced image compression techniques used for big data. These techniques involve the discussion about traditional techniques as well as advanced techniques discussed by different researchers in this direction.

The third section, "Various Applications of Image Processing," discusses the application of image processing using the big data techniques in different fields. Chapter 7 discusses the use of image processing in remote sensing by taking and discussing different techniques used for remote sensing purpose, whereas Chapter 8 discusses the use of image processing and data science in medical applications where most of the researchers are working these days. Chapter 9 discusses about applications of image processing and data science in management of traffic. With implementation of smart cities, the smart traffic management is the need of the hour, and this chapter provides different approaches for smart traffic management. Chapter 10 discusses the use of image processing and data science in the field of education. Thus, it discusses how image processing with data science has changed the scene of education across the globe. Chapter 11 discusses the role of image processing and data science in the field of agriculture. Thus, this section discusses about different approaches of image processing and data science in different fields.

**Dr. Ankur Dumka**
**Alaknanda Ashok**
**Parag Verma**
**Poonam Verma**

MATLAB® is a registered trademark of The Math Works, Inc. For product information, please contact:

The Math Works, Inc.
3 Apple Hill Drive
Natick, MA 01760-2098
Tel: 508-647-7000
Fax: 508-647-7001
E-mail: info@mathworks.com
Web: http://www.mathworks.com

# Acknowledgments

First of all, I would like to thank the Almighty.

Acknowledgement when honestly given is a reward without price. I am thankful to the publishing team at Taylor & Francis Group (CRC Press) for accepting to publish this authored book. I thank Daniel Kershaw and Richard O'Hanley, development editor, for helping me in bringing this project to a successful end. I would also like to thank all other editorial team members behind the scene who helped us in completing and bringing this book to the market.

Writing this part is probably the most difficult task. Although the list of people to thank heartily is long, making this list is not the hard part. The difficult part is to search the words that convey the sincerity and magnitude of my gratitude and love.

I express my deep gratitude to my parents for their moral support, blessings, and encouragement throughout my life. I am greatly indebted to my wife (Monika) for her constant support in every aspect of life who was also responsible for encouraging me to complete this book. She has paid the real cost for this work by sacrificing many of her desires and carrying out our combined social responsibilities alone. I want to acknowledge her contributions and convey my sincere thankfulness. I am also heartily thankful to Naina and Siddhi, my loving daughters and inspiration, blessed by God. They always generate enthusiasm and spark in my work by their warm welcome and blossom smile at home. They also sacrifice their valuable time with their father for completing the book in due time. Last of all, I would like to thanks my co-authors (Alaknanda Ashok, Parag Verma, and Poonam Verma) without whom the completion of this work will be impossible. Their day and night effort for completion of this book is beyond par.

In addition, the authors would like to thank the anonymous reviewers Yuvayana Tech and Craft (P) Ltd. and Tech Counsellor for their valuable comments and suggestion to improve the quality of the content of the book and all people who directly or indirectly contributed.

# Authors

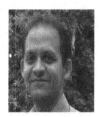

**Dr. Ankur Dumka** is working as associate professor in Women Institute of Technology, Dehradun, India. He has more than 10 years of experience with academic and industry exposure. He has published more than 50 research papers in reputed journals and conferences. He contributed three books with publishers such as Taylor & Francis Group and IGI global. He has nearly 15 book chapters with different publishers. He has published 3 patents under his name. He is also associated with many journals in the capacity of editor, editorial board member, and guest editor. He is also a coordinator and member of smart city Dehradun, Uttarakhand, India.

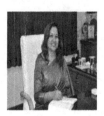

**Dr. Alaknanda Ashok** is working as professor and dean, College of Technology, G.B.Pant University of Agriculture and Technology, Pantnagar. She has a long administrative experience as the director, Women Institute of Technology and the controller of examiner of Uttarakhand technical University. She has published more than 50 research papers in reputed journals and conferences of repute. She also has many book chapters. She has published three patents. She has completed many research projects and undertaken many under her supervision. She is also associated with many journals and conferences in the capacity of editor, editorial board member, and chair of conferences.

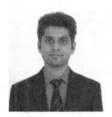

**Mr. Parag Verma** is working as assistant professor at Uttaranchal University, Dehradun. He has a long experience of 8+ years in the field of industry and academics. He has published 15+ international papers in reputed conferences and journals. He has contributed two books with publishers such as Nerosa and Alpha, and is currently working on two more accepted books. He had also contributed four chapters for reputed publishers. He is also an editorial board member of many reputed conferences and journals including Scopus. He is also a guest editor of IJNCDS (Scopus Indexed inderscience Journal) and many more. He is associated with many societies and organizations for the welfare of educationalist societies.

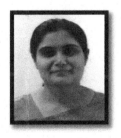

**Poonam Verma** is a Ph.D. student of the Computer Science Department of Graphic Era Deemed to be University at Dehradun. She received Master's Degree from AKTU, Uttarpradesh in Computer Science and Engineering. She has qualified UGC NET in 2017. Her areas of research interest are Deep Learning and Blockchain. She is currently working as assistant professor in GEHU, Dehradun.

# Part I

## Concept and Background of Image Processing, Techniques, and Big Data

# 1 Introduction to Advanced Digital Image Processing

## 1.1 INTRODUCTION

Digital image processing is being used ubiquitously in various fields, which has been increasing exponentially. This is majorly due to extensive use of digital images in the fields of remote sensing, medicine, machine vision, video processing, microscopic imaging, and so on. Image processing requires manipulation of image data using various electronic devices and softwares. Along with devices, digital image processing requires the application of different algorithms as per the requirements to convert a physical image into a digital image to fetch desired information or features (Figure 1.1).

A digital image is a representation of two-dimensional images as a finite set of digital picture elements termed as pixels. These pixel values represent various parameters like gray levels, height, colors, opacities, etc. of an image in the form of binary digits, and the binary digits can be represented in the form of mathematical equations. The digital image size can be determined by the matrix used to store the pixels based on their size. In order to access a particular pixel in the digital image, the relevant coordinates at x and y axis are defined. Each pixel has its own unique intensity and brightness. Pixels in an image will have different values as per an image or else the images may not appear different from each other. Various mixtures of colors will produce a color image. Pixel dimensions are the horizontal and the vertical measurements of an image. Each pixel is defined using the bit depth which is determined by the number of bits. Resolution is the spatial scale of digital images, is the indicator of the spatial frequency with which the images have been sampled, and can be measured in lpi, ppi, and dpi.

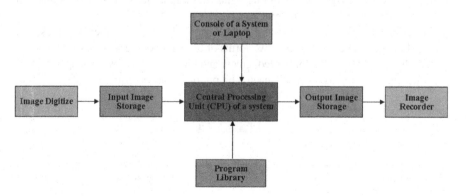

**FIGURE 1.1** Process of digital image processing.

Lpi stands for lines per inch and is used generally for magazine printing. Ppi stands for pixels per inch and refers to the pixel arrays depicting the real-world image. Dpi stands for dots per inch and is used to describe the printer's resolution.

## 1.2 CATEGORIZATION OF DIGITAL IMAGES

Digital images may be categorized as shown in Figure 1.2.

### 1.2.1 BINARY IMAGE

Binary images are images whose pixels have only two possible values normally as 0 ad 1 displayed as black and white. This image is termed as monochrome or bitonal. Binary images are represented by pixels that can represent only one shade where each pixel consists of 1 bit each. It is an image that is composed exclusively of shades of only one color with the varying range from the brightest to the darkest hues.

### 1.2.2 BLACK AND WHITE IMAGE

This image consists of only two colors, i.e black and white color and is termed as black and white image. It combines black and white in a continuous fashion creating different ranges of gray. The color range is represented in 256 different gray values. These different shades lie between 0 and 255, where 0 refers to black, 255 refers to white (also known as panchromatic images), and intermediate shades refer to the neutral tonal values of black and white, which are commonly termed as grayscale image, whereas 127 stands for gray. Previous versions of monitors used 4 bits that could display only 16 shades of color between white and black. However, in present-day scenario, 8-bit grayscale is used to indicate that only 8 bits are used to store different shades of gray, thereby permitting 256 different intensities of black and white in each pixel.

### 1.2.3 8-BIT COLOR FORMAT

This image format consists of 256 different shades of colors. This method requires storing the image information in the computer's memory where each pixel is represented by using one byte, that is, 8 bits. Thus, maximum numbers of colors that can be displayed are not more than 256.

Color image is basically formed by three colors red, blue, and green to represent a coloured image. There are basically two forms of the 8-bit color graphics. One form utilizes each of the 256 entries for the red, green, and blue color thereby forming shades of 16,777,216 colors. In this approach, each 8 bit out of 24 bits describes the shades of red,

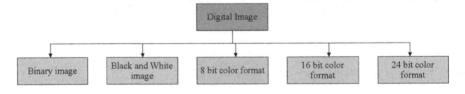

**FIGURE 1.2**    Categorization of digital images.

green, and blue. Sometimes 18 bits or 12 bits can be used to define the shades of the color where 18 bits utilizes 6 bits for red, green, blue (RGB) forming a palette of 262,144 colors and 12 bits utilizes 4 bits for each RGB thereby forming a color palette of 4096 colors.

The other form of the 8-bit color format is three bits for red, three bits for green, and two bits for blue. This second form is often called 8-bit truecolor, as it does not use a palette at all. Most 8-bit image formats store a local image palette of 256 colors, as the graphics hardware's global color palette will be overwritten with the local image palette, due to which it is highly possible to have distorted colors of the images. This is one of the major reasons that the 8-bit hardware programs are written along with the web browsers to be able to display images from various sources; each image may consist of its own palette, which will be finally mapped to a local palette, thereby causing some form of dithering. The popular file formats that consist of 8-bit formats are GIF, PNG, and BMP. In case the 24-bit image is converted into the 8-bit image, the image loses its quality and sharpness.

## 1.2.4 16 COLOR FORMAT

In this type of image format, there are 65,536 types of different colors, and hence, it is termed as high color format. The 16-bit format is divided into three primary colors of red, green, and blue, and the distribution of the RGB can be 5 bits for red, 6 bits for green color, and 5 bits for representing the blue color. Generally, the distribution is like the above stated, and one extra bit is allocated to the green color, as it is soothing to the eyes among the three colors.

## 1.2.5 24-BIT FORMAT

24-bit color format is also known as true color format. Like 16-bit color format, in a 24-bit color format, the 24 bits are again distributed in three different formats of red, green, and blue. Since 24 bits are equally divided on 8, they have been distributed equally between three different color channels. Their distributions are as follows:

- 8 bits for R (red),
- 8 bits for G (green),
- 8 bits for B (blue).

Compared to indexed color images, true color images lack a color lookup table. A pixel does not have an index referring to a specific color in the color lookup table. Every pixel has its own (RGB) color value and, depending on the file format, may also consist of a value for transparency (RGBA). The main advantage of true color images is the availability of an unlimited amount of colors.

Some of the important image attributes to be considered can be listed as follows:

a. Width: This represents the number of columns in the image.
b. Height: It represents the number of rows in the image.
c. Class: It represents the data type used by the image such as uint8.
d. Image type: It represents the type of image such as intensity, true color, binary, or indexed.

e. Minimum intensity: This is used to define the intensity of image which represents the lowest intensity value of any pixel, whereas for indexed images, it represents the lowest index value into the color map. (This attribute not included for "binary" or "true color" images.)

f. Maximum intensity: This attribute represents the highest intensity value of any pixel for intensity images and for indexed images, and it represents the highest index value into a color map. (This attribute not included for "binary" or "true color" images.)

g. Image intensity: It refers to the amount of light which is available per pixel in an image. It can also be considered as the data matrix that records the values of light for each pixel in the image. However, it is difficult to detect the intensity of an individual pixel. More high-resolution images require a larger number of pixels per unit, thereby producing an image which represents pixels in such a way that the individual pixels are not detectable easily.

h. Image brightness: Image brightness is a relative term where the number of pixels in an image can be considered brighter in comparison to other neighboring pixels. Image brightness depends on the wavelength as well as amplitude, for example, supposing an image with pixel values having intensity of 6, 80, 150 and 180 then pixel value of 180 will be the brightest. Hence higher the intensity, brighter the pixel.

## 1.3 PHASES OF DIGITAL IMAGE PROCESSING

Image processing is an expensive yet important method to perform unique operations to be able to develop an enhanced image from the original image or in order to be able to extract minute details from the original image so that it can be used for some important interpretations. It is a type of signal processing that may take an input in the form of an image and may result in an image with typical features as required. Image processing remains one of the trending technologies being pursued for the research area.

Image processing basically consists of multiple tasks; however, it includes the following four main steps:

- Capturing an image using image acquisition tools
- Analyzing and manipulating an image
- Image enhancement and restoration
- Refined image that can be used for required task/information.

Image processing may occur either in the form of analog or digital image processing. Analog images are captured using photographic sensors, and they detect the variation of the energy intensity of the objects, whereas digital images are captured using electro-optical sensors and consist of the arrays of pixels with varied intensities.

Analog image processing can be used for hard copies like printouts and photographs. Image analysts use various fundamentals of interpretation while using these visual techniques. Digital image processing techniques help in manipulation of the digital images by using computers. Digital image processing applied on digital images i.e. images having matrix of small pixels and it is done using software. The three general phases that all types of data have to undergo while using the digital technique are

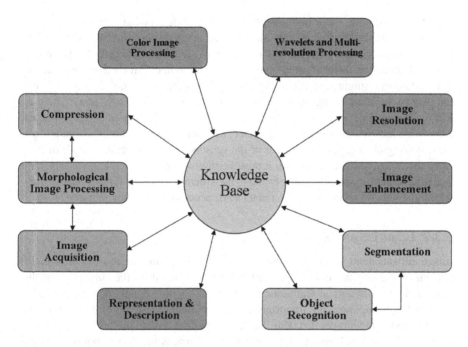

**FIGURE 1.3** Different phases of image processing.

pre-processing, enhancement, display, and information extension. Digital signal processing system is used to convert analog signals to digital signals or vice-versa with the help of converter. It is faster and easy to retrieve any image and of good quality.

As shown Figure 1.3, the different phases of image processing can be described as follows:

## 1.3.1 ACQUISITION OF AN IMAGE

The process of image processing cannot begin unless the image has been captured. It is invariably the first step of the image processing procedure. Image acquisition is a hardware-independent process. In the image acquisition step, basically an optical image is captured by the camera and is converted into an array of the numerical data in the form of bits.

Images are acquired using cameras or different forms of sensors that can capture various features of the energy reflected by the surface of an object. Image acquisition can be divided into three steps, where the camera lenses focus that object, and when the object reflects the entire energy, it is captured by the sensors of the camera. Different types of cameras are available for different applications. The images are generated by the combination of illumination of the source of light and the reflection or the absorption of the light by the object of interest. The illumination can be generated by different energy sources and to sense the image, a sensor depending on the nature of illumination is selected. This complete process of image capturing is known as image acquisition. Generally, the sensor named as the charged coupled device (CCD) or CMOS is used in the cameras. The cameras using the CMOS generally would acquire images with noise and uses more power to capture an image. However, the cameras with a CCD are more capable of producing more high-quality images, with less power consumption. CCD cameras are single IC devices that consist of an array of photosensitive cells, where each cell produces an electric current when a light ray falls on the cells. CCD cameras have less geometric distortion and give a linear video output. Image acquisition can be acquired using a single sensor; however, it is a slow method to acquire images. Images can also be acquired arranging individual sensors in the form of a 2D array. There are five fundamental parameters to be borne in mind while capturing an image, and these parameters are view of the capturing device, distance of an object to be captured from the acquiring device, resolution, size of the sensors in the device, and depth of field. Once the image has been captured, it must be digitized by a device known as a frame store that stores the samples of the frame in own memory, and the frame is easily transferred to a file or a memory location that can be accessed later when required.

### 1.3.2 IMAGE ENHANCEMENT

Image enhancement is the procedure of improving the quality and the information content of the original data before processing. It is based on the subjective quality criteria. The enhancement technique is used to extract the details of images that are obscured or to highlight the important features of images that are of due importance while applying the images in a field. Thus, image enhancement provides more suitable results of the original image. It accentuates or sharpens the edges, boundaries, and contrast of image in order to make graphic display more helpful for analysis purposes. In order to achieve the above properties, image enhancement increases the dynamic range of chosen features in order to detect them easily and more effectively.

Contrast is an important factor in any subjective evaluation of image quality. Contrast is created by the difference in luminance reflected from two adjacent surfaces. It will not be wrong to describe contrast as one of the important visual properties that can make an object distinguishable from the surrounding objects and the background. Basically, contrast can be determined by the difference in the brightness and the color of the target object from the other objects. The eyes of humans are more sensitive to the property of the contrast than the absolute luminance. Many algorithms have been proposed and developed to handle the contrast feature of an image in the image processing tasks. However, there is a possibility of losing information in the areas of an image where the contrast is near to black. Thus, there is a need to develop such an algorithm that can help to optimize the contrast of an image, in order to represent all the information in the given input image. Some of the techniques that have been popularly used for the image contrast are given as follows:

- Noise clipping
- Window slicing
- Histogram modeling/equalization
- Filtering
- Unsharp masking
- Median filtering
- Linear filter
- Root filter

- Fourier transform
- Mean filter
- Gaussian smoothing and filter

Image enhancement emphasizes the important features while reducing the noise. The image enhancement process involves steps like contrast, changing of brightness of image, etc. Image enhancement methods are point processing, spatial filtering, transform operation, and image coloring. The point processing or operation includes the operations like contrast stretching, noise clipping, window slicing, and histogram modeling, whereas spatial filtering includes operations like noise smoothing, median filtering, low-pass (LP), high-pass (HP), and band-pass filtering, and zooming of images. Transform operation includes linear filtering, root filtering, and homomorphic filtering. Image coloring or pseudocoloring includes steps like false coloring and pseudo coloring.

The image enhancement method can be categorized based on spatial or frequency domain frequencies. Spatial domain techniques are performed to image plane itself which are based on direct manipulation of pixels in an image. The operation can be formulated as $g(x,y) = T[f(x,y)]$, where g is the output, f is the input image, and T is an operation on f defined over some neighborhood of $(x,y)$. As per the operations on image pixels, it can be further divided into two categories: point operations and spatial operations.

The frequency domain method enhances an image by convoluting the image with a linear, position invariant operator.

Enhancement types and their categorization are as follows (Figure 1.4):

1. Spatial
   a. **Point operation:** This process method focuses on the intensity of single pixels.
      **a.1. Simple intensity transformation**
         **a.1.1. Image negatives:** In this, the negatives of images are used in applications such as medical images and photographing a screen with a monochrome positive film with the idea of using the resulting negatives as normal slides.
         **a.1.2. Contrast stretching:** It focuses on increasing the dynamic range of gray levels in the image being processed. This technique focused on low-contrast images which can be caused because of low illumination or lack of a dynamic range in the image sensor or due to wrong setting of lens aperture during image acquisition.
         **a.1.3. Compression of dynamic range:** This method compresses the dynamic range of the image which may exceed the capability of display devices where only the brightest part of the image is visible on display screens.
         **a.1.4. Gray level slicing:** It is performed highlighting a specific range of gray levels in an image; this technique can be used to enhance features such as masses of water in satellite imaginary or enhancing flaws in X-ray images.

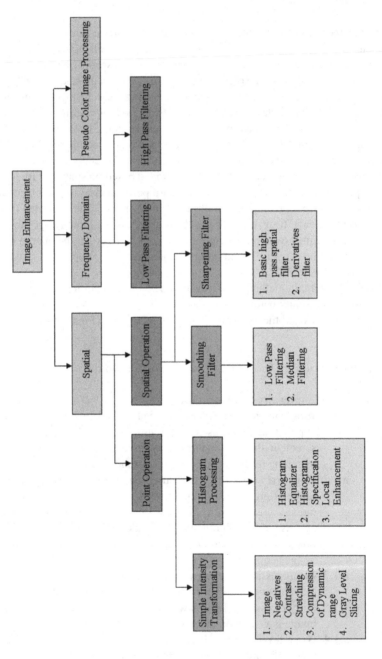

**FIGURE 1.4**    Types and categorization of image enhancement.

**a.2. Histogram processing:** Histograms of digital images are used to find the probability occurrence of the gray level, where the shape of a histogram of an image is used to provide information about possibility for contrast enhancement, where the shape of the histogram tells about the image; for example, a narrow-shaped histogram indicates little dynamic range corresponding to a low-contrast image.

**a.2.1. Histogram equalization:** It equalizes or uniformity in the histogram by mapping an input image to output image.

**a.2.2. Histogram specification:** It makes use of the histogram created in order to highlight gray-level ranges in an image.

**a.2.3. Local enhancement:** This is used to enhance details of a small area.

b. **Spatial operation (linear and non-linear):** It makes use of a spatial mask for image processing. These spatial masks are termed as spatial filters.

**b.1. Smoothing filter:** Smoothing filters are used for blurring and reduction of noise, where blurring is a pre-processing step which removes small details from the image prior to object extraction and bridging of small gaps in lines or curves, whereas reduction of noise is achieved by blurring with linear or non-linear filtering.

**b.1.1. LP filtering:** It is used for blurring edges and other sharp details in an image.

**b.1.2. Median filtering:** It is a non-linear operation which is used to reduce noise rather than burring. It is useful when the noise pattern consists of strong, spike-like components, and the characteristic to be preserved is edge sharpness.

**b.2.2. Sharpening filters:** It is used to highlight the fine details of image or to enhance the details that are blurred. This image sharpening concept can be used in applications such as electronic printing and medical imaging to industry inspection and autonomous target detection in smart weapons.

**b.2.3. Basic HP spatial filters:** This process involves scaling and/or clipping to make the final result of the gray level within the specified range.

**b.2.4. Derivative filters:** They are used to blur details in an image and to sharpen an image and able to detect edges. They use the method of gradient to achieve the objectives.

2. **Frequency domain:** This method computes the Fourier transform of an image which needs to be enhanced and is used for multiplying the result by a filter transfer function and then taking the inverse transform in order to produce an enhanced image.

a. **LP filtering:** Edges and sharp transitions in the gray levels contribute to the high-frequency content of its Fourier transform, so a LP filter smoothes an image.

b. **HP filtering:** A HP filter attenuates the low-frequency components without disturbing the high-frequency information in the Fourier transform domain which can sharpen edges.

3. **Pseudo color image processing:** It is applied on a monochrome image, which is enhanced using color to represent different gray levels or frequencies.

   a. **Image restoration:** Image restoration is used to improve the appearance of an image. Image restoration uses a mathematical or probabilistic model. The basic purpose of image restoration is to remove the defects on the original image caused by motion blur, noise, or camera miss-focus and to predict a clean original image. Image restoration can be performed by reversing the process that caused the blurring of the image, and such process is performed by imaging a point source and uses the point source image, which is called the point spread function (PSF) to restore the image information lost to the blurring process.

   Image restoration techniques are performed either in the image domain or the frequency domain. The most straightforward and conventional technique for image restoration is deconvolution, which is performed in the frequency domain and after computing the Fourier transform of both the image and the PSF and undoes the resolution loss caused by the blurring factors. This deconvolution technique, because of its direct inversion of the PSF, typically has a poor matrix condition number, amplifies noise, and creates an imperfect deblurred image. In addition, conventionally, the blurring process is assumed to be shift-invariant. Hence, more sophisticated techniques, such as regularized deblurring, have been developed to offer robust recovery under different types of noises and blurring functions.

Different restoration techniques are as follows (Figure 1.5):

1. **Median filter:** It is used to remove random noise by sliding the window over the image. In this approach, the filtered image is obtained by placing the median of the values in the input window, at the location of the center of that window, at the output image.
2. **Adaptive filter:** It uses color or gray space for removing the impulsive noise from the image. It is achieved by using a transfer function, which is controlled by variable parameters.
3. **Linear filter:** It includes the sharpening, smoothening, and edge enhancement to remove noise from an image. It is achieved by replacing each pixel with linear combination of its neighbor.

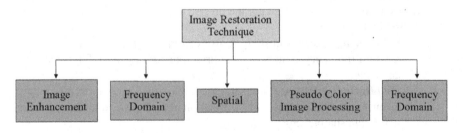

**FIGURE 1.5**   Different techniques for image restoration.

4. **Iterative Blind Deconvolution:** This approach was proposed by Ayers and Dainty (1988) which is used in blind deconvolution. This method is based on Fourier transform which provides high resolution and better quality.

5. **Nonnegative and Support Constraints Recursive Inverse Filtering:** This algorithm was proposed by Ong and Chambers (1999) where the given image makes an estimation of the target image. This estimation is made by minimizing an error function which contains the domain of the image and nonnegative information of pixels of the image.

6. **Super-resolution restoration algorithm based on gradient adaptive interpolation:** It works in three steps, namely, registration, fusion, and deblurring. In the registration process, it utilizes the frequency domain registration algorithm to estimate the motion of low-resolution images. In the fusion process, it maps a low-resolution image to a high-resolution grid and then the gradient-based adaptive interpolation is used to form a high-resolution image. In the deblurring step, a wiener filter is applied to reduce the effects of blurring and noise caused by the system.

7. **Block matching:** It is used to find blocks that contain high correlation because its accuracy is significantly impaired by the presence of noise. In this approach, block-similarity measurements are used by performing coarse initial denoising in the local 2D transform domain. In this method, the image is divided into blocks and noise or blur is removed from each block.

8. **Color image processing:** The human visual system can distinguish hundreds of thousands of different color shades and intensities, compared to only dozen shades of gray. Therefore, in an image, a great deal of extra information may be contained in the color, and this extra information can then be used to simplify image analysis, for example, object identification and extraction based on color.

   Color image processing includes color modeling and processing in digital images. Digital color processing includes processing of colored images and different color spaces that are used. For example, some color models are RGB model, HSI (hue, saturation, and intensity) model, and CMY (cyan, magenta, and yellow).

   A color model is an abstract mathematical model which describes the way colors can be represented as tuples of numbers as three or four values or color components. Each color model is hardware oriented (RGB, CMY, and YIQ) or image processing application based (HIS).

   The RGB model consists of three image planes which are independent in nature, and each one consists of primary colors red, green, and blue. In this model, a particular color is specified by specifying the amount of each primary component present. This model can be used in color monitors or color video cameras.

   The CMY model is a subtractive model which is appropriate for the absorption of color. It differs from RGB as RGB focuses on what is added to black for getting a particular color, whereas CMY focuses on what is subtracted from white to get a particular color.

   The HSY model specifies color through three qualities, namely, hue, saturation, and intensity. The RGB model can be converted to HSY using the following formula:

$$I = R + G + B,$$

where I = intensity, R = amount of red, G = amount of green, and B = amount of blue normalized to range [0,1].

In simple words, the intensity is the average of red, green, and blue components, whereas the saturation is given as follows:

$$S = 1 - \text{Minimum}$$

Pseudo color processing assigns color to the base value by means of certain criteria. Intensity slicing and color coding are some of the simplest types of pseudo image processing. It works by considering the image as a 3D function which maps spatial coordinates to intensity and then consider placing planes at certain levels parallel to the coordinate plane. If the value is one side of such plane, it is rendered in one color else different colors.

9. **Wavelets and multi-resolution processing:** Wavelets are used for representation of images in various degrees of resolution. Images subdivide successively into smaller regions for data compression and for pyramidal representation. Theoretically, it can be said that signals processed by wavelets can be stored in a more efficient manner as compared to Fourier transform.

Wavelet transform decomposes an image into small waves of varying frequencies and limited duration and thus makes the information available that when the frequency appears. This technique can be used in images for the purpose of compression, transmission, and analysis.

The wavelets can be constructed by rough edges in order to have a better approximation to real-world signals. Wavelets do not remove any information rather move it around by separating noise and averaging the signal. There are two important properties of wavelets, namely, admissibility and regularity. Wavelet transform provides information about frequency as well as wavelets and thus is far better than Fourier transform. It also leads to multi-resolution analysis of the signals with more than one form of resolution or scaling features; thus, if features are not available in one resolution form, then they can be detected using another resolution.

10. **Image compression:** Compression is used to minimize the size of storage, without affecting or degrading its quality to a greater extent, for saving an image or saving the bandwidth to transmit it. Image compression is defined as the process of reducing the amount of data needed to represent a digital image. This is achieved by removing the redundancy within the data by using the compression algorithm or codec. The criteria for development of these algorithms are based on the following logic:

- Specifying all similarly colored pixels by the color name, code, and the number of pixels. This way one pixel can correspond to hundreds or thousands of pixels.
- The image is created and represented using mathematical wavelets.
- Splitting the image into several parts, each identifiable using a fractal.
- Digital images can be compressed using either lossless or lossy compression.

Image compression can be categorized into two parts as lossless compression and lossy compression. Image compression can be compressed based on the following reasons: within a single image, there exists significant correlation or redundancy among neighboring samples or pixels. This correlation is termed as spatial correlation or redundancy. In case of satellite images where images are acquired from different sensors, there exists a correlation or redundancy among samples received from these sensors, and this redundancy is termed as spatial correlation or redundancy. The compression technique makes use of this redundancy for compression. Removing this redundancy before compression will make an effective compression within an image.

Image compression consists of two parts, that is, a compressor and decompressor. A compressor compresses the data and hence is a pre-processor which is used for encoding, whereas a decompressor is a post-processing stage which is used for decoding. In the pre-processing stage, the data are reduced by the gray-level and/or spatial quantization and can also be used to remove noise. The next step of the pre-processing stage is the mapping process, which maps the original image data into another mathematical space which makes it easy to compress the data. Next is the quantization stage which takes continuous data from the mapping stage and puts it in discrete form. The final stage is coding of the resultant data. The compression technique may consist of all the stages or combination of one or two stages.

Decompression is also divided into two stages, where in the first stage the decoder takes the compressed file and reverses the original coding by mapping the codes to original, quantized values. In the next stage, the original mapping process is reversed to process the value that performs an inverse mapping. Finally, the image may be post-processed to enhance the look of the final image (Figure 1.6).

**Lossless compression:** This compression technique can be used to reduce the size of an image making sure that the quality of the image is maintained. The intensities per pixel should be maintained although the space complexity should be dramatically

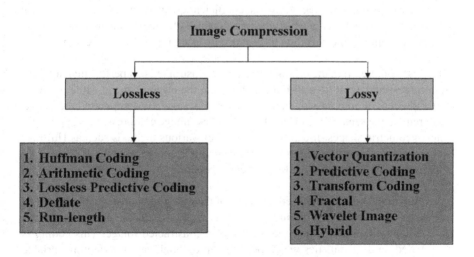

**FIGURE 1.6** Image compression classification and techniques.

reduced. In a digital single-lens reflex (DSLR) camera, the images can be either stored as RAW or JPEG. The RAW files will not have any compression and may consume large space to be stored. However, a DSLR camera may also result in Joint Photographic Experts Group (JPEG) file format, which is a better format than RAW. The basic types of file formats that fall into the category of the lossless images can be listed as follows:

- **RAW** – This file format is lossless, because it maintains the information of the light information as received from the camera's sensors. However, the issue is that the RAW file format consumes larger space to store the images, and typical software can help to edit such images, which may further occupy space in the system.
- **PNG** – In this file format, the recurring pattern is searched and if there is any recurring pattern in the image, it is compressed together and kept in a required loop, thereby reducing the space to occupy the image files. The PNG file format is reversible, making it quite popular format among the professionals using images.
- **BMP** – This file format is lossless file format exclusively defined by Microsoft to enable different devices to exchange images. It has a predefined structure to store the different intensities of each pixel.
- **GIF** – GIF is one of the unique file formats as it permits animated images. Moreover, it permits a separate palette of 256 colors for each frame. It utilizes the Lempel-Ziv-Welch data compression technique to reduce the file size without degrading the quality observed.
- **JPG** – It is a file format that is lossy compression although the quality of an image is not degraded to be visible to the casual observer. This format reduces the image file size by removing some of the redundant data. The basic procedure that it adopts is: The RGB color scheme of the file is converted into the YCbCr color scheme. The complete image is then divided into the blocks of 8*8 pixels and then the discrete cosine transformation is carried out on the matrix prepared for each block. Then, the coefficient quantization is carried out using the JPEG quantization table where each table is for the luminance and chrominance. Finally, the encoding takes place by using the Huffman encoding.

In lossless compression, the original image is reconstructed in a perfect manner from the compressed data. It uses all information from the original image while performing the process of compression, and hence when we again decompressed the image, it will remain the same as the original one. Lossless image compression is applied for simple geometric shapes. It can be performed by various methods such as Huffman coding, arithmetic coding, entropy coding, run length coding, etc.

**Different methods used for lossless compression:**

1. **Huffman coding:** This method is one of the oldest methods which was named after its inventor (Huffman, 1952). This method reduces the coding redundancy without degrading the quality of reconstructed image. This coding is based on data statistics which provides an optimal way of assigning variable length codewords to an alphabet of symbols with a known probability

distribution. Huffman coding is optimal only if the probability distribution of a source is known, and each source symbol is encoded in integral number of bits. It is mostly used in JPEG and other standards.

2. **Arithmetic coding:** This method also reduces coding redundancy as Huffman coding by using a variable length coding procedure. It gives optimum results when all symbol probabilities are an integral power of ½ (Clarke, 1996). The arithmetic coding used in this method was proposed by Glen and Langdon (1984). Arithmetic coding divides the interval between 0 and 1 and denotes the range of the input message, into a number of smaller intervals corresponding to the probabilities of the message symbols. Each probability is represented by a two-end interval; the left end is closed, while the right end is open. The next input symbol selects one of these intervals, and the procedure is repeated. In this way, the selected interval narrows with every symbol, and at the end, any number inside the final interval can be used to represent the message.

This method has disadvantages that arithmetic coder produces only one codeword, a real number in the interval [0, 1], for the entire message to be transmitted. We cannot perform the decoding process until we received all bits representing this real number and also this method is an error-sensitive compression scheme. A single bit error can corrupt the entire message. It is mostly used in JBIG (Joint Bi-level Image Experts Group) and JPEG.

3. **Lossless predictive coding:** This method was proposed by Gonzalez and Woods (1992), which removes the redundancies within interpixel by predicting the value of current pixel using closely spaced pixel values and generating new values for coding. The generated new value is used to represent error generated by subtracting the predicted value from the original value. The image compression is performed using variable length coding where redundancy in coding is removed and prediction operation provides the elimination of the interpixel redundancy.

4. **Deflate:** Deflate is a lossless data compression algorithm that can be used for PNG images, and it utilizes both LZ77 and Huffman encoding to achieve the compression of the data without causing the deterioration of the image quality. The Deflate technique consists of encoding of the blocks using 3-bit headers, where 1 bit is either 1 or 0. One in the first bit header indicates that the sequence is over and presence of zero in the first bit header indicates that there are more sequences that are required to be encoded. The second and the third bits of the header file consist of either of the values of 00, 01, 10, and 11, describing the technique used for the encoding purposes. One of the most popular encoding techniques is 10 that is dynamic Huffman encoding (Oswal et al., 2016).

5. **Run length:** Run length encoding is a form of the lossless data compression technique that stores the recursive patterns of the content into one single unit. If there is an image that consists of a number of blocks of blue and green color and there are 10 green pixels with 14 blue pixels, the long sequence of the data GGGGGGGGGGGBBBBBBBBBBBBBB can be represented as 10G and 14B. Although the data reduce considerably the meaning, the output remains unchanged (Martinez, 2011).

**Lossy compression:** The other type of compression is the lossy compression that discards few data in the image to reduce the size of the image. Some of the popular algorithms used for lossy compression are transform coding, discrete wavelet transformation, fractal compression, discrete cosine transformation, etc. It works on the inability of lossless compression to produce a low bit rate as desired. In lossy compression, there is always a trade-off between the bit rate and quality of image.

**Different methods used for lossy compression:**

1. **Vector quantization (VQ):** This method reduces the bitrate and minimize communication channel capacity or digital storage memory requirements while maintaining the necessary fidelity of the data (Gray, 1984). This method has a high compression ratio with relatively small block sizes (Al-Fayadh et al., 2008).

   VQ is a clustering method, where grouping similar vectors (blocks) into one class occurs. It maps features extracted from the sampled input image using pre-processing operations. In the most direct application of VQ to image compression, the source samples (pixels) are blocked into vectors so that each vector describes a small segment, or subblock, of the original image. This method has a fast decompression by making use of a small size lookup table and hence can be used in places where the image compression is done once, whereas decompression many times.

2. **Predictive coding:** This method is based on prediction which allows compact representation of data by means of encoding the error between data and information predicted from past observations. Based on the predictor, the predicted samples are similar to the actual input, and the prediction error is relatively small. Predictive coding is used to remove the mutual redundancy by means of decorrelating the data in order to obtain efficient and better compressed coding of signals.

   This coding predicts the value of next pixel based on the sequence of reproduced or previous pixel values which are obtained during scanning of images. It then encodes or quantizes the difference between actual and predictive values which is the error signal (Umbaugh, 2005). Better the prediction, smaller will be transmitted error and thus better will be the coding process. If the current reproduced pixel is taken as a combination of the predicted pixel value and quantized error value between current and predicted pixels, then in such cases the prediction method is termed as differential pulse code modulation (Al-Fayadh et al., 2007; Kim and Lee, 1992).

   The predictive coding encoder consists of two parts, namely, predictor and quantizer. A predictor is used to predict the next value of the image signal by using previous coding elements, whereas a quantizer quantizes the difference between predicted and original values where the order of predictor is the number of previous elements used in prediction. The predictors are classified into linear and non-linear types. For linear predictors, the previous samples are linearly coded to predict the current value, while non-linear predictors use non-linear functions for coding the previous samples. The prediction can be one dimensional or two dimensional. A one-dimensional predictor uses the previous pixel values in the same row. A two-dimensional predictor uses pixels in the same row and in the previous rows to predict the current pixel value.

3. **Transform coding:** This method makes use of the transformation technique which transforms the pixels in the image domain into another domain in order to prepare a set of coefficients with more natural and compact representation. In order to achieve this, transform coding makes use of Fourier transform which maps the image into a set of coefficients which are later quantized and coded. Better transformation merges as many data as possible into a small number of transform coefficients. After this process, the process of quantization eliminates those coefficients that carry least information. In the transform coding approach, an $N \times N$ input image first is divided into a number of $n \times n$ nonoverlapping subimages (blocks), which are then transformed to generate $(N/n)^2$ subimage transform arrays, each of size $n \times n$, and the transform is applied separately to each of these blocks.

The three mechanisms involved in transform coding make this method a highly compressed method. These three mechanisms work as follows: in the first stage, the coding process transforms a block of data rather than a single element of image. In the second stage, the process of quantization of the transformed coefficients results in removing the correlation defined among the pixels of each subimage. In the third stage, all the coefficients that are transformed are not quantized or transmitted to the receiver which favors for a high compression rate.

The transform coding system also consists of two parts, namely, encoder and decoder, where the encoder works in four stages as subimage decomposition, transformation, quantization, and coding. These are used for transformation of the values of gray levels in each block. Larger values which can be responsible for influencing the energy of the system will be quantized, whereas other values set to zero. All the processes of encoder in reverse order except the quantization process are decoded.

4. **Fractal:** The fractal compression technique is a lossy compression technique. Fractals are patterns that can be repeated over and over again. In other words, fractals are considered to be self-similar patterns. Fractals are considered to be best suited for the natural scenes or textures. They are used to recreate the encoded image. The fractal compression technique has a unique feature that it is resolution independent, which indicates that if a particular size image requires to be resized, then the quality of the image is not compromised; however, the quality of the images is affected by the panel size. The values of the gamma or values of gamma and beta can be used to change the intensity of each pixel.

5. **Wavelet image lossy compression technique:** Wavelet transformation is usually a process of changing data from time-space domain to time-frequency domain in order to have a better compression result. Wavelet image compression uses five stages for image compression and decompression. As all the steps are invertible except the quantization step, hence it is lossless compression. The steps for compression are imaging, wavelet transform, quantize,

encode, and compress image, whereas steps for decompression are compressed image, decode, approximate wavelet transform, inverse wavelet transform, and round off to integral values to create images.

There are many algorithms proposed under wavelet based lossy compression, namely, the embedded zerotree wavelet algorithm, set partitioning in hierarchical trees algorithm, wavelet difference reduction algorithm, and adaptively scanned wavelet difference reduction algorithm which further reduce error per compression rate and highest perceptual quality.

6. **Hybrid coding:** It consists of a combination of two or more lossy compression methods.

**Chroma subsampling**

Chroma subsampling is used to compress images within video. It is based on the concept that images are made up of pixels, and each pixel contains two types of information: luminance or luma, which is brightness, and chrominance or chroma, which is color. Because our eyes are less sensitive to color detail than to brightness detail, chroma subsampling is used to reduce the amount of data in a video signal while having little or no visible impact on image quality.

The video created with chroma subsampling still includes brightness information for every single pixel, but not color information. Color information is shared among adjacent pixels. The number of pixels that share the same color information is determined by the type of chroma subsampling. To describe the extent of subsampling, video professionals use a numerical shorthand in the form of a ratio that references a block of 8 pixels, 4 across and 2 high. This ratio has three numbers separated by colons. The first number indicates the number of pixels within the sample is (usually 4). The second number tells you how many of the pixels in the top row will have color information, that is, chroma samples. The third number tells you how many pixels in the bottom row will have chroma samples.

7. **Morphological processing:** It deals with tools that are used for extracting image components that are useful for representation and description of shapes. Morphological image processing is a collection of non-linear operations related to the shape or morphology of features in an image. The operations in morphological image processing depends on relative ordering of values of the pixel rather than on their numerical values and hence is useful for processing of binary images. Morphological operations can also be applied to grayscale images such that their light transfer functions are unknown, and therefore, their absolute pixel values are of no or minor interest.

Morphological techniques probe an image with a small shape or template called a structuring element. The structuring element is positioned at all possible locations in the image, and it is compared with the corresponding neighborhood of pixels. Some operations test whether the element "fits" within the neighborhood, while others test whether it "hits" or intersects the neighborhood. A morphological operation on a binary image creates a new binary image in which the pixel has a non-zero value only if the test is successful at that location in the input image.

The structuring element is a small binary image, that is, a small matrix of pixels, each with a value of zero or one:

- The matrix dimensions specify the size of the structuring element.
- The pattern of ones and zeros specifies the shape of the structuring element.
- An origin of the structuring element is usually one of its pixels, although generally the origin can be outside the structuring element.

When a structuring element is placed in a binary image, each of its pixels is associated with the corresponding pixel of the neighborhood under the structuring element. The structuring element is said to fit the image if, for each of its pixels set to 1, the corresponding image pixel is also 1. Similarly, a structuring element is said to hit, or intersect, an image if, at least for one of its pixels set to 1 the corresponding image pixel is also 1.

8. **Segmentation:** This step partitions the image into sub-parts or objects. It includes processes like autonomous segmentation, rugged segmentation, etc. Segmentation is an integral component in digital image processing which divides the image into different segments and discrete regions. The image segments are used for locating the objects and boundaries within an image. The image segmentation is thus used to divide the image into a group of segments that jointly enclose the whole image.

The image segmentation is divided into two types of techniques as contextual and non-contextual techniques. For instance, methods based on compression techniques propose that the best method of segmentation is the one which minimizes data's coding length and the general probable segmentations. Methods based on histograms are known to be extremely well-organized to evaluate additional segmentation schemes as they need only single exceed in the progression of the pixels. In this scheme, all of the pixels of an image are taken into consideration to figure the histogram, and the valleys and peaks in the histogram are utilized for establishing the clusters in an image. Inside-image processing, edge detection is a robust field on its own. Region edges and boundaries are connected directly since there is often a quick modification in strength at the area of boundaries.

One of the simplest methods of image segmentation is thresholding which is based on the clip level or threshold value in order to turn a gray scale image into binary image. This method is based on selecting a threshold value or values. Some of the algorithms and techniques proposed in this regard are the maximum entropy method, Otsu's method (maximum variance), and k-means clustering. This forms its basis based on luminance or color value whose threshold value is of two types as bilevel luminance thresholding and multilevel luminance thresholding. In bilevel luminance thresholding, images have only the luminance level such as a printed page having black letters on white background whereas in multilevel luminance, the thresholding image has multiple levels of luminance. Color thresholding is based on a nonstandard color component, loosely called intensity.

Image segmentation can also be achieved using fuzzy clustering techniques. There are many algorithms proposed by different researchers in this direction but one of the most common algorithms in this direction is the Fuzzy c-Means (FCM) algorithm which uses objective functions to define the relationship between pixels within an image. In this approach, pixels are considered as data points and the fuzzy classification matrix denotes the memberships of pixels in clusters. Some researchers who proposed different approaches in this direction are Trivedi and Bezdek (1986) who proposed a fuzzy set theoretic image segmentation algorithm for aerial image segmentation and Huntsberger et al. (1986) who applied FCM in image segmentation with refined iterative manner. Keller et al. (2011) used a modified version of FCM in image segmentation.

9. **Image representation and description:** This is done after segmentation of objects which is used for successful detection and recognition of objects in a scene to represent the characteristic features during pattern recognition or in quantitative codes for efficient storage during image compression. Image representation and description techniques can be categorized into two classes of methods as contour-based methods and region-based methods. This classification is based on whether the image is extracted from contour only from the entire shape region.

Contour shape techniques are used to exploit only information of the boundary of the shape. The contour shape technique uses two types of approaches as **continuous approach** or **global approach** or **discrete approach** or **structural approach** (Figure 1.7). The continuous approach does not divide the image into sub-parts, in order to describe the shape it derived the feature vector from the integral boundary of the image, whereas the discrete approach divides

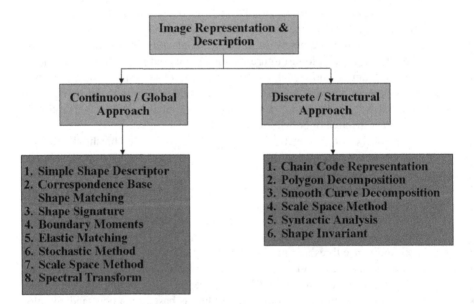

**FIGURE 1.7**  Classification and techniques for image representation and description.

the shape boundaries into segments based on certain criteria; these segments are termed as primitives. It produces the final results as a string or a graph or tree. There are two types of approaches to achieve this as follows:

1. **Global method:** This method takes entire image contour for image representation which performs the matching between images either in space or feature domain. In image description, there is a trade-off between accuracy and efficiency.

    a. **Simple shape descriptors:** This method includes global descriptors as area, circularity (perimeter$^2$ = area), eccentricity (length of major axis/ length of minor axis), major axis orientation, and bending energy used as filters to eliminate false hits or combined with other shape descriptors to discriminate shapes. Other global contour shape descriptors have been proposed by other researchers like Peura and Iivarinen (1997) which include descriptors like convexity, ratio of principle axis, circular variance, and elliptic variance.

    b. **Correspondence-based shape matching:** This method works in space domain which measures the similarity between shapes using point-to-point matching. In this method, each point on an image is treated as a feature point. This matching is performed in 2D space. Some of the examples for this method are as the hausdorff distance which is used to locate objects in an image and measure similarity between shapes (Chetverikov and Khenokh, 1999). The matching between two shapes is performed by mapping the context map of the two images. In order to reduce the matching overhead, it samples the boundary at a number of points and uses the shortest augmenting path algorithm for the matrix matching.

    c. **Shape signature:** It represents shape by a one-dimensional function derived from shape boundary points. There are many shape signatures such as the centroidal profile, complex coordinates, centroid distance, tangent angle, cumulative angle, curvature, area, and chord-length. Shape signatures are usually normalized into being translation and scale invariant. In order to compensate for orientation changes, shift matching is needed to find the best matching between two shapes. It has high matching cost and is sensitive to noise and also prone to large error in matching in case of slight change in boundary.

    d. **Boundary moments:** This method is used to reduce the dimensions of boundary representations. This method is easy to implement but difficult to associate order moments with physical interpretation.

    e. **Elastic matching:** Bimbo (1997) have proposed the use of elastic matching for shape-based image retrieval. According to this approach, a deformed template is generated as the sum of the original template $\iota(s)$ and a warping deformation V(s).

$$\varphi(s) = \iota(s) + V(s);$$

    f. **Stochastic method:** It uses the stochastic modeling of a 1-D function f obtained from the shape. It uses autoregressive (AR) modeling to achieve the same (Das et al., 1990). A linear AR model expresses a value of a function as the linear combination of a certain number of preceding value. Specifically, each function value in the sequence has some correlation with previous function values and can therefore be predicted through a number. This method is not suitable for complex boundaries as a small number of AR parameters are not sufficient for adequate description.

g. **Scale space method:** This method is used to deal with the problem of noise sensitivity and boundary variation in most space domain shape methods. The scale space representation of a shape is created by tracking the position of inflection points in a shape boundary filtered by LP Gaussian filters of variable widths which help in creating an interval tree termed as "fingerprint" which consist of these inflection points. The result produced by this method is hard to interpret.

h. **Spectral transform:** This method deals with the problem of noise sensitivity and boundary variations by means of analyzing shapes of images in spectral domain by making use of the Fourier descriptor and wavelet descriptor.

2. **Structural method:** Structural image representation is another image analysis process which breaks the image into boundary segment termed as primitives. In order to select and organize these primitives for representation of images, there are many structural methods as discussed below.

a. **Chain code representation:** This method was proposed by Freeman (1961), which is used to describe an object by a sequence of unit-size line segments with a given orientation by encoding of arbitrary geometric configurations. In this approach, an arbitrary curve is represented by a sequence of small vectors of unit length and a limited set of possible directions, thus termed the unit-vector method. In the implementation, a digital boundary of an image is superimposed with a grid, the boundary points are approximated to the nearest grid point, and then a sampled image is obtained. From a selected starting point, a chain code can be generated by using a four-directional or eight-directional chain code. The chain code usually has high dimensions and is sensitive to noise. It is often used as an input to a higher level analysis

b. **Polygon decomposition:** Polygon approximation is used to break the boundary of the image into line segments. The polygon vertices are used as primitives. The feature for each primitive is expressed as a four-element string which consists of internal angle, distance from the next vertex, and its x and y coordinates. The similarity between any two shapes is the editing distance of the two feature strings. For efficiency and robustness reason, only a fixed number of sharpest vertices are selected from each shape. Therefore, a collection of features belonging to all models in the database is generated for the feature index. The features are then organized into a binary tree or m-nary tree. The matching between shapes involves two steps, that is, feature-by-feature matching in the first step and model-by-model matching in the second step. In the first step, given a data feature of a query shape, the feature is searched through the index tree, if a particular model feature in the database is found to be similar to the data feature, the list of shapes associated with the model feature are retrieved. In the second step, the matching between the query shape and a retrieved model is matched based on the editing distance between the two strings of primitives.

c. **Smooth curve decomposition:** This approach is given by Berretti et al. (2000), who extended the work of Groskey and Mehrotra (1990) where in this approach Gaussian smoothed boundaries are used to obtain primitives which are termed as tokens. The feature for each token is its maximum curvature and its orientation, and the similarity between two tokens is measured by the weighted Euclidean distance.

d. **Scale space method:** This method is proposed by Dudek and Tsotsos (1997), who analyzed the image in scale space and employed a model-by-model matching scheme. In this method, the curvature-tuned smoothing technique is used for obtaining image primitives. A segment descriptor consists of the segment's length, ordinal position, and curvature tuning value extracted from each primitive. A string of segment descriptors is then created to describe the image. To increase robustness and to save matching computation, the shape features are put into a curvature scale space so that shapes can be matched in different scales.

e. **Syntactic analysis:** This method is based on the logic that the composition of a natural scene is an analog to the composition of a language, that is, sentences are built up from phrases, phrases are built up from words, and words are built up from alphabets (Fu, 1974). In this method, shape is represented by a set of predefined primitives. The set of predefined primitives is called the code book, and the primitives are called codewords. The matching between shapes can use string matching by finding the minimal number of edit operations to convert one string into another. Syntactic shape analysis is based on the theory of formal language (Chomsky, 1957). It attempts to simulate the structural and hierarchical nature of the human vision system. However, it is not practical in general applications because it is not possible to infer a pattern of grammar which can generate only the valid patterns. In addition, this method needs a priori knowledge for the database in order to define code words or alphabets. The knowledge is usually unavailable for general applications.

f. **Shape invariants:** This method represent shapes based on boundary primitives. This approach is based on the logic that shape representation techniques are invariant under similarity transformations (rotation, translation and scaling) which depend on viewpoint (Sonka et al., 1993) and hence invariants attempt to represent properties of the boundary configurations which remain unchanged under an appropriate class of transformations. This invariant theory is based on a collection of transformations that can be composed and inverted. Invariant is usually named according to the number of features used to define it. An order one invariant is defined on a single feature and is called an unary invariant; an order two invariant is defined between two features and is called a binary invariant; similarly, ternary invariant, quaternary invariant, and so on.

10. **Object recognition:** Object recognition is used to determine the identity of an object being observed in an image from a set of known tags. It is used to find objects in the real world from an image of the world by using object model which is known in advance. Different components required for object recognition are:

    a. model database or modelbase

    b. feature detector

    c. hypothesizer

    d. hypothesis verifier.

        a. **The model database:** It contains the entire model which is known to system. The information in the model database depends on the approach used for the recognition. It can vary from a qualitative or functional description to precise geometric surface information.

        b. **Feature detector:** Feature is attributes of an object which are considered to be important in describing and recognition the object in relation to other objects. Examples are size, color, shapes, etc. which are some common features. Feature detector identifies the location of features which help in forming object hypothesis by applying operators to images. Depending upon the type of object to be recognized and organization of model database, these systems can be used by the system.

        c. **Hypothesizer:** The hypothesizer assigns likelihoods to objects present in the scene by using the detected feature in the image which helps in reducing the search space for recognizer using certain features.

        d. **Hypothesis verifier:** Hypothesis verifier makes use of the object model to verify the hypothesis and refine the likelihood of objects. The system then selects the object with the highest likelihood, based on all the evidence, as the correct object.

Object recognition systems use models either explicitly or implicitly and employ feature detectors based on these object models. The hypothesis formation and verification components vary in terms of their importance in different approaches to object recognition. Some systems use only hypothesis formation and then select the object with the highest likelihood as the correct object.

## REFERENCES

Al-Fayadh, A.J., Hussain, P.L., and Al-Jumeily, D. (2007). A hybrid classified vector quantisation and its application to image compression. *IEEE Int. Con. ICSPC07*, Nov. 24–27, 2007, Dubai, pp. 125–128.

Al-Fayadh, A.J., Hussain, P., and Lisboa, D.A., and Al-Jumaily, M. (2008). An adaptive hybrid image compression method and its application to medical images. *IEEE Int. Symp. Biomedical Imaging (ISBI "08)*, May 14-17, 2008, France.

Ayers, G.R. and Dainty, J.C. (1988). Iterative blind convolution method and its application. *Optical Society of America* 13(7), 547–549.

Berretti, S., Bimbo, A.D., and Pala, P. (2000). Retrieval by shape similarity with perceptual distance and effective indexing. *IEEE Trans. Multimedia* 2(4), 225–239.

Chetverikov, D. and Khenokh, Y. (1999). *Matching for Shape Defect Detection*, Lecture Notes in Computer Science, Vol. 1689, Springer, Berlin, pp. 367–374.

Chomsky, N. (1957). *Syntactic Structures*, Mouton, The Hague, Berlin.

Clarke, R.J. (1996). *Digital Compression of Still Images and Video*, 2nd edn., Academic Press, London.

Das, M., Paulik, M.J., and Loh, N.K. (1990). A bivariate autoregressive modeling technique for analysis and classification of planar shapes. *IEEE Trans. Pattern Anal. Mach. Intell.* 12(1), 97–103.

Del Bimbo, P. (1997). Visual image retrieval by elastic matching of user sketches. *IEEE Trans. Pattern Anal. Mach. Intell.* 19(2), 121–132.

Dudek, G. and Tsotsos, J.K. (1997). Shape representation and recognition from multiscale curvature. *Comput. Vision Image Understanding* 68(2), 170–189.

Freeman, H. (1961). On the encoding of arbitrary geometric configurations. *IRE Trans. Electron. Comput.* EC-10(1961), 260–268.

Fu, K.S. (1974). *Syntactic Methods in Pattern Recognition*, Academic Press, New York.

Glen, G. and Langdon, J. (1984). An introduction to arithmetic coding. *IBM J. Res. Develop.* 28(2), 135–149.

Gonzalez, R.C. and Woods, R.E. (1992). *Digital Image Processing*, Addison-Wesley, Reading, pp. 307–411.

Gray, R.M. (1984). Vector quantization. *IEEE ASSP Magazine* 1, 4–29.

Groskey, W.I. and Mehrotra, R. (1990). Index-based object recognition in pictorial data management. *Comput. Vision Graphics Image Process.* 52, 416–436.

Huffman, D.A. (1952). A method for the construction of minimum redundancy codes. *Proc. IRE* 40, 1098–1101.

Huntsberger, T., Rangarajan, C., and Jayaramamurthy, S. (1986). Representation of uncertainty in computer vision using fuzzy set. *Computers, IEEE Transactions on* C-35, 145–156. 10.1109/TC.1986.1676732.

Keller, B., Nathan, D., Wang, Y., Zheng, Y., Gee, J., Conant, E., and Kontos, D. (2011). Adaptive multi-cluster fuzzy C-means segmentation of breast parenchymal tissue in digital mammography. *Medical image computing and computer-assisted intervention: MICCAI ... International Conference on Medical Image Computing and Computer-Assisted Intervention* 14(Pt 3), 562–569. https://doi.org/10.1007/978-3-642-23626-6_69.

Kim, J.W. and Lee, S.U. (1992). A transform domain classified vector quantizer for image coding. *IEEE Trans. Circuits and Systems for Video Technology* 2(1), 3–14.

Martinez, I. (2011). Guadalajara and Mexico (2011). *Using the Run Length Encoding Features on the MPC5645S*, pp. 1–8.

Ong, C.A. and Chambers, J.A. (1999). An enhanced NAS-RIF algorithm for blind image deconvolution. *IEEE Transactions on Image Processing* 8(7), 988–992.

Oswal, S., Singh, A., and Kumari, K. (2016). Deflate compression algorithm. *International Journal of Engineering Research and General Science* 4(1), 430–436.

Peura, M. and Iivarinen, J. (1997). Efficiency of simple shape descriptors. *Proceedings of the Third International Workshop on Visual Form*, Capri, Italy, May 1997, pp. 443–451.

Sonka, M., Hlavac, V., and Boyle, R. (1993). *Image Processing, Analysis and Machine Vision*, Chapman & Hall, London, UK, NJ, pp. 193–242.

Trivedi, M. and Bezdek, J.C. (1986). Low level segmentation of aerial images with fuzzy clustering. *IEEE Transaction on System, Man, Cybernate* 16(4), 589–598.

Umbaugh, S.E. (2005). *Computer Imaging: Digital Image Analysis and Processing*, CRC Press.

# 2 Different Techniques Used for Image Processing

## 2.1 INTRODUCTION

Image processing is a technique used to process images and is used for improving the images received from various sources such as cameras, satellites, sensors, etc. There are various techniques developed and also developing from the past years to the current years in order to extract image in an efficient and best manner. Thus, image processing can be termed as a technique used for analyzing and manipulating the digitized images to improve the quality of images. The techniques proposed can be applied in various applications such as diagnosis of an image analysis, object detection and matching, localization of tumors, surgical planning, background removal in videos, traffic control system, measuring the volume of tissues, location of objects such as roads, forests, etc. in satellite images, iris recognition, medical and agriculture imaging, object localization in face recognition, etc. (Rajkomar et al., 2019) The various techniques of digital image processing primarily focus on issues such as loss in the quality of images or enhancing the degraded image.

Image processing can be classified into two parts as follows:

1. Analog image processing
2. Digital image processing

Analog image processing is a process of processing of images by electrical means. Example of such processing is television images. As the television signal is a voltage level, hence they vary in terms of amplitude in order to represent brightness by means of image. Displayed image appearance can be altered by varying these electrical signals. The brightness and contrast controls on a TV set serve to adjust the amplitude and reference of the video signal, resulting in the brightening, darkening, and alteration of the brightness range of the displayed image.

Digital image processing on the other hand uses digital computers for processing of images. This technique uses a digital conversion method for converting the image into digital form in order to process the image in digital format. Now most of the image processing methods are based on digital image processing only and in this chapter, we focus on different techniques used in digital image processing only.

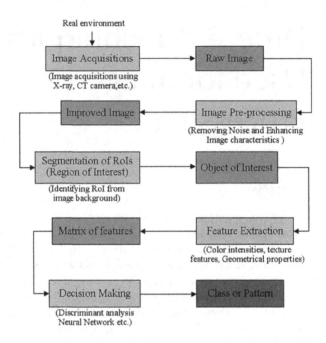

**FIGURE 2.1**   Operational steps of image processing.

We can broadly divide the entire digital image processing into four components as represented in Figure 2.1:

1. Acquisition of images
2. Image pre-processing
3. Processing of images
4. Decision making

Diagnostic image analysis, surgical planning, object detection and matching, background subtraction in video, localization of tumors, measuring tissue volumes, locating objects in satellite images (roads, forests, etc.), traffic control systems, locating objects in face recognition, iris recognition, agricultural imaging, and medical imaging all these application fields consist of different approaches for image processing such as feature extraction, classification, pattern matching, decision making, and validation that finally lead to the desired output.

### 2.1.1 ACQUISITION OF AN IMAGE

The procedure of image preparation cannot start except if the image has been caught. It is perpetually the initial step of any strategy used for image processing. Image acquisition is an equipment autonomous procedure. In this step, fundamentally an optical image is caught by the camera and is changed over into a variety of numerical information as bits.

An image is obtained utilizing cameras or various types of sensors that can catch different features of the energy that was reflected by the object surface. The acquisition process of images can be categorized into three stages, where the camera focal points center that object, and when the item mirrors the whole energy, it is caught by the sensors of the camera. Various sorts of cameras are accessible to diverse applications. The images are produced by the blend of a brightening of the wellspring of light and the reflection or the assimilation of the light by the object of intrigue. The enlightenment can be produced by the diverse energy source and to detect the image, a sensor relying upon the idea of brightening will be chosen. This total procedure of image catch is known as image securing. By and large, the sensor named the charged coupled gadget or complementary metal-oxide semiconductor (CMOS) image sensors start at the same point of capturing the image and able to convert light into electrons is utilized in the cameras. The cameras utilizing the CMOS, for the most part, would get images with commotion and use a greater amount of capacity to catch an image. Anyway, the cameras with a charge coupled device (CCD) are more equipped for creating all the more great images, with less force utilization. CCD cameras are single IC gadgets that comprise a variety of photosensitive cells, where every cell delivers an electric flow when a light beam falls on the cells. CCD cameras have less mathematical twisting and give a linear visual output. Image obtaining can be done utilizing a solitary sensor; anyway, it is a moderate technique to secure images. Images can likewise be obtained orchestrating singular sensors as an array of two dimensional (2-D) form. (Zhu et al., 2019). There are five principal boundaries to be borne as a main priority while catching an image, and these boundaries are perspective on the catching gadget, separation of an article to be caught from the gaining gadget, goal, size of the sensors in the gadget, and profundity of field. When the image has been caught, it must be digitized by a gadget known as an edge store that stores the examples of the casing in its own memory, and the edge is handily moved to a record or a memory area that can be gotten to later when required.

## 2.1.2 IMAGE PRE-PROCESSING

Major pre-processing techniques are (Figure 2.2):

### 2.1.2.1 Image Enhancement

Image enhancement is enhancing the part of image which is of use in order to have a better understanding of the image so that various operations can be performed on the selected image. Enhancement programs make information more visible by redistributing the intensities of the image in the 256 gray scale levels or by carrying out the unsharp masking by emphasizing intensity changes.

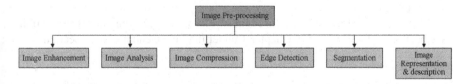

**FIGURE 2.2**   Techniques used under image pre-processing.

### 2.1.2.2 Image Analysis

This section deals with analysis of images in order to extract the required information from the image by means of various methods.

### 2.1.2.3 Image Compression

Image compression is used to remove the redundancy within an image and store or transmit data in its best suited format. This is done by encoding the original image with bits. Thus, image compression is used to compress the image as much as possible such that the original feature of the image will retained.

### 2.1.2.4 Edge Detection

The edge detection method is used to find the edges where the brightness of an image changes sharply.

### 2.1.2.5 Segmentation

Segmentation is segmenting the image when needed to extract the required component from the image.

### 2.1.2.6 Image Representation

Image representation is a process of representation of images which can be in 2-D or three-dimensional. Based on these representations, only the processing operations can be decided.

Image representation can be of many forms in computer science. In basic terminology, image representation refers to the way which is used to convey information about the image and its features such as color, pixels, resolution, intensity, brightness, how the image is stored, etc.

Some important techniques discussed in more detail are as follows:

*Image Enhancement*

Image enhancement is a procedure that is utilized for performing calculation inside the images by utilizing diverse heuristic strategies, so as to extract significant data from the image. This procedure improves the quality and data substance of the first image before image processing. There are different enhancement techniques that can be utilized so as to extricate the subtleties of a concerned image as to highlight the significant features of the image that are of due significance. It emphasizes or hones the edges and boundaries and does differentiation of images so as to make realistic showcase more accommodating for display and examination purposes. So as to accomplish the above properties, image enhancement expands the dynamic range of selected features so as to identify them without any problem.

The details of these techniques used under image enhancement and classification have been already discussed in Chapter 1 under the image enhancement section.

*Image Analysis*

Image analysis is a tool used for differentiating, recognizing, and quantifying different types of images. Image analysis helps in providing the numerical values

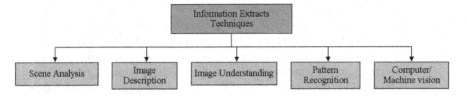

**FIGURE 2.3** Information extraction techniques used for image analysis.

and/or graphical information of the characteristics of images that can be used for classification, detection of any defect, or prediction of some of the properties of imaged objects. Thus, image analysis is used to provide output in a form of number or decision which can be used to provide some important information (Sarkar et al., 2019).

Thus, image analysis extracts information from an image by using different techniques as follows (Figure 2.3):

Image analysis can be used in different applications such as optical character recognition, analysis of medical images, industrial robots, cartography, geology, biometry, and military applications. In terms of optical character recognition, image analysis can be used for sorting of mail, reading of labels, product billing, processing of bank-cheque, reading of text, etc. However in medical images, image analysis can be used for detection of tumors, measurement of organs in terms of their shape and size, analysis of chromosomes, counting of blood cells, etc. (Rajkomar et al., 2019) In industrial robots, it can be used for recognizing and interpretation of objects in a scene and motion control by means of visual feedback. In cartography and geology, it can be used for preparation of maps from photos, plotting of weather maps, exploration of oil, etc. It can also be used in military and other applications as recognition of fingerprint and face, detection and identification of targets, guidance of helicopter and aircraft in times of landing, remote guidance of missiles, etc.

Techniques of image analysis can be divided into three parts as follows (Figure 2.4):

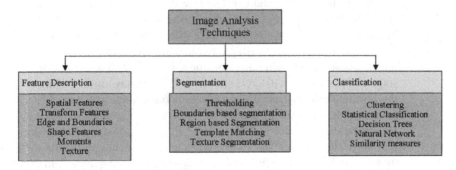

**FIGURE 2.4** Classification of image analysis.

**Image segmentation:** Image segmentation is used to segment an image into sub-components in order to distinguish object of interest from background. Different methods of segmentation are thresholding, boundary-based segmentation, region-based segmentation, template matching, and texture segmentation. In threshold-based segmentation, a threshold is the one which acts as a segmentation parameter such that any image point which is higher to the selected threshold will be selected and considered as object and other points are considered as background. Boundary-based segmentation considered specific boundaries as a parameter to select the object from images, whereas region-based segmentation selects a particular region which can be considered as an object. Template matching uses an image correlation technique for finding matches of a searched pattern of specific size within an image of larger size. Texture segmentation selects the object based on texture within an image.

**Image compression:** Image compression is accustomed to limiting the size of memory capacity, without influencing or corrupting its quality indeed, sparing an image or sparing the data transmission to communicate it. Image compression is characterized as the way toward decreasing the measure of information expected to express to a computerized image. Image compression can be compressed dependent on the accompanying reasons: inside a solitary image, there exists a noteworthy connection or repetition among neighboring examples or pixels. This connection is named spatial relationship or excess. On account of satellite images where images are obtained from various sensors, then there exists a connection or excess among tests got from these sensors, and this repetition is named spatial relationship or excess. The compression strategy utilizes this excess for compression. Expelling this excess before compression will make a successful compression inside an image. Image compression comprises two sections as a blower and decompressor. The blower packs the information and consequently is a pre-processor that is utilized for encoding though the decompressor is a post-preparing stage that is utilized for disentangling. In the pre-preparing stage, the information is diminished by the dim level as well as spatial quantization and can likewise be utilized to expel commotion. The following stage of the pre-processing stage is the planning procedure, which maps the first image information into another scientific space which makes it simple to pack the information. Next is the quantization stage which takes nonstop information from the planning stage and places it in a discrete structure. The last stage is the coding of the resultant information. The compression procedure may comprise a considerable number of stages or a mix of a couple of stages. Decompression is additionally isolated into two phases, wherein the first stage the decoder takes the compacted document and inverts the first coding by planning the codes to unique, quantized qualities. In the following stage, the first planning process is switched to process the worth that plays out backward planning. Finally, the image might be present handled on improvement of the appearance of the final image.

Image compression can be divided into sub-categories as lossless and lossy image compression. The details of these compression techniques have been already discussed in Chapter 1 under the image compression section.

**Edge detection:** Edge detection is used to detect the edges of the image of concern. Where the edges can be defined as the area of an image characterized by a sharp change in gray level or brightness. The edge detection process is used to attenuate high fluctuation in color within an image.

**Segmentation:** This progression segments the images into different objects or sub-parts. It incorporates processes such as autonomous segmentation, rugged segmentation, and so on. The segmentation is an indispensable segment in computerized image preparation which partitions the image into various sections and discrete areas. The image fragments are utilized for finding the object and limits inside an image. The segmentation of an image is in this manner used to partition the image into a gathering of portions that together encase the entire image.

The image segmentation is separated into two sorts of strategies as relevant that mean contextual and non-contextual procedures. These strategies have been explained in chapter 1 section image segmentation.

**Image representation and description:** This progression step taken part after the image segmentation of objects has been done which is utilized for effective discovery and acknowledgment of items in a scene to define the quality features during design acknowledgment or in quantitative codes for proficient capacity during image compression. Image portrayal and depiction strategies can be sorted into two classes of techniques as shape-based strategies and locale-based techniques. This classification depends on whether the image is extricated from the contour part that forms the whole shape area.

The procedures for the contour shape are utilized to misuse just data of the shape boundary. The contour shape technique utilizes two sorts of contour approaches named continuous approach and discrete approaches also known as global approach and structural approach, respectively. Both of these techniques have been explained in chapter 1 in section Image representation and description.

**Some other pre-processing techniques are as follows:**

1. **Image editing:** Image editing is alteration in images by means of graphics software tools.
2. **Image restoration:** Image restoration is extraction of the original image from the corrupt image in order to retrieve the lost information.
3. **Independent component analysis (ICA):** This method is used to separate multivariate signals computationally into additive subcomponents.
4. **Anisotropic diffusion:** This is also known as Perona–Malik Diffusion which is used to reduce noise of an image without removing any important part of an image.

5. **Linear filtering:** This technique is used to process time varying input signals and produce output signals which are subject to constraint of linearity.
6. **Pixelation:** This process is used to convert printed images into digitized ones.
7. **Principal component analysis (PCA):** This technique is used for feature extraction.
8. **Partial differential equations**: These techniques deal with effectively denoising images.
9. **Hidden Markov model:** This technique is used for image analysis in two dimensional models
10. **Wavelets:** It is a mathematical model which is used for image compression.
11. **Self-organizing maps:** This technique is used to classify images into a number of classes.
12. **Point feature mapping:** It is used to detect a specified target in a cluttered scene.
13. **Histogram:** The histogram is used to plots the number of pixels in the image in the form of curve.

**Image editing:** Image editing is a process used for editing within an image by altering digital images or chemical images/illustrations. Earlier this technique was recognized as photo retouching. Recent advancement in image processing will enable grouping computer graphics into vector graphics editor, raster graphics editor, and 3D modelers which are primary tools that can be used for manipulation, enhancement, and transformation of images. Raster images can be stored in form of pixels consisting of information regarding color of images and information of brightness of images. These pixels can be altered by using different graphics software such as Adobe Illustrator, Corel Draw, Xara Designer Pro, or Inkscape. The digital images are stored as descriptions of lines, Bézier curves, and text instead of pixels. It is easier to rasterize a vector image than to vectorize a raster image. Vectorizing a raster image can be achieved using computer vision. Vector images can be modified more easily because they contain descriptions of the shapes for easy rearrangement. They are also scalable, being rasterizable at any resolution. The features of Image editor are selection, layers, image size alteration, cropping an image, and cutting a part of the image.

**Image restoration**: Image restoration is a process of restoring the image by removing the corrupt and noisy image from the original image and restores the original image. These noises are in form of motion blur, noise, and camera mis-focus. Image restoration is performed by reversing the process that blurred the image and such is performed by imaging a point source and using the point source image, which is called the Point Spread Function to restore the image information lost to the blurring process. Image restoration is different from image enhancement in that the latter is designed to emphasize features of the image that make the image more pleasing to the observer, but not necessarily to produce realistic data from a scientific point of view.

    The objective of image restoration techniques is to reduce noise and recover resolution loss. The most common and conventional technique used for image restoration is deconvolution, which is performed in the frequency domain and after computing the Fourier transform of both the image and the point spread function (PSF) and undo the resolution loss caused by the blurring factors. This deconvolution technique, because of its direct inversion of the PSF which typically has a poor matrix condition number, amplifies noise, and creates an imperfect deblurred image. Also, conventionally the blurring process is assumed to be shift-invariant. Hence, more sophisticated techniques, such as regularized deblurring, have been developed to offer robust recovery under different types of noises and blurring functions which can be further divided based on their working as geometric correction, radiometric correction, and noise removal.

**ICA:** ICA is used to project the image on the basis of its components. The watermarks in the images are the part of the representation of the data in an encoded format, which is the key of the steganography problem. One of the examples of ICA is anisotropic diffusion. In image processing and computer vision, anisotropic diffusion also called Perona–Malik diffusion, is a technique aimed at reducing image noise without removing significant parts of the image content, typically edges, lines, or other details that are important for the interpretation of the image. Each of the resulting images in this family is given as a convolution between the image and a 2D isotropic Gaussian filter, where the width of the filter increases with the parameter. This diffusion process is a linear and space-invariant transformation of the original image. Anisotropic diffusion is a generalization of this diffusion process: it produces a family of parameterized images, but each resulting image is a combination between the original image and a filter that depends on the local content of the original image. As a consequence, anisotropic diffusion is a non-linear and space-variant transformation of the original image.

**Linear filtering:** Filtering is a technique used for modifying or enhancing an image. You can filter an image to emphasize certain features or remove other features. Filtering is a *neighborhood operation,* in which the value of any given pixel in the output image is determined by applying some algorithm to the values of the pixels in the neighborhood of the corresponding input pixel. A pixel's neighborhood is some set of pixels, defined by their locations relative to that pixel. *Linear filtering* is filtering in which the value of an output pixel is a linear combination of the values of the pixels in the input pixel's neighborhood.

**Pixelation:** Pixelation is a term used to describe the act of turning a printed image into a digitized image file (such as the GIF file that is used to display an image on a Web page). As the image is captured, it is processed into a vectorized or rasterized file that can be used to illuminate color units called pixels on a display surface. Pixelation is used to display a digitized image where the individual pixels are apparent to a viewer. This can happen unintentionally when a low-resolution image designed for an ordinary computer display is projected on a large screen and each pixel becomes separately viewable.

**PCA:** PCA is a popular dimensionality reduction technique used in Machine Learning applications. PCA condenses information from a large set of variables into fewer variables by applying some sort of transformation onto them. The transformation is applied in such a way that linearly correlated variables get transformed into uncorrelated variables. Correlation tells us that there is redundancy of information and if this redundancy can be reduced, then information can be compressed. For example, if there are two variables in the variable set which are highly correlated, then, we are not gaining any extra information by retaining both the variables because one can be nearly expressed as the linear combination of the other. In such cases, PCA transfers the variance of the second variable onto the first variable by translation and rotation of original axes and projecting data onto new axes. The direction of projection is determined using eigen values and eigen vectors. So, the first few transformed features (termed as principal components) are rich in information, whereas the last features contain mostly noise with negligible information in them. This transferability allows us to retain the first few principal components, thus reducing the number of variables significantly with minimal loss of information.

**Principal differential equation:** Partial differential equations (PDEs) have become one of the significant mathematical methods that are widely used in the current image processing area. One of its common applications is in image smoothing which is an essential preliminary step in image processing. Smoothing is necessary because it affects the result of further processes in image processing. It can be used to provide better image quality as compared to conventional filters, such as the median filter and Gaussian filter.

**Hidden Markov Model:** In simpler Markov models (like a Markov chain), the state is directly visible to the observer, and therefore, the state transition probabilities are the only parameters, while in the hidden Markov model (HMM), the state is not directly visible, but the output (in the form of data or "token") dependent on the state is visible. Each state has a probability distribution over the possible output tokens. Therefore, the sequence of tokens generated by an HMM gives some information about the sequence of states; this is also known as pattern theory, a topic of grammar induction.

A HMM can be considered a generalization of a mixture model where the hidden variables (or latent variables), which control the mixture component to be selected for each observation, are related through a Markov process rather than being independent of each other. Recently, HMMs have been generalized to pairwise Markov models and triplet Markov models which allow consideration of more complex data structures and the modeling of nonstationary data.

**Wavelets:** A wavelet is a mathematical function useful in digital signal processing and image compression.

**Self-organizing map (SOM):** A SOM or self-organizing feature map is a type of artificial neural network (ANN) that is trained using unsupervised learning to produce a low-dimensional (typically 2-D), discretized representation of the input space of the training samples, called a map, and is therefore a method to do dimensionality reduction. Self-organizing maps differ from other ANNs as they are used for competitive learning as related to error-correction learning like backpropagation with gradient descent and hence use a neighborhood function in order to preserve the topological properties of input space.

**Point feature matching:** Point feature matching is an effective method to detect a specified target in a cluttered scene. This method detects single objects rather than multiple objects. For instance, by using this method, one can recognize one specific person in a cluttered scene, but not any other person. The algorithm is based on comparing and analyzing point correspondences between the reference image and the target image. If any part of the cluttered scene shares correspondences greater than the threshold, that part of the cluttered scene image is targeted and considered to include the reference object there.

Histogram: Digital editors have capacities that can be used to create the curves from the given images. The histogram plots the number of pixels in the image (vertical axis) with a particular brightness value (horizontal axis). Algorithms in the digital editor allow the user to visually adjust the brightness value of each pixel and to dynamically display the results as adjustments are made. Thus, it can be used to improve the brightness and contrast within an image.

Some common approaches for image processing are as follows:

Selection: It is a process which is able to select a part of an image, one of the important prerequisites for various applications using image processing. Most graphics software packages have a marquee tool or a lasso tool for rectangular and freehand selection of a region. A Magic wand tool selects objects or regions on the basis of the color and luminance. Edge detection and color- and channel-based extraction also refer to the selection of a part of an image. The border of a selected area in an image with some different effects can help the users to distinguish the border of an image from the image background.

Layers: Another common feature is of layers that can contain separate elements of the picture on separate transparent layers that can help to stack the elements on the top of each other with the elements being capable of being individually positioned, altered, and blended with the layers without the need to reposition any other element on other layer. Portable Network Graphics (PNG) is a raster-graphics file format one of the formats of the images that help to enable this flexibility for the user.

Image size alteration: Image editors can resize images in a process often called image scaling, making them larger or smaller. High image resolution cameras can produce large images which are often reduced in size for Internet use. Image editor programs use a mathematical process called resampling to calculate new pixel values whose spacing is larger or smaller than the original pixel values. Images for Internet use are kept small; say 640 x 480 pixels which would equal 0.3 megapixels.

Cropping an image: Editors are generally used to crop the images by selecting a rectangular region of the image. The remaining part of the image is discarded. Image cropping will not reduce the quality of the images that have been cropped. Some of the best results are obtained when the images that are being cropped are presented to the software with high resolution. One of the main reasons for the cropping of an image is to improve the composition or selection of a particular region of an image.

Image orientation: Image editors have the potential to change the orientation of the image in any required direction at any specified degree. The mirror images can be easily created by altering the angle of the images by 180 degrees.

Math process program: Math processes programs perform a variety of functions such as adding two images together pixel-by-pixel, subtracting the second image from the first image, pixel by pixel, exponential or logarithm-Raises e to power of pixel intensity, or takes log of pixel intensity. Nonlinearly accentuates or diminishes intensity variation over the image, scaler add, subtract, multiply, or divide-Applies the same constant values as specified by the user to all pixels, one at a time. Scales pixel intensities uniformly or non-uniformly, dilation-Morphological operation expanding bright regions of image and Erosion-Morphological operation shrinking bright regions of image.

**Processing of images:** The preprocessed image in a preprocessed form is processed in this stage. This stage includes the mining of image data after the preprocessing process. Generally, this stage is divided into four models as follows:

a. Regression model
b. Classification model
c. Clustering model
d. Association rules

**Regression model:** The regression model is used for predicting a continuous quantity. It may predict the discrete value but it should be in the form of integer quantity. Regression is a special application of classification rules which is used when the value of variable is predicted based on tuple rather than mapping a tuple of data from a relation to a definite class. Thus, regression is defined as a process of finding a model or function used for distinguishing the data into continuous real values instead of making use of classes. Thus, regression problem will help to find the function approximation with minimum error deviation. In this approach, the data numeric dependency is predicted in order to distinguish it.

Thus, the regression model can be used for the purpose of analysis in order to predict the numeric data instead of labels. This model can also be used for identifying the distribution movement depending on available or historic data. Most of the common algorithms used in these methods are random forest, linear regression, etc. The details of this approach are in subsequent chapters.

**Classification model:** Classification is a learning process model which elucidates different predetermined classes of data. It is a two-step process, consisting of learning and classification steps. Where in the learning step, a classification model is constructed and it prefigures the class labels for given data.

The classification model is used to classify the data set into two or more classes by approximating a mapping function from input variables to discrete output variables. The output variables obtained are often termed as labels or categories, whereas the mapping function is used to predict the class or category for a given observation. The classification model can take a real or discrete value as input variables. This model then classifies the problem into two classes termed as two-class or binary classification problem. If a problem is classified into more than two classes, then it is termed as a multiclass classification approach. A problem where an example is assigned, multiple classes are termed as a multilabel classification problem. This model predicts a continuous value as the probability of given example belonging to each output class. The probabilities can be interpreted as likelihood or confidence of a given example belonging to each class. These predicted probabilities can be converted into class values by means of selecting a class label having the highest probabilities. There are many approaches to predict the skill of classification predictive model but the common approach is calculating the classification accuracy, in which the percentage of classifying correctly examples out of all prediction is made. Some common classification algorithms are decision tree, neural network, logistic regression, etc. (Paiva et al., 2019) The details of this approach are explained in subsequent chapters in the book.

**Clustering Model:** Clustering is an unsupervised method which is used with unlabeled data. Clustering is a process of dividing the data into groups such that each group shares some similarity with each other. There are many clustering schemes available for the clustering approach which will be discussed in detail in subsequent chapters. Some of the most common clustering techniques are k-mean clustering and hierarchical clustering. The k-mean clustering method describes the k-mean method which is used to cover a wide range of used cases. In this approach, the observations are partitioned into a pre-specified number of clusters, where the number of clusters is limited by means of the k-mean algorithm. The clusters are set in such a manner that each cluster shares some specific properties among them so that a specific approach can be used to abstract data or implement some approach to the cluster.

**Association model:** The association model is used to find the probability of relationship between data items with large data sets in different types of database. This approach finds its maximum application in medical science. This model can be used to show the number of frequency of occurrence of an item set in a transaction.

**Decision making:** Decision making is the last step or stage of image processing which is used for making the decisions based on the preprocessing and processing steps discussed above (Dubey, 2019).

Artificial intelligence (AI) and its sub categories have an exponential growth in its use for the various tasks. The corporate, academics, and government federal organizations have been making use of the AI algorithms for making various decisions. Machine learning or deep learning allows the machines to process a large amount of data that makes it better for the decision making as no fact will be left unturned. AI helps to not only process the data, but also automate the cognitive and physical tasks that further help to make better decisions. AI has been helpful in solving many new problems. Machine learning as per a survey conducted by DZone described that 14% of the task of AI is of making recommendations which is primarily helpful in the decision making. (Gharsellaoui et al., 2020; Hong et al., 2019)

Machine learning is able to augment the human intelligence with the accuracy of the machine thereby helping in the decision making. With the availability of the open frameworks of python, the machine learning algorithms are being written for different tasks and are being adopted with ease by the companies. It has been majorly used in the predictive analysis, automation tasks, and optimizations (Nieto et al., 2019).

Machine learning can be used for regression, classification, or clustering purposes. Supervised learning is the machine learning algorithms that can be used on the datasets consisting of the labels or the target classes and can carry out classification or regression (Cavalcante et al., 2019) Classification can be further categorized into binary or multi-class classification. Regression can be also popularly classified into two further categories of linear and logistic regression. Unsupervised learning can be used on the datasets without the target class. Clustering and association analysis are some of the popular algorithms that can be used as the unsupervised learning algorithms. Reinforcement learning is implemented on the agents, who can be made to learn the patterns of implementation of an algorithm using the penalties or rewards. Semi-supervised learning algorithms are becoming popular as the large datasets consist of data without labels with few records with complete target labels.

Machine learning has been successfully implemented in various places to carry out the decisions. In the customer driven markets, the decisions are to be taken after understanding the audience requirements. Dependent on the requirements and feasibility, the production of the products has to be decided. Machine learning helps to understand the past trends and based on those trends, it helps the authorities to predict the possible trend (Brown et al., 2020). Machine learning can also help in the customer relationship management by managing various factors and likings of the customers. The complex algorithms make it easier to process multimodal data and then provide the decisions with better accuracy.

Recommendation systems are in vogue, and machine learning algorithms have been successfully implemented on the various data inputs thereby helping to recommend products or other contents to the users. Feedbacks and backpropagation algorithm of neural networks help to understand the likings and disliking of the user. This can help the organizations to be more inclined toward the customized content for their users, thereby increasing the business opportunities.

Many expert systems have been developed to replicate the domain knowledge of the experts. Thus, these systems help to provide the reasoning as per the experts, thereby improving the decision-making capabilities. (Khosravi et al., 2019; Qolomany et al., 2019)

New machine learning techniques when combined with the big data carry out survey of feedbacks in various ways from the users, thereby analyzing the data and making sure that the opinions of the users help them to get better services from the service providers, which ultimately helps the corporate to take better decisions for implementing innovative ideas to better serve the customers. As more and more feedbacks are added to the data, the augmented analysis is carried out by the organizations.

## REFERENCES

Brown, L.A. et al. (2020). Machine learning algorithms in suicide prevention: clinician interpretations as barriers to implementation. *Journal of Clinical Psychiatry* 81.3, e12970–e12970.

Cavalcante, I.M. et al. (2019). A supervised machine learning approach to data-driven simulation of resilient supplier selection in digital manufacturing. *International Journal of Information Management* 49, 86–97.

Dubey, A. (2019). *Detection of liver cancer using image processing techniques.* 0315–0318. 10.1109/ICCSP.2019.8698033.

Gharsellaoui, S. et al. (2020). Multivariate Features extraction and effective decision making using machine learning approaches. *Energies* 13(3), 609.

Hong, H. et al. (2019). Landslide susceptibility assessment at the Wuning area, China: A comparison between multi-criteria decision making, bivariate statistical and machine learning methods. *Natural Hazards* 96(1), 173–212.

Khosravi, K. et al. (2019). A comparative assessment of flood susceptibility modeling using multi-criteria decision-making analysis and machine learning methods. *Journal of Hydrology* 573, 311–323.

Nieto, Y. et al. (2019). Supporting academic decision making at higher educational institutions using machine learning-based algorithms. *Soft Computing* 23(12), 4145–4153.

Paiva, F.D. et al. (2019). Decision-making for financial trading: A fusion approach of machine learning and portfolio selection. *Expert Systems with Applications* 115, 635–655.

Qolomany, B. et al. (2019). Leveraging machine learning and big data for smart buildings: A comprehensive survey. *IEEE Access* 7, 90316–90356.

Rajkomar, A., Dean, J., and Kohane, I. (2019). Machine learning in medicine. *New England Journal of Medicine* 380(14), 1347–1358.

Sarkar, S. et al. (2019). Application of optimized machine learning techniques for prediction of occupational accidents. *Computers & Operations Research* 106, 210–224.

Zhu, B., Jiang, H., and Cong, W. (2019). *A three-dimensional image processing method based on data layered two-dimensional normalization.* 1–4. 10.1109/ICSPCC46631.2019.8960913.

# 3 Role and Support of Image Processing in Big Data

## 3.1 INTRODUCTION

Images can be defined as a set of signals sensed by human eyes and processed by means of visual cortex in the brain, thus creating intensely deep experience of a scene, which is closely associated with objects and concepts perceived previously and recorded in the memory of a human brain. For computers, images can be raster images or vector images, where raster images are a sequence of pixels with discrete numerical values for color, whereas vector images are a sequence of color-annotated polygons. In order to analyze the image or video, geometric encoding needs to be transformed into constructs used to depict physical features, objects, and movement represented by the image or video. These constructs are analyzed in a logical manner by a computer through various image-processing techniques.

Big data analytics can be used for identifying underlying patterns and intrinsic inter-relationships among large volumes of data sets. Big data analytics is governed by two factors, that is, quantity of data and quality of data, where the amount of data helps in uncovering recurring data patterns, whereas the quality of data is used to find the reliability of data patterns. Thus, it can be concluded that the quality of data defines the fitness of data to be used in any form or as an application for modeling or predictive purposes (Agrawal and Srikant, 1994).

The role of big data analytics has been increasing in various fields of image processing from medical image processing to processing of satellite images. As most of the medical, satellite, and agriculture data are in huge amounts, which need fast processing for faster results, the need for big data analytics comes into existence (Sudhir, 2020).

Image processing needs innovative techniques to process images. With advancement in image processing, it is being used in many areas such as industries, organization, social organization, administrative divisions, healthcare, defense, etc. In image processing, images are taken as the input and then processed using different techniques to obtain a modified image or a video as the output. Collection of a large dataset of images and videos can be processed in a faster and efficient manner using the concept of big data application which stores the data as structured or unstructured data as a result of processing images using the concept of computing techniques. These processed data or big data that were integrated with image processing are used in the fields where the data in the form of image and video are large, such as education, healthcare, manufacturing, retail business, banking, finance, etc., thus showing greater potential in various fields.

In terms of latest updates, Google is working on integration approach of image processing with big data application by simulating the ability of the human brain to compute, evaluate, and choose the course of action by using massive neural networks. This makes the analytics of image and video science scalable using machine vision, rule-based decision engines, and multi-lingual speech recognition. Thus, image analytics can be considered as a potential solution for economic, social, industrial, and political issues.

## 3.2 BIG DATA MATHEMATICAL ANALYSIS THEORIES

Data can be collected in a collective manner or an individual manner. Some of the examples of collective data collection are data of smart cities, national geographic condition monitoring data, and earth observation data (Li et al., 2014). These collective data were gathered using sampling strategies and hence the quality of data is high, whereas the examples of individual data collection are data from social media in the Internet, electronic business data, etc. (Shaw and Fang, 2014).

With the advancement, most of the data are digital in nature and with the increase in storage capacity and methods of data collection, huge amounts of data are easily available. More and more data are created on every second basis, and in order to extract the information of concern from this huge amount of data, there is a need for good analytical methods.

Big data is a tool that is used to scale, distribute, and diversify and/or with timeliness requires the use of new technical architectures, analytics, and tools to enable the insight in order to unlock the new sources of business value.

Data are a set of values of quality and quantity variables which need some mathematical approaches for the analysis of big data. There are two mathematical theories for the analysis of big data as given in Figure 3.1.

### 3.2.1 INDEPENDENT AND IDENTICAL DISTRIBUTION THEORY (IID)

Big data science is an extension of statistics and machine learning which is used for data sampling and inferences. Thus, data science can be considered to provide an optimal decision about sample estimation of population in asymptotic theory along with function approximation in specific domain criteria. IID is used to simplify the underlying mathematics of many statistical inferences. The IID theorem states that the probability distribution of the sum (average) of IID variables with finite variance approaches a normal distribution or Gaussian distribution, which is an elementary

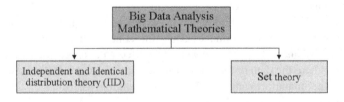

**FIGURE 3.1**    Mathematical theories for the analysis of big data.

probability distribution that can be extended into mixed Gaussian distribution and generalized distribution. Mixed Gaussian distribution and generalized distribution are used to solve complex problems, which are correspondingly related to non-linear models in algebra.

### 3.2.2 Set Theory

In the relational database, a relation is a set of tuples with the same attributes or fields. Thus, a tuple defines an object and its information, whereas a domain is a set of possible values for given attributes and hence can be considered as a constraint on values of attributes. Relational algebra consists of a set of tuples with five sets of operations, that is, as union, intersection, joining, projection, and selection, where union combines the tuples of two relations by removing the redundant tuples from the relation while intersection produces a combined result of tuples that share some relationship in common. The joint operation is the Cartesian product of two relations restricted by the same join criteria, whereas the projection operation is used for extracting useful information or attributes from tuples. Selection operation is used for selecting some tuples from the relation or table by limiting the results which fulfill the criteria. A mathematical space can be defined as a set assigned with added structure.

## 3.3 CHARACTERISTICS OF BIG DATA

The characteristics of big data can be defined by 3 Vs, namely, volume, variety, and velocity, where volume is the size of data which defines how much are the data in terms of gigabyte, petabyte, etc. The variety of data defines the different format and types of data as well as their different types of uses and different ways of analyzing the data, whereas the velocity of data refers to the rate of changing of data and their rate of creation. Some researchers also added the fourth V as veracity, which defines the quality of data that is used to characterize the big data as good, bad, or undefined data based on data inconsistency, latency, incompleteness, deception, ambiguity, and approximations.

The data volume can be quantified in terms of size as terabyte, petabyte, etc. as well as it can be quantified in terms of number of records, tables, transactions, and number of files. The reason for a large amount of data can be justified by the number of sources they come from such as logs, clickstream, social media, satellite data, etc. Data can be divided as unstructured, semi-structured, and structured data. The unstructured data are data such as text, human languages, etc., whereas the semi-structured data are data such as eXtensible Markup Language (XML) or Rich Site Summary feeds, and when these unstructured and semi-structured data are converted in a form that can be processed by a machine, then it is termed as structured data. There are some data which are hard to be categorized such as audio or video data. There are also streaming data which are available on real-time basis. There is also another type of data which is multi-dimensional data that can be drawn from a data warehouse to add historic context to big data. Thus, with big data, variety is just as big as volume. The velocity of data is the speed or frequency of generation or delivery of data.

## 3.4 DIFFERENT TECHNIQUES OF BIG DATA ANALYTICS

Raw or unprocessed data are a collection of numbers and characters. Data sampling and analytics is a method of extracting decision support information, whereas knowledge is derived from large experience on subjects. Thus, data can be considered as an observation about real phenomena. There are basically seven techniques used for big data analytics which are given in Figure 3.2 and are discussed below.

### 3.4.1 Ensemble Analysis

Ensemble data analysis can be used for a whole data set or large volume of data and hence be termed as multi-dataset analysis or multi-algorithm analysis. The whole dataset can be resampling data, labeled or unlabeled data, and prior and posterior data. The word ensemble comes from the concept of machine learning which uses supervised and unsupervised data for processing purpose. So, the machine learning approach ensemble analysis can be used for the analysis of data sets extracted from rough data sets using certain algorithms or a group of algorithms in order to provide an efficient analysis of the dataset. Ensemble analysis uses bootstrapping, boosting, stacking, bagging, and random forest learning approaches.

### 3.4.2 Association Analysis

This analysis is based on the logic that the relationship among set members corresponds to association in big data. Thus, association analysis can be used for multi-type, multi-sourcing, and multi-domain analysis of data. Association analysis is exemplified with association rule algorithms in data mining (Agarwal and Srikant, 1994) and data association in target tracking and link analysis in networks.

### 3.4.3 High-Dimensional Analysis

Mathematically, the dimension of objects is the information defined as the minimum number of coordinates needed to specify any point within it, whereas the dimension of vector space is the number of coordinates needed for specifying a vector. Thus, the dimension of an object is an intrinsic property which is independent of space where the object embeds. Thus dimensions can be defined as the number of perspectives from which the real world can be recognized. The issue with dimensionality in big data is that as the dimensionality increases, the volume of space increases in such a

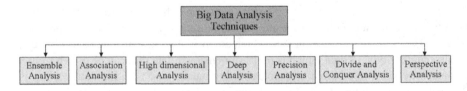

**FIGURE 3.2**     Different Big Data analysis techniques.

manner that available data become sparse; this sparsity leads to a statistically significant error and dissimilarity between objects in high-dimensional space.

In order to keep the variability of original variables as such by using the metrics of distance or variance, dimension reduction is used for reducing the number of random variables and finding a subset of the original variables, which leads to transformation of linear and non-linear dimension reduction. High-dimensional analysis uses the same concept for analysis of such high-dimension data.

### 3.4.4 DEEP ANALYSIS

The deep analysis technique uses the concept of deep learning for the analysis of a high amount of data. Thus, deep analysis is used for exploring complex structure properties of big data. Thus, deep analysis can be used for analyzing unobservable variables, hidden hierarchies, local correlations, hidden parameters, and the complex distribution of random variables. Deep analysis is thus defined as a deterministic or stochastic transform function from input to output.

### 3.4.5 PRECISION ANALYSIS

Precision is defined as resolution of the representation defined by the number of decimal or binary digits. It is also related to accuracy, which is defined as nearness of the calculated value to original value. A measurement system can be either accurate or precise, but not be both. When an experiment contains a systematic error, then increasing the size of samples generally increases precision but does not improve accuracy. Eliminating the systematic error improves accuracy but does not change precision. Thus, both of them are alternatives to each other.

Precision analysis is used for evaluating the veracity of data from the perspective of data utility and data quality. In order to form a relationship between big data and linguistics, the veracity is analogous to the semantics, and the utility is analogous to the pragmatics.

### 3.4.6 DIVIDE AND CONQUER ANALYSIS

Divide and conquer analysis is a computational strategy which is used for increasing the efficiency of solving the problem and velocity of big data computation. This analysis breaks a problem in a recursive manner into two or more sub-problems until the problem becomes simple enough to be solved directly in the stage of conquering. Upon completion, the solutions to sub-problems are combined into a solution to the original problem. Divide and conquer analysis gives better performance in multi-processor machines, and distinct sub-problems can be executed on different processors. Information is exchanged by passing messages between the processors.

### 3.4.7 PERSPECTIVE ANALYSIS

Perspective analysis is defined as a set of operations to process the structured and unstructured data by means of intermediate representations to create a set of prescriptions. These operations produce essential changes to variables, and variables influence target metrics over a specified time frame. Thus, perspective analysis can be used for representation of time series, detected patterns, and relationships between different sets of variables and metrics. A predictive model can be used for predicting the future time series of metric through forecast influencing variables. It first transforms the unstructured and structured data into analytically prepared data. Then this image analytics is used for providing real-time analysis and for future prediction in different sectors.

## 3.5 STEPS OF BIG DATA PROCESSING

Various processes involved in data analytics, from data collection to virtualization, in a phase-wise manner are as follows (Figure 3.3):

### 3.5.1 DATA COLLECTION

The collection process depends on the type of data from where we had to collect it and also on the type of data sources. Social sites usually produce unstructured data. In order to collect data from various sources, we have different tools available, and some of the common tools are as follows:

1. semantria
2. opinion Crawl
3. open Text
4. trackur

Semantria is used for text and sentiment analysis. It is an NLP (Natural language processing that have the ability to program a computer system to understand human language as it is spoken, it used technical techniques such as tokenization, parsing, tagging parts-of-speech, identifying sentiments or semantic relationships) based analysis engine which can be deployed in web, cloud, API (Application Programming Interface provide set of programming code that enables data transmission between one software product and another), etc. This is a propriety tool. Opinion Crawl is used for sentiment analysis with sense bot-based analysis engine. This tool can be deployed in web only and is an open source tool which is readily available. OpenText tool is used for content management and analysis which uses Red Dot and Captive analysis engine. It can be used for window-based server application and is at the enterprise level not an open source. Trackur is used for influence and sentiment

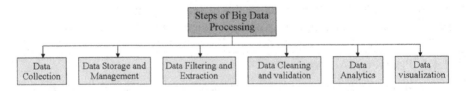

**FIGURE 3.3**   Various steps for data processing.

analysis which uses trackur as the analysis engine. This can be used for web or social media-based application and is a propriety tool (Komal, 2018).

### 3.5.2 DATA STORAGE AND MANAGEMENT

Storage of these large data is also a challenging task; some of the traditional methods of data storage are relational databases, data marts, and data warehouses. The data are uploaded to the storage from operational data stores using Extract, Transform, Load (ETL), or Extract, Load, Transform, tools which extract the data from outside sources, transform the data to fit operational needs, and finally load the data into the database or data warehouse. Thus, it can be concluded that any data which are stored are first cleaned, transformed, and cataloged before they are made available for mining purpose or analytical purpose. Some of the common data storage and management tools available are as follows:

1. Apache HBase (Hadoop database)
2. CouchDB
3. MongoDB
4. Apache Cassandra
5. Apache Ignite
6. Oracle NoSQL Database

Apache Hbase (Hadoop database) is a column-oriented data model which provides zero downtime during node failure and thus provides good redundancy. It provides concurrency by means of optimistic concurrency. CouchDB is a document-oriented data model which also provides concurrency by means of optimistic concurrency and also provides secondary indexes. MongoDB is also a document-oriented data model which provides nearly the same features as CouchDB. Apache Cassandra is a column-oriented data model which provides zero downtime on node failure and hence provides good redundancy to the system. It also provides concurrency to the system. Apache Ignite is a multi-model data model which provides nearly all the features such as zero downtime on node failure, concurrency, and secondary indexes and hence mostly in use. Oracle NoSQL Database is a key-value-based data model which provides concurrency and secondary indexes.

### 3.5.3 DATA FILTERING AND EXTRACTION

The data filtering and extraction process is used for creating structured data from unstructured data collected from previous steps. Various tools that are used for data filtering and extraction purposes are as follows:

1. Pentaho
2. OctoParse
3. ParseHub
4. Mozenda
5. Content Grabber

Pentaho is used to produce a structured output from unstructured data. This tool has ETL and data mining capabilities. It is available as a free and enterprise version based on the number of functionalities of the tool in use. OctoParse is used for spreadsheets to produce structured spreadsheets. It has a feature of webscrapping. It is also available as a free and unpaid version. The ParseHub tool can be used for preparing structured data of Excel, CSV (comma-separated values file), and Google sheets. It is a cloud-based desktop application. Mozenda is used for producing the structured data for JSON (JavaScript Object Notation is a lightweight data-interchange format), XML, and CSV file. It also has a feature of webscrapping. However, Content Grabber is used for preparing structured data for CSV, XML, and databases. It also has an additional feature of webscrapping with debugging and error handling.

### 3.5.4 DATA CLEANING AND VALIDATION

The next step after data filtering and extraction is data cleaning and validation. Data cleaning is used to reduce the processing time and computational speed of analytical tools and engines. It is not a mandatory condition to use this tool. Some of the latest and mostly used cleaning tools are as follows:

1. Data Cleaner
2. Map Reduce
3. Rapidminer
4. OpenRefine
5. Talend

Data Cleaner is used for record and field processing with additional features of data transformation, validation, and reporting. This tool is integrated with the Hadoop database. Map Reduce is a parallel data-processing model which has additional features of searching, sorting, clustering, and translation. This tool is also a part of the Hadoop database. Rapidminer is a graphical user interface and a batch-processing model with additional features of filtering, aggregation, and merging. It is used for internal database integration. OpenRefine is a batch-processing model with additional features of transforming data from one form to another. It can be used with web services and external data. Talend is a streaming and batch-processing model with an additional feature of data integration. It can be used with numerous databases.

### 3.5.5 DATA ANALYTICS

Collection of large data is not the only solution for taking efficient decision at right time; there is a need for faster and efficient methods for analyzing large data in a faster and efficient manner. Since traditional methods are not so efficient for analyzing such large data, developing new tools and techniques for big data analytics along with advanced architecture for storing and managing such large data is the need of hour. Elgendy et al. (2016) proposed a big data analytics and decision framework, which integrates big data analytics tools with a decision-making process to provide efficient results in an optimized time period. In recent years, a large number of tools, which provide many additional properties apart from analytics, have been developed. Some of the tools discussed below are as follows:

1. Hive
2. Apache Spark
3. Apache Storm
4. Map Reduce
5. Qubole
6. Flink

Hive is a streaming processing model which supports structured query language (SQL) and provides a high latency to the system. Apache Spark is a mini/micro-batch, streaming model which uses scala java and python language for operation and integration. Apache storm is another version of Apache which is a record at a time-processing model which uses any language for integration and operation and provides better latency than Apache Spark. Map Reduce is a parallel-processing model which uses languages like Java, Ruby, Python, and C++ for its operation. Qubole is a stream-processing and ad-hoc query-based processing model which supports languages like Python, Scala, R, and Go. Flink is a batch and stream-processing model which supports languages like scala, java, and python for its operation.

### 3.5.6 Data Visualization

Now when analytics of data is performed, one of the last operations requires visualization of these analyzed data in a readable format. The data visualization process involves visualizing the data in a form that can be readable. There are various tools used for the data visualization process but most of them are integrated versions of data extraction, analysis, and visualization. Some of the common tools used for data visualization are as follows:

1. Data Wrapper
2. Tableau
3. Orange
4. Qlik
5. Google fusion table
6. CartoDB
7. Chartio
8. Gephi

Data wrapper is an open source tool which is compatible with CSV, PDF, Excel, and CMS. It has ready-to-use codes which produce output in the form of bar charts, line charts, maps, and graphs. Tableau is also an open source tool which is compatible with the database and API which produce output in the form of maps, bar charts, and scatter plots. Orange is also an open source tool with data source compatibility of Apache Cassandra files, SQL tables, and data tables or can paint random data which need no programming and can be used to produce output as scatter plots, bar charts, trees, dendrograms, networks, and heat maps. Qlik is licensed software with data source compatibility of databases, spreadsheets, and websites. It produces the output as dashboard and app. Google fusion table is a Google's web service which supports data source compatibility of comma-separated value file formats. It produces the output in the form of pie charts, bar charts, line plots, scatter plots, and timelines. CartoDB is also an open source tool with data source compatibility of location data, plenty of data types which use CartoCSS language, and results in the form of maps. Chartio is again an open source tool with multiple data sources as data source compatibility which uses its own visual query language and produces output as line, bar, pie charts, and dashboard sharing as PDF reports. Gephi is again an open source tool which uses CSV, GraphML, GML, and GDF spreadsheet as data source compatibility and produces the output as graphs and networks.

## 3.6 IMPORTANCE OF BIG DATA IN IMAGE PROCESSING

Image processing uses the computer proficiency in analyzing the digital images. Image technology is nowadays used in various applications like oceanography, medical imaging, remote sensing, currency recognition, etc. Images and videos are of large size consisting of large data sets because of a large set of pixels, hence processing of such a large set of data demands bid data techniques for fast processing and analyzing of these large size images and videos. These digitized images are analyzed and manipulated in order to improve the domineering phase in image processing, popularly termed as "image segmentation." The process of image segmentation is used to extract the required object of concern from the existing image. Thus, image segmentation is used to extract that part of image which is of concern and any user will focus only on this part rather than the entire image. There are many image-processing techniques that are used for separating different color levels of images in order to make them two-dimensional signals. Image processing can also be used for processing of distinct color levels into three-dimensional signals with the third dimension. The resultant signal extracted by means of image processing is used to analyze some knowledge and help in the decision-making process.

In order to process large data, there is a need for powerful software as well as hardware. There are different techniques proposed by different researchers in the field of image processing and big data analytics which can be used for processing of such large data. But in order to interact with such large data, there is a need for obtaining the insight of interaction and integration of these two broader fields in order to explore and exploit the best benefits from these two techniques.

There are many researchers who use the techniques of big data in the field of image processing; some are discussed in this section. Sudhir et al. (2020) introduced the concept of image mining which includes the phases such as image segmentation. Image mining deals with mining of hidden data, image data, and its supplementary configurations that are accrued indistinctly in the image. Image mining involves various steps which make it complex such as data mining, image retrieval, pattern recognition, indexing scheme, etc. This method provides a space for storage of images in an efficient manner along with convenient access and can also be used for distinguishing the system of data configurations and makes information lesser than the representation of the given image. This technique combines functions like storage of images, extraction of features from images, indexing of images, processing of images, pattern knowledge and discovery, and image retrieval.

Mohan and Porwal (2015) focused their study on image analysis methods using multispectral where they focused on availability of spatial aspects of the particular objects of interest, that is, their shape, texture, and spectral properties with few wavelength bands. They suggested that the spectral technique can be used for obtaining the images.

## 3.7 HADOOP

Hadoop is a framework which allows storage and processing of big data in a distributed environment using a simple programming model. Hadoop uses the cluster approach where different nodes are arranged in a cluster format to process data in distributed fashion. Hadoop is an open source tool with advantages of scale-out storage and distributed processing. Hadoop uses Map Reduce which is a programming model of Hadoop. Hadoop also provides redundancy using distributed storage and transferring code. Thus, Hadoop can recover itself in case of failure of a single node. The programming approach in Hadoop is also easy as it uses the Map Reduce framework which is easier to code. Hadoop performs automated partition of data and allocation of task to different nodes and provides communication among nodes. Thus, it makes the programmer free from the fear of code, and the programmer can just focus on the logic implementation of the system.

Hadoop is managed by Apache Software foundation and is open source in nature designed to handle large data. Map Reduce of Hadoop uses a batch-processing technique for analyzing the big data and historic data sets. Map Reduce breaks big data into small sets across multiple machines to perform this task. The user can scale the network to multiple nodes in a cluster in Hadoop. These multiple nodes can act in parallel to give better throughput of the system to process a large data set. Some of the features of Hadoop are as follows:

1. Reliable
2. Economical
3. Flexible
4. Scalable

Hadoop is termed as reliable in the sense that it can recover itself in case of failure; that is, it keeps the backup of data or replication of data and also of nodes such that in case of failure it can use these backup data to provide the reliability to the system. It is also economical as it is an open source tool which is readily available and hence the distribution of Hadoop is free; you need to pay only for its services. Flexibility and scalability are related to each other. Hadoop is termed as flexible due to its scalable nature as it is free from the number of nodes. Any nodes can be added or removed from Hadoop without affecting the entire system which adds to the flexibility of the system and also it supports *n* number of nodes that can be added to the system which adds to the scalability of the system.

## 3.8 PARTS OF HADOOP ARCHITECTURE

The main architecture of Hadoop consists of two parts:

1. Hadoop Distribution File System (HDFS)
2. Map Reduce

### 3.8.1 HDFS

The HDFS is used for storage purpose; it consists of a set of machines in a cluster format which is used together for storing data. The cluster is divided into two types of nodes as the namenode and datanode. The namenode is the admin of the system, whereas the datanode is used for storage purpose. Thus, the HDFS provides a distributed file system design for better efficiency. The HDFS provides redundancy to the system as removal of any system will not cause the failure of the system. It also supports large data due to its distributed architecture. It processes the data in a parallel manner for providing better efficiency. In the HDFS, to increase the capacity of storage, the data are partitioned based on criteria and these partition data are sent across different machines. They store large files based on streaming data access patterns using cluster commodity hardware. The streaming data pattern follows write once and read many-times pattern for providing efficient processing of data. Thus, breaking large data into small chunks of data helps large data to be stored in small segments termed as disk to reduce the cost of seek. These data are in the form of blocks which are integral multiples of disk block size. The default size of each block in the HDFS is 64 MB. Thus, this fixed size block makes calculation of data easier that can be stored on given disk and eliminates metadata concern.

Hadoop creates two types of nodes which are arranged in a client–server manner. Here, the server node is termed as namenode, whereas the client node works as a datanode as shown in Figure 3.4. The purpose of the namenode is to manage the file system namespace by means of maintaining the file system tree and metadata for all the files and directories in the tree. It stores the information of architecture persistently on local disk in two-file format as namespace image and edit log. The namenode is responsible for managing this file system and for regulating the datanode access to these files, and it is also responsible for executing the file system operations like opening, renaming, and closing of files and directories. On the other hand, the datanode is responsible for read-write operations on a file system as per the request from users. The datanode is also responsible for operations such as block creation, deletion, and replication as per the instruction of the namenode. Based on the request from the user or namenode, the datanode stores and retrieves blocks and reports back the results to the namenode with the list of blocks they are storing in a

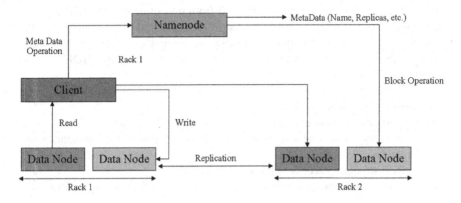

**FIGURE 3.4**   HDFS architecture.

periodic manner. As the dependency is on the namenode as without namenode there would be no way to reconstruct the files from the blocks on the datanode if lost; in order to avoid this, a backup is maintained. This backup is maintained by means of installing a secondary namenode which periodically merges the namespace image with edit logs to prevent edit logs from being large enough. This secondary namenode runs on different machines as it needs complete central processing unit (CPU) for processing, and it also requires more memory to perform the merge operation. Any request from the user will be accessed by communicating with the namenode and datanode.

Figure 3.4 shows the architecture of the HDFS, from which we can see that all metadata operations are performed in the namenode. Metadata are data, which contain information about a list of files, blocks for each file, and a list of nodes for each block file attributes like time, replication factor, etc. Thus, these metadata are somewhat like an index of a book and contain all information about the book that which content is located at which place. They also store transaction logs like record of file creation, file deletion, etc. Thus, the entire structure of file directory and location of data block is located in the namenode, whereas the metadata store in the main memory of namenode. Thus, the namenode contains only metadata not the actual data. Any request from the user will first interact with the namenode for metadata operations which helps in extracting information from the datanode which contains actual information. Thus, the datanode is considered as book chapters which contain actual information about the subject. Any user can perform read or write operation to datanode by means of java interface or the HDFS command line. In order to make this read and write operation in the datanode, the use of the namenode will be there by means of metadata operations. Thus, any request will be directed from the namenode through metadata operation to that particular datanode in order to access information from a particular datanode.

Datanodes act as a client of the system and are deployed on each machine in order to provide actual storage. These datanodes make the read/write request for client. Cheap replica can be made for the datanode and can be in any number. Thus, it can be inferred that datanodes act as a database for the file system which stores and retrieves blocks as per the request from user or namenode and responds to these requests by means of sending a list of blocks stored under them. Thus, the HDFS is used to provide fault detection and recovery and stores a large data set by means of the clustering approach. The other advantages of the HDFS are as follows:

1. Support distributed storage and processing
2. Support command interface for interacting with the HDFS
3. Provide easy status checking of cluster using built-in servers of namenode and datanode
4. Support streaming access to file system data
5. Support permission and authentication based feature for security of files.

### 3.8.2 MAP REDUCE

Map Reduce is a programming model which is used for processing of data. The Map Reduce algorithm is divided into two important tasks, that is, Map and Reduce where a map is used for taking the data as per user requirement and then these raw data are converted into a set of data in a processed form where individual elements are broken down into tuples. On the other hand, the output of this Map function is fed into Reduce function and those tuples are combined into a small set of tuples to reduce data into formatted data as per instructions from users. Thus, Map Reduce is used for scaling data processing over multiple computing nodes. The working of Map Reduce is divided into three stages as follows:

1. Map Stage: In this stage, the map processes the input data in the form of file or directory and stores it in the HDFS.
2. Reduce Stage: This stage combines the shuffle stage and reduction stage. This stage processes the data that come as input from map stage.
3. Inputs and Outputs: This stage takes the input from the reduction stage and processes it using key values as per request from the user and based on these key values which can be scalar or composite forms the output as per requirement of the user (Figure 3.5).

Map Reduce performs its task by means of Job Tracker and Task Tracker, where Job Tracker distributes the task-to-task tracker, whereas Task Tracker runs these

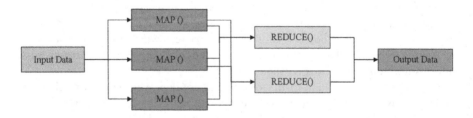

**FIGURE 3.5**    Map Reduce architecture.

programs on datanodes. Job Tracker is associated with the namenode, whereas the Task Tracker is associated with the datanode. Thus, it can be concluded that the namenode and datanode are machines, whereas Job Tracker and Task Tracker are programs that run on these machines to make the task complete.

## 3.9 WORKING OF HADOOP ARCHITECTURE

Technology advancement makes all the data to be migrated from the file-based system to computer-based systems. Handling such large data is a challenging task for IT professionals. In order to solve the problem of large data, there are multiple techniques and technology available and proposed by many researchers, but to explain the working of big data, we are explaining the working of Hadoop. The Hadoop architecture framework consists of four modules as follows:

1. Hadoop Common
2. Hadoop Yarn
3. HDFS
4. Hadoop Map reduce

Hadoop common consists of java utilities and libraries that are required by Hadoop modules. Hadoop yarn is defined as the framework for searching jobs and is responsible for cluster resource management. The HDFS is a distributed file system used to provide large throughput access to the application data, whereas Hadoop Map reduce is used for parallel processing of large data sets to process information in a faster manner.

Map Reduce and the HDFS are defined as two most important pillars of the Hadoop system as shown in Hadoop architecture in Figure 3.6, where map reduce is used for processing of whole data sets for whole query and thus has the ability to process as ad-hoc queries to provide results. It performs such activity by means of a programming model which is used for abstracting the problem from the disk reads

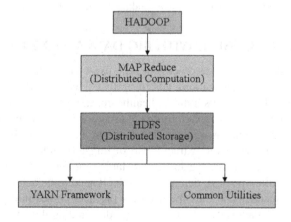

**FIGURE 3.6**  Hadoop architecture.

and writes and then transforming it into computation over set of keys and values. Thus, Map Reduce is defined as programming model which is used for processing and generating large data sets in parallel processing using a distributed algorithm in a cluster manner. Map Reduce thus helps in unlocking the data which was previously achieved on tape or disk.

The HDFS, on the other hand, is used for storing the data in an organized manner. Thus, Hadoop in combination with Map Reduce and the HDFS is used for providing a reliable storage with efficient analysis systems for big data sets.

Hadoop runs application using a map-reduce algorithm which processes data parallels on different CPU nodes. The working of Hadoop can be categorized into three stages as follows:

1. In the first stage, user by means of application can submit a job to Hadoop for specific process by means of specifying variables like location of input and output files within a file system. This stage consists of java classes in the form of jar file which contains implementation of map and reduce functions.
2. In the second stage, Hadoop job client submit the job and configuration to job tracker which is responsible for distribution of the work to the slave, scheduling tasks, and monitoring of this job.
3. In the third stage, the task tracker at different nodes executes the task as per Map Reduce implementation and the output of this reduce function is stored in output files in the file system.

Thus, Hadoop is more beneficial than the traditional file system in the following manner:

1. Hadoop makes writing and testing of distributed system in a faster manner.
2. Hadoop makes process independent of hardware.
3. Hadoop makes dynamic addition and removal of server from the cluster without affecting the operation.
4. Hadoop being implemented in java makes it compatible on all platforms.

## 3.10 IMAGE PROCESSING WITH BIG DATA ANALYTICS

With more inventions in image processing, the use of image processing has been extended to industries, organizations, administrative divisions, various social organizations, economic/business institutions, healthcare, defense, etc. Image processing takes images as input and using various image-processing techniques produces modified and enlarges images as output. The image processing can be applicable to images as well as on videos to extract a part of image or video which needs to be addressed. The image processing involves a large amount of data in the form of images from satellite, medical, defense, etc. which need to be addressed in an efficient and faster manner and thus the need for big data comes into picture. Image processing with big data is used to process large data and used to store this data in a structured or unstructured format as a result of processing images by means of different computation techniques. This big data analytics integrating with image processing can be used for mining knowledge from the data created which can be used in different sectors like medical, education, defense, agriculture, satellite mapping, etc.

Image processing processes the images by means of applying different computation techniques. It takes images as input and enhances the properties of image to extract the features of importance in order to make it less complex for the purpose of study. Different image-processing techniques are as follows:

1. **Visualization:** This is technique used to set up a communication by means of messages using images, diagrams, and animation. One of the visualization techniques is visual imagery. Image visualization can be performed by two methods. One is abstract visualization and another is model-based scientific visualization, where abstract visualization uses 2D and 3D techniques, whereas model-based scientific visualization uses digitally constructed real images for its purpose.

2. **Image restoration:** Image restoration is used for clearing noise and recovering the loss of resolution. Thus, it is used to recover the original image from the degraded image. This can be achieved by various software such as paint, Adobe Photoshop, NET, etc.

3. **Image retrieval:** It is a process of retrieving image from a large database. It involves different techniques such as Content-based Image Retrieval, Human-oriented Image Retrieval, Document-based Image Retrieval, Content-based Visual Information Retrieval, etc.

4. **Image recognition:** It is used to recognize the image object. It takes input as image and gives the recognized object as output.

5. **Image Enhancement:** It is used to enhance the required object of concern to high quality which can be addressed easily. There are different techniques used for image enhancement such as morphology, filtering, etc.

## 3.11 IMAGE PREPROCESSING

Image preprocessing enhances the image by means of modifying the value of pixel either in terms of its brightness or contrast for its visual impact which may occur due to blurriness due to capturing from low conventional/digital cameras or from the images obtained from the satellite pictures. Image preprocessing can be divided into two types as follows:

i. Static Thresholding
ii. Dynamic Thresholding

The above-mentioned techniques of image processing with big data techniques can be used for processing and analytics of big data received from satellites, cameras, etc.

Digitized images are analyzed and manipulated for the eminence of image. There is a process of image segmentation which contributes for this integration. The image segmentation process is used to separate the object of concern from the original image which can be used for the purpose of analysis. There are different techniques that are being used in the field of image processing and big data analytics which is discussed in the chapters in the subsequent section.

Authors like Wang et al. (2008) proposed an algorithm for denoising and extraction of contour. The proposed algorithm uses features such as feature extraction, smoothing of images, image reconstruction, enhancement of quality of images, etc. These features along with canny edge detection, median filtering, contour tracing, and wavelet transform help in processing of images captured which have spatial redundancy and high noise. Hu et al. (2014) classified a big data framework into four components as data analytics, data acquisition, data generation, and data storage. He used Hadoop as a tool of data analytics to perform his research and conclude his result. Paulchamy et al. (2017) performed image detection, classification, and recognition on vehicle on the road using MATLAB software. In his experiment, he suggested that the existing model involves the region of interest (ROI) and pixel classification technique which requires a large amount of database. He uses other techniques like raspberry pi, E-speak, etc. for slowing the vehicle at road sign such as speed break, school zone, etc. Pandian and Balasubramanian (2017) revealed that use of image processing is increasing and gathering the data of image leads to generation of gigabyte of space which needs to be handled. The need for organizing, examining, retrieving, and recovering of images from these large data is the demand for computer vision with database management system. Goutam et al. (2016) studied the role of big data and its technologies in the field of map reduce. He defined that map reduce plays an important role in creating key and value. He focused his research on structured and unstructured data, whereas in unstructured data he focused on data of images which got erroneous due to noise and other factors. For augmenting the quality of a tainted image, the mapper function could accomplish acceptably and precisely in creating the data related to key and value pair. This program again can be used as a reducer function for the auxiliary dispensation of major prominence. The author also proposes histogram technique for equalization which can be used for image improvement. This technique in combination with map reduce can be used for effectual and precise process.

Thus, it can be concluded that with advancement in image processing, various applications are there in image processing which process the data of images and videos which produce a large amount of data and which need to be stored and processed in an efficient manner for better results. Image processing application in areas such as medical, remote sensing, defense, etc. where there is a need of faster image processing as the data in these cases are very high and the processing and result require to be in an efficient manner, accurate and faster. Thus, the need for big data analysis comes into picture which helps in processing large data of image and video in a faster and effective manner so that the result can be achieved in a short span of time with effective results. The big data are also used for efficient storing of data in an organized manner. The big data application with image processing can be integrated with other tools such as machine learning, fuzzy logic, etc. for increasing the efficiency of the system which provides the result in an efficient manner in terms of accuracy and time involved.

# REFERENCES

Agrawal, R. and Srikant, R. (1994). Fast algorithms for mining association rules in large databases. In *Proceedings of the 20th International Conference on Very Large Data Bases*, pp. 487–499.

Archana, B.P.K., Bruno, A.D., and Gopala, I.D.M. (2017). *A novel approach towards road safety based on investigational survey using image processing and user interface system*, pp. 105–108.

Buddhiraju, K. M. and Alok, P. (2015). Hyperspectral image processing and analysis. *Current Science* 108, 833–841.

Elgendy, N. and Elragal (2016). Big data analytics in support of the decision making process. *Procedia Computer Science* 100, 1071–1084. 10.1016/j.procs.2016.09.251.

Goutam, D.S. and Gupta, S.D. (2016). Big data analytics: Image enhancement based approach. *International Journal Advanced Research Computer Science Software Engineering* 6(5), 570–573.

Hu, H., Wen, Y., Chua, T.-S., and Li, X. (2014). Toward scalable systems for big data analytics: A technology tutorial. *Access, IEEE* 2, 652-687. 10.1109/ACCESS.2014.2332453.

Komal, M. (2018). *A review paper on big data analytics tools*.

Pandian, A. and Ramasamy, B. (2017). *Performance analysis of texture image retrieval in curvelet, contourlet, and local ternary pattern using DNN and ELM classifiers for MRI brain tumor images*. 10.1007/978-981-10-2104-6_22.

Sudhir, R. (2020). *A Survey on Image Mining Techniques: Theory and applications*.

Wang, Y. Zheng, J., Zhou, H., and Shen, L. (2008). Medical image processing by denoising and contour extraction. In *Proceedings of the 2008 IEEE International Conference on Information and Automation, ICIA 2008*, pp. 618–623. 10.1109/ICINFA.2008.4608073.

# Part II

## Advanced Image Processing Technical Phases for Big Data Analysis

# 4 Advanced Image Segmentation Techniques Used for Big Data

## 4.1 INTRODUCTION

An image is one of the best outcomes from rendering data, and it contains heaps of helpful data. Understanding the image and collecting or extracting important information from the image to perform some work is a significant area of utilization in computerized image technology. The initial phase in understanding the image is image segmentation. In practical approaches, we are frequently not intrigued by all pieces of the image, however just by specific areas that have similar qualities. Image segmentation is one of the best strategies in image processing and computer vision technology. It is likewise a significant reason for image recognition. It depends on specific models to partition an input information image into quantities of similar nature of the category so as to remove the areas which individuals are keen on. It is also the fundamental strategy for image analysis and comprehension of images feature extraction and image recognition.

Numerous image segmentation algorithms are usually utilized. This chapter fundamentally depicts some of the accompanying advanced algorithms for basic examination. Among them, the first is the threshold segmentation technique. Threshold segmentation is one of the best generally utilized segmentation techniques in the list of region-based segmentation algorithms (Haralick and Shapiro, 1985). Its quintessence is to naturally decide the ideal threshold as indicated by a specific basis and utilize these pixels as indicated by the growth level to accomplish clustering. The essential thought of regional growth algorithms is to join pixels with comparable properties to frame the region, that is, for every region to be separated first to discover a seed pixel as a growth point and afterward combine the encompassing neighborhood with comparable properties of the pixel in its zone. At that point, it is the edge detection segmentation method. The edge detection segmentation algorithm alludes to the utilization of various locales of the pixel gray or shading intermittence recognition area of the edge so as to accomplish image segmentation (Marr & Hildreth, 1980). The following is the cluster-based segmentation technique. The algorithm is dependent on clustering based on the closeness between things as the standard of class division; that is, it is separated into a few subclasses as per the interior structure of the example set with the goal that a similar set of tests are as comparable as could reasonably be expected, and the distinctions are not as comparative as could reasonably be expected (Wu and Leahy, 1993). The latter is weakly supervised learning in CNN-based image segmentation. It alludes to the issue of doling out a semantic mark to each pixel in the image and comprises three states (Lin et al., 2016).

1. Providing an object specific image.
2. Providing an object boundary.
3. Object area of an image is marked with a partial pixel.

At present, advanced image segmentation techniques are used to enhance the smoothness and efficiency of image processing. Some of the specific operations of the segmentation method are assorted and complex, and there is no unified standard. This chapter closely describes and compares the over-selected advanced image segmentation strategies and gains from the weaknesses to dissect better arrangements and make future gauges.

## 4.2 CLASSIFICATION OF IMAGE SEGMENTATION TECHNIQUES

Several existing image segmentation techniques which are used are covered in this section. These techniques have their own significance. These techniques can be drawn closer to two essential methodologies of segmentation, for example, region-based and edge-based methodologies. Each procedure can be applied to various images to perform the required segmentation. Portions of the propelled image segmentation technique are as follows (Figure 4.1):

### 4.2.1 REGION-BASED SEGMENTATION

Region-based image segmentation methods are methods that segment the image into numerous regions that have similar proprieties. There are three basic techniques used in this method (Senthilkumaran and Rajesh, 2009; Angelina et al., 2012; Khokher et al., 2013) (Figure 4.2).

#### 4.2.1.1 Threshold Segmentation

Threshold segmentation is the least difficult technique for image segmentation and furthermore one of the most widely used parallel segmentation techniques. It is a basic segmentation algorithm that legitimately separates the image grayscale data, which is dependent on the gray estimation of various targets. Threshold segmentation

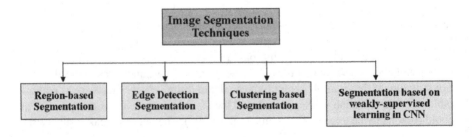

**FIGURE 4.1** Classification of image segmentation techniques.

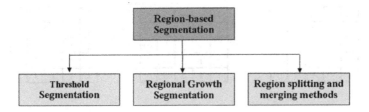

**FIGURE 4.2** Basic techniques of region-based segmentation.

can be separated into local and global threshold methods. The global threshold method isolates the image into two districts of the objective and the foundation by a solitary threshold (Davis, 1975). The local threshold method needs to choose various segmentations of the threshold and partitions the image into numerous objective districts and foundations by different edges.

The most generally utilized threshold segmenting algorithm is the biggest interclass difference strategy, which chooses an all-inclusive ideal threshold by augmenting the fluctuation between classes. Furthermore, there are techniques such as entropy-based threshold segmentation strategies, the error minimization technique, co-occurrence matrix strategy, moment preserving strategy, basic statistical strategy, probability relaxation strategy, fuzzy set technique, and threshold strategies joined with different strategies (Kohler, 1981).

The threshold segmentation technique holds various advantages. The advantages are that the computation is straightforward and the operation performance rate is high. Specifically, when the objective and the foundation have high complexity, the division impact can be acquired. The disadvantage is that it is hard to obtain precise outcomes for image segmentation issues where there is no noteworthy grayscale distinction or a large overlapping of the grayscale esteems in the images. Because it just considers the gray data of the image without thinking about the spatial data of the image, it is delicate to the commotion and grayscale unevenness, causing it to be regularly joined with different strategies (Pal and Pal, 1993).

## 4.2.1.2 Regional Growth Segmentation

The regional growth method of image segmentation is typically based on serial region segmenting algorithms. Its fundamental thought is to have comparable properties of the pixels together to shape a region (Wani and Batchelor, 1994). The technique requires first choosing a seed pixel and afterward blending the comparable pixels around the seed pixel into the locale where the seed pixel is found.

Figure 4.3 shows a case of a realized seed point for the region developed. Figure 4.3(a) demonstrates the need to part the image. There are two known seed pixels (set apart as gray squares) which are set up for regional development. The rule utilized here is that if the total estimation of the gray worth distinction between the pixel and the seed pixel is viewed as not exactly a specific threshold value T, the pixel is remembered for the area where the seed pixel is found. Figure 4.3(b) shows the regional growth results at T = 3, and the entire plot is all around separated into two regions. Figure 4.3(c) shows the aftereffects of the region growth at T = 6, and the entire plot is in a zone. Along these lines, the decision of the threshold value is significant (Tang, 2010).

| 1 | 0 | 4 | 7 | 5 |
|---|---|---|---|---|
| 1 | 0 | 5 | 7 | 7 |
| 0 | 1 | 5 | 5 | 5 |
| 2 | 0 | 5 | 6 | 5 |
| 2 | 2 | 5 | 6 | 4 |

(a)

| 1 | 1 | 5 | 5 | 5 |
|---|---|---|---|---|
| 1 | 1 | 5 | 5 | 5 |
| 1 | 1 | 5 | 5 | 5 |
| 1 | 1 | 5 | 5 | 5 |
| 1 | 1 | 5 | 5 | 5 |

(b)

| 1 | 1 | 1 | 1 | 1 |
|---|---|---|---|---|
| 1 | 1 | 1 | 1 | 1 |
| 1 | 1 | 1 | 1 | 1 |
| 1 | 1 | 1 | 1 | 1 |
| 1 | 1 | 1 | 1 | 1 |

(c)

**FIGURE 4.3**  Examples of regional growth.

The regional growth techniques have several advantages that regional growth as a rule isolates the associated region with similar attributes and gives worthy boundary data and segmenting results. The possibility of regional growth is straightforward and requires just a couple of seed focuses to finish. The development rules in the developing procedure can be openly indicated. Finally, it can pick different standards simultaneously. The impediment is that the computational expense is enormous (Angelina et al., 2012). Additionally, the noise and grayscale unevenness can prompt voids and over-division. The latter is the shadow impact on the image which is regularly not generally excellent (Ugarriza et al., 2009).

### 4.2.1.3 Region Splitting and Merging Methods

The region splitting- and merging-based image segmentation techniques utilize two essential procedures, for example, parting and merging for partitioning an image into different regions. Parting represents iteratively partitioning an image into districts having comparable attributes, and merging contributes to the contiguous comparable regions. In Figure 4.4(a), the graph shows the division dependent on the quad tree. The fundamental calculation ventures for region growth and merging are (Kaganami and Beiji, 2009):

Let "$p$" be the original image and "$T$" be the particular predicate.

- First of all the $R_1$ is equal to $p$.
- Each region is divided into quadrants for which $T(R_i) = False$.
- If for every region, $T(R_j) = True$, then merge adjacent regions $R_i$ and $R_j$ such that $T(R_i \cup R_j) = True$.
- Repeat step 3 until merging is impossible.

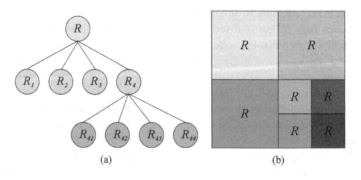

(a)          (b)

**FIGURE 4.4**  Region split and merging technique based on the quad tree.

## 4.2.2 Edge Detection Segmentation

The object edges are considered as broken local attributes of the images, that is, the most significant piece of the image changes in nearby brightness, for example, the gray estimation of the transformation, color shading change, surface changes, etc. (Davis, 1975). The utilization of discontinuities to distinguish the edges in the image is done in order to accomplish the motivation behind image segmentation.

There is consistently a gray edge between two adjoining regions with various gray qualities in the image, and there is a situation where the gray worth is not constant. This brokenness can regularly be identified utilizing subordinate tasks, and subsidiaries can be determined to utilize differential administrators (Senthilkumaran and Rajesh, 2009). Parallel edge identification is frequently done by methods for a spatial area differential administrator to perform image segmentation by tangling its format and image. Parallel edge recognition is commonly utilized as a technique for image preprocessing. The general first-request differential administrators are the Prewitt operator, Roberts' operator, and Sobel operator (Kundu and Pal, 1986). The second-order differential equation of operator has nonlinear operators, for example, Laplacian operator, Kirsch operator, and Wallis operator.

### 4.2.2.1 Sobel Operator

The Sobel operator is predominantly utilized for detecting edges, and it is in fact a discrete differential operator used to ascertain the estimate of the angle of the image luminance work. The Sobel operator is a run of the mill edge identification operator dependent on the primary subordinate. Because of the operator in the presentation of a comparative nearby normal activity, the noise has a smooth impact and can successfully take out the effect of commotion. The impact of the Sobel operator on the situation of the pixel is weighted, which is superior to the Prewitt operator and the Roberts operator.

The Sobel operator comprises two arrangements of 3 × 3 matrixes, which are transverse and longitudinal layouts, and are plotted with the image plane, separately, to acquire the contrast between the flat and the longitudinal distinctions. For genuine use, the accompanying two formats are utilized to distinguish the edges of the image.

$$G_x = \begin{bmatrix} -1 & 0 & 1 \\ -2 & 0 & 2 \\ -1 & 0 & 1 \end{bmatrix}$$

Detect horizontal edge (transverse template)

$$G_y = \begin{bmatrix} 1 & 2 & 1 \\ 0 & 0 & 0 \\ -1 & -2 & -1 \end{bmatrix}$$

The horizontal and vertical gradient approximations of each pixel of the image can be combined to calculate the size of the gradient using the following formula:

$$G = \sqrt[2]{G_x^2 + G_y^2}$$

The gradient can then be calculated using the following formula:

$$\theta = \arctan\left(\frac{G_y}{G_x}\right)$$

In the above example, if the above angle $\theta$ is equal to zero, that is, the image has a longitudinal edge, and the left is darker than the right.

### 4.2.2.2 Laplacian Operator

The Laplace operator is a kind of isotropic operator in addition to being a second-order differential operator. It is progressively suitable when it is concerned about the situation of the edge paying little heed to the pixel grayscale contrast around it (Haddon, 1988). The Laplace operator's reaction to separated pixels is more grounded than the edge or line and is consequently applied just to noise-free images. Within the sight of noise, the Laplacian operator needs to perform low-pass sifting before distinguishing the edge. In this manner, the segmentation algorithm joins the Laplacian operator with the smoothing operator to create another layout.

The Laplacian operator is likewise the least difficult isotropic differential operator with rotational invariance. The Laplace change of a two-dimensional image work is an isotropic second subsidiary, which is progressively appropriate for computerized image handling, and the draw operator is communicated as a discrete structure:

$$\nabla^2\left(f\right) = \frac{\partial^2 f}{\partial x^2} + \frac{\partial^2 f}{\partial y^2}$$

In addition, the Laplace operator can also be expressed in the form of a template.

$$\begin{bmatrix} 0 & 1 & 0 \\ 1 & -4 & 1 \\ 0 & 1 & 0 \end{bmatrix}$$

Discrete Laplacian garlic template

$$\begin{bmatrix} 1 & 1 & 1 \\ 1 & -8 & 1 \\ 1 & 1 & 1 \end{bmatrix}$$

Extended template

The Laplacian operator is used to enhance the blurring effect as it conforms to the descent model. Diffusion effects often occur in the imaging process (Figure 4.5).

### 4.2.3 CLUSTERING-BASED SEGMENTATION

There is no broad hypothesis of image segmentation. Be that as it may, with the presentation of numerous new speculations and strategies for different controls, there

Original Image

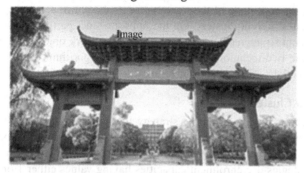

Sobel Operator

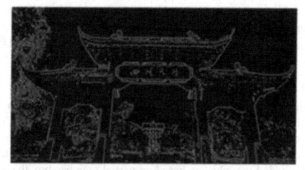

Laplacian Operator

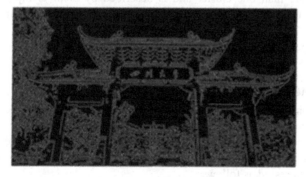

**FIGURE 4.5** Examples of different operator images.

have been many image division techniques joined with some particular hypotheses and strategies. The purported class alludes to the assortment of comparative components. Clustering is as per certain prerequisites and laws of the arrangement of things all the while. The clustering method of the feature space is utilized to fragment the pixels in the image space with the compared highlight space focuses. As per their total in the feature space, the feature space is segmented, and afterward they are mapped back to the first image space to obtain the segmented result. There are two fundamental classifications of clustering techniques: hierarchical strategy and partition-based technique. Various hierarchical techniques depend on the idea of trees. In this, the root node of the tree represents the entire database, and the inner nodes represent different clusters. On the opposite side, partition-based techniques use enhancement strategies iteratively to minimize a work objective function. In the middle of these two techniques, there are different algorithms to discover clusters. There are essentially two sorts of clustering (Dehariya et al., 2010).

### 4.2.3.1 Hard Clustering

Hard clustering is a basic grouping strategy that partitions the image into a lot of groups with the end goal that one pixel can just have a place with just one cluster. As it were, it is also defined as that every pixel can have a place with precisely one cluster. These strategies use enrolment capacities having values either 1 or 0; for example, one either certain pixel can have a place with a specific cluster or not. A case of a hard clustering-based strategy is one k-mean clustering-based method known as hard clustering mean. In this method, above all, the focuses are figured, and then every pixel is relegated to the closest focus. It stresses on augmenting the intra-cluster similitude and furthermore limiting the between cluster balance.

### 4.2.3.2 Soft Clustering

Soft clustering is a progressively specific type of clustering because precise segmentation in real life is not possible due to the occurrence of noise. Thus, the soft clustering technique is most useful for image segmentation in which segmentation is not strict. An example of such a technique is fuzzy c-means clustering. In this technique, the pixels are divided into clusters based on partial membership, that is, a pixel can belong to more than one cluster and is described by membership values of this degree. This technique is more flexible than other techniques (Yamal and Gupta, 2013).

Some types of clustering techniques are most commonly used in image segmentation.

### 4.2.3.3 K-Means Clustering Technique

K-means is one of the most commonly used clustering algorithms. The basic idea of K-means is to collect samples in different groups according to the distance. The closer the two points are to achieving compact and independent clusters as close as the intended targets (Suleiman and Isa, 2010). The implementation process of K-means is expressed as follows:

1. randomly select K initial clustering centers;
2. calculate the distance of each cluster center from each sample and return each sample to the nearest clustering center;
3. for each cluster, through all samples as clusters of new clustering centers;
4. repeat steps (2) to (3) until the cluster center no longer reaches or reaches the specified number of changes (Kumar and Singh, 2013).

The advantage of the K-means clustering algorithm is that the algorithm is fast and simple and is highly efficient and scalable to other data sets. Its time complexity is close to linear and suitable for large-scale data set mining. The disadvantage of K-means is that its clustering number K has no clear selection criteria and is difficult to estimate (Chuang et al., 2006). Secondly, it can be seen from the K-means algorithm framework that each iteration of the algorithm traverses all samples, so the algorithm time is very expensive. Finally, the K-means algorithm is a distance-based segmentation method (Celebi et al., 2013). This only applies to the data set that is convex and not suitable for adding nonwave convex groups (Figures 4.6 and 4.7).

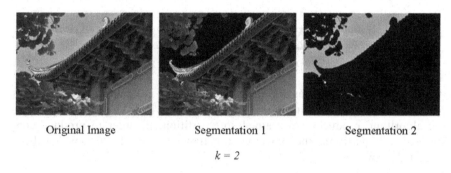

| Original Image | Segmentation 1 | Segmentation 2 |

$$k = 2$$

**FIGURE 4.6** Examples of different K-means images ($k = 2$).

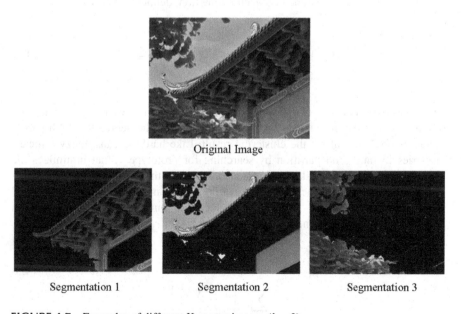

Original Image

| Segmentation 1 | Segmentation 2 | Segmentation 3 |

**FIGURE 4.7** Examples of different K-means images ($k = 3$).

#### 4.2.3.4 Fuzzy C-Means Clustering Technique

The fuzzy c-means algorithm is an unheard fuzzy clustering algorithm. The traditional clustering algorithm finds a "hard partition" of a given dataset based on certain criteria that evaluate the goodness of the partition. By "hard partition," we mean that each datum belongs to exactly one cluster of partitions, whereas the soft clustering algorithm finds the "soft partition" of a given dataset. In "soft partitions," the datum may be partially related to several groups. A soft partition is not necessarily a fuzzy partition because the input space can be larger than the dataset. However, most soft clustering algorithms generate a soft partition that also creates a fuzzy partition. A type of soft clustering of particular interest is one that ensures the degree of membership of point x for one, that is, in all groups.

$$\sum_j \mu_{cj}\left(x_i\right) = 1 \quad | \, \forall x_i \in X \tag{4.1}$$

A soft partition that satisfies this additional condition is called a constrained soft partition. The fuzzy c-means algorithm, which is the best-known fuzzy clustering algorithm, produces constrained soft partition. In order to produce constrained soft partition, the objective function $J_1$ of hard c-means has been extended in two ways:

1. The fuzzy membership degree in cluster has been incorporated in the formula.
2. An additional parameter m has been introduced as a weight exponent in fuzzy membership. The extended objective function, denoted by $J_m$, is:

$$J_m\left(P,V\right) = \sum_{i=1}^{k} \sum_{x_k \in X} \left(\mu_{C_i}\left(x_k\right)\right)^m \| x_k - v_i \|^2 \tag{4.2}$$

where $P$ is fuzzy partition of dataset $X$ formed by $C_1, C_2, \ldots\ldots, C_k$ and $k$ is the number of clusters. The parameter m is weight that determines the degree to which partial members of cluster affect the clustering result. Like hard c-means, fuzzy c-means also tries to find good partition by searching for prototype $v_i$ that minimizes the objective function $J_m$. Unlike hard c-means, however, the fuzzy c-means algorithm also needs to search for membership function $\mu_{C_i}$ that minimizes $J_m$. A constrained fuzzy partition $\{C_1, C_2, \ldots\ldots., C_k\}$ can be the local minimum of the objective function $J_m$ only if the following conditions are satisfied:

$$\mu_{C_i}\left(x\right) = \frac{1}{\sum_{j=1}^{k} \left(\frac{\| x - v_i \|^2}{\| x - v_j \|^2}\right)^{\frac{1}{m-1}}} \tag{4.3}$$

Where $1 \leq i \leq k, x \in X$

$$v_i = \frac{\sum_{x \in X} \mu_{C_i}(x)^m x}{\sum_{x \in X}^{n} \mu_{C_i}(x)^m} \qquad (4.4)$$

where $1 \leq i \leq k$

Few important points regarding the FCM algorithm: It guarantees converge for $m > 1$. It finds local minimum of the objective function $J_m$. The result of applying FCM to a given dataset depends not only upon the choice of parameter m and c but also on the choice of the initial prototype.

The fuzzy c-means clustering algorithm is applied on a MRI cerebral image. The segmentation output presented in the figure below Figure 4.8(a) corresponds to a human cerebral cut; it is the original input image of the program which is split into ($m \times n$) elementary images as in Figure 4.8(b). Figures 4.8(c)-(e) are the segmented output images where each of them corresponds to a specific class: the gray matter, the cerebrospinal fluid, and the white matter.

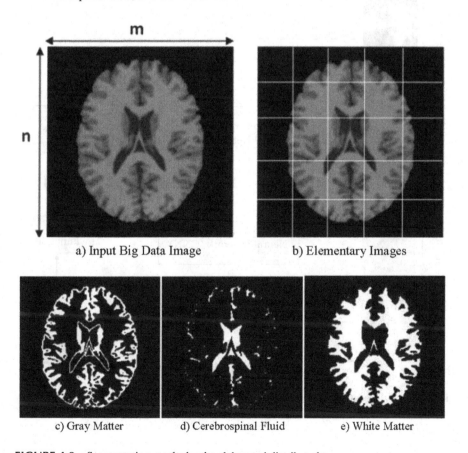

a) Input Big Data Image    b) Elementary Images

c) Gray Matter  d) Cerebrospinal Fluid  e) White Matter

**FIGURE 4.8** Segmentation results by the elaborated distributed program.

### 4.2.4 SEGMENTATION BASED ON WEAKLY SUPERVISED LEARNING IN CNN

In recent years, image classification, detection, segmentation, high-resolution image formation, and many other fields have found breakthrough results in deep learning (Zhang et al., 2013). In the aspect of image segmentation, an algorithm has been proposed that is more effective in this area, which is the weakest and semi-fabricated learning of DCNN for arithmetic image segmentation. Google's George Papandreou and UCLA's Liang-Chieh Chen studied the use of bounding boxes and image-level labels as markup training data based on DeepLab and the expected maximization algorithm to estimate predicted pixel squares and CNN parameters (Em) used. The DeepLab method is divided into two phases, the first step is still using FCN to obtain a coarse score map and project the size of the original image, and then the second stage is the CRF fully connected to the FCN Borrowing to obtain the details of segmentation refinement (Chen et al., 2017) (Figure 4.9).

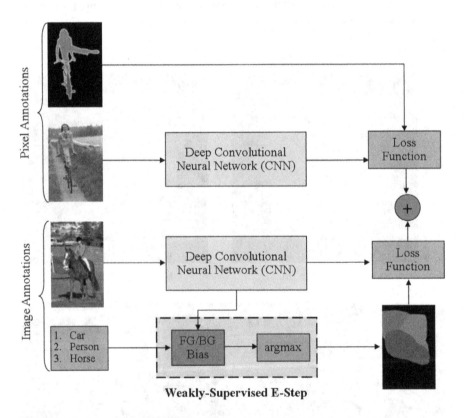

**FIGURE 4.9**   DeepLab model training using image-level labels.

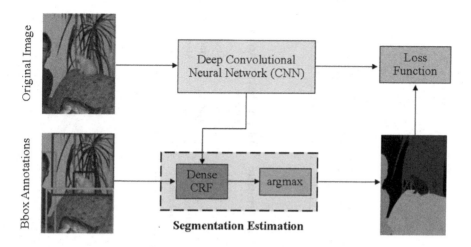

**FIGURE 4.10** DeepLab model training from bounding boxes.

For image-level tagged data, we can observe the image's pixel value x and the image-level mark $z$ but do not know the label y for each pixel, so y is considered as a hidden variable. Use the following probability graph model:

$$P(x, y, z; \theta) = P(x)\left(\prod\nolimits_{m=1}^{M} P(y_m | x; \theta)\right) P(z|y) \qquad (4.5)$$

Use the EM algorithm for estimation and y. The E step is fixed with the value of Y expected, and the M step is fixed to calculate Y using SGD (Papandreou et al., 2015) (Figure 4.10).

The training image that returns the bounding box mark uses the CRF to automatically segment the training image and then perform full supervision based on segmentation. Experiments show that using the image level of the bus sign to achieve the segmentation effect is poor, but better results (Fu & Mui, use of bound box training data, 1981) can be found.

### 4.2.4.1 Comparative Study of Image Segmentation Techniques

These methods are comparatively studied using some standard parameters such as spatial information, field continuity, speed, computation complexity, automaticity, noise resistance, multiple object detection, and accuracy. Table 4.1 presents an analysis of all methods.

**TABLE 4.1**
**Comparison of Image Segmentation Methods**

| Parameters | Spatial Information | Region Continuity | Speed | Computation Complexity | Automaticity | Noise Resistance | Multiple Object Detection | Accuracy |
|---|---|---|---|---|---|---|---|---|
| Threshold | Ignored | Reasonable | Fast | Less | Semiauto | Less | Poor | Moderate |
| Region-based | Considered | Good | Slow | Rapid | Semiauto | Less | Fair | Fine |
| Cluster | Considered | Reasonable | Fast | Rapid | Automatic | Moderate | Fair | Moderate |
| Fuzzy C-mean | Considered | Good | Moderate | Moderate | Automatic | Moderate | Fair | Moderate |

## 4.3 DISCUSSION

The different techniques developed for image segmentation compare well with the methods used in practice. The result of the image segmentation method is dependent on many factors such as intensity, texture, and image content. Therefore, neither single segmentation applies to all types of images nor does all segmentation methods perform well for a particular image.

## REFERENCES

Angelina, S., Suresh, L.P., and Veni, S.K. (2012, March). Image segmentation based on genetic algorithm for region growth and region merging. In *2012 International Conference on Computing, Electronics and Electrical Technologies (ICCEET)* (pp. 970–974). IEEE.

Celebi, M.E., Kingravi, H.A., and Vela, P.A. (2013). A comparative study of efficient initialization methods for the k-means clustering algorithm. *Expert Systems with Applications* 40(1), 200–210.

Chen, L.C., Papandreou, G., Kokkinos, I., Murphy, K., and Yuille, A.L. (2017). Deeplab: Semantic image segmentation with deep convolutional nets, atrous convolution, and fully connected CRFS. *IEEE Transactions on Pattern Analysis and Machine Intelligence* 40(4), 834–848.

Chuang, K.S., Tzeng, H.L., Chen, S., Wu, J., and Chen, T.J. (2006). Fuzzy c-means clustering with spatial information for image segmentation. *Computerized Medical Imaging and Graphics* 30(1), 9–15.

Davis, L.S. (1975). A survey of edge detection techniques. *Computer Graphics and Image Processing* 4(3), 248–270.

Davis, L.S., Rosenfeld, A., and Weszka, J.S. (1975). Region extraction by averaging and thresholding. *IEEE Transactions on Systems, Man, and Cybernetics* (3), 383–388.

Dehariya, V.K., Shrivastava, S.K., and Jain, R.C. (2010, November). Clustering of image data set using k-means and fuzzy k-means algorithms. In *2010 International Conference on Computational Intelligence and Communication Networks* (pp. 386–391). IEEE.

Fu, K.S., and Mui, J.K. (1981). A survey on image segmentation. *Pattern Recognition* 13(1), 3–16.

Haddon, J.F. (1988). Generalised threshold selection for edge detection. *Pattern Recognition* 21(3), 195–203.

Haralick, R.M. and Shapiro, L.G. (1985). Image segmentation techniques. *Computer Vision, Graphics, and Image Processing* 29(1), 100–132.

Kaganami, H.G. and Beiji, Z. (2009, September). Region-based segmentation versus edge detection. In *2009 Fifth International Conference on Intelligent Information Hiding and Multimedia Signal Processing* (pp. 1217–1221). IEEE.

Khokher, M.R., Ghafoor, A., and Siddiqui, A.M. (2013). Image segmentation using multilevel graph cuts and graph development using fuzzy rule-based system. *IET Image Processing* 7(3), 201–211.

Kohler, R. (1981). A segmentation system based on thresholding. *Computer Graphics and Image Processing* 15(4), 319–338.

Kumar, S. and Singh, D. (2013). Texture feature extraction to colorize gray images. *International Journal of Computer Applications* 63(17), 10–17.

Kundu, M.K. and Pal, S.K. (1986). *Thresholding for edge detection using human psycho visual phenomena*.

Lin, D., Dai, J., Jia, J., He, K., and Sun, J. (2016). Scribblesup: Scribble-supervised convolutional networks for semantic segmentation. In *Proceedings of the IEEE Conference on Computer Vision and Pattern Recognition* (pp. 3159–3167).

Marr, D. and Hildreth, E. (1980). Theory of edge detection. *Proceedings of the Royal Society of London. Series B. Biological Sciences* 207(1167), 187–217.

Pal, N.R., and Pal, S.K. (1993). A review on image segmentation techniques. *Pattern Recognition* 26(9), 1277–1294.

Papandreou, G., Chen, L.C., Murphy, K.P., and Yuille, A.L. (2015). Weakly-and semi-supervised learning of a deep convolutional network for semantic image segmentation. In *Proceedings of the IEEE International Conference on Computer Vision* (pp. 1742–1750).

Senthilkumaran, N. and Rajesh, R. (2009, October). Image segmentation-a survey of soft computing approaches. In *2009 International Conference on Advances in Recent Technologies in Communication and Computing* (pp. 844–846). IEEE.

Sulaiman, S.N. and Isa, N.A.M. (2010). Adaptive fuzzy-K-means clustering algorithm for image segmentation. *IEEE Transactions on Consumer Electronics* 56(4), 2661–2668.

Tang, J. (2010, April). A color image segmentation algorithm based on region growing. In *2010 2nd International Conference on Computer Engineering and Technology* (Vol. 6, p. V6-634). IEEE.

Ugarriza, L.G., Saber, E., Vantaram, S.R., Amuso, V., Shaw, M., and Bhaskar, R. (2009). Automatic image segmentation by dynamic region growth and multiresolution merging. *IEEE Transactions on Image Processing* 18(10), 2275-2288.

Wani, M.A. and Batchelor, B.G. (1994). Edge-region-based segmentation of range images. *IEEE Transactions on Pattern Analysis and Machine Intelligence* 16(3), 314–319.

Wu, Z. and Leahy, R. (1993). An optimal graph theoretic approach to data clustering: Theory and its application to image segmentation. *IEEE Transactions on Pattern Analysis and Machine Intelligence* 15(11), 1101–1113.

Yambal, M. and Gupta, H. (2013). Image segmentation using fuzzy C means clustering: A survey. *International Journal of Advanced Research in Computer and Communication Engineering* 2(7).

Zhang, L., Gao, Y., Xia, Y., Lu, K., Shen, J., and Ji, R. (2013). Representative discovery of structure cues for weakly-supervised image segmentation. *IEEE Transactions on Multimedia* 16(2), 470–479.

# 5 Advance Object Detection and Clustering Techniques Used for Big Data

## 5.1 INTRODUCTION

Object detection is a procedure for determining object's class instance to which it belongs to and also for determining the object location by outputting the bounding box around the object. Object detection can be classified into two groups as single-class object detection and multiclass object detection. Single-class object detection is a process of detecting a single instance of a class from the image, whereas multi-class object detection is a process of detecting classes of all objects in an image. Object detection can be used in video surveillance for monitoring the cloud in order to prevent any riots and terrorist attack, count the number of people, etc. In order to understand object detection, we have to start with image classification which answers the question "What is in this picture?" Image classification is used to classify image into different categories. After classification, we have to locate our object within the image which answers our question "Why it is and where it is?" which is a combination of object classification and localization. After this process, the process of object detection comes into picture which is used to detect or locate multiple objects in a single image. Let's understand it in detail taking example of a self-driven car where real-time video stream has to find multiple objects as the location of other cars, humans, signs, and traffic lights in a single image, and accordingly, we have to take appropriate actions. Once the objects are detected, the segmentation of images is carried out in order to extract useful information from the image (Figure 5.1).

Segmentation of images is used to analyze the interior of an image. Image segmentation is used for separating and analyzing each object individually in order to retrieve the information inside it. Image segmentation is partitioning of digital images into multiple different regions, where each region consists of a set of pixels known as superpixels with similar attributes. Image segmentation is used for representation of images into a meaningful and easier-to-analyze object. As discussed earlier, image segmentation is a pre-process, and then pattern recognition, feature extraction, and compression of images are carried out. Thus, in simple words, we can say that image segmentation is classification of images into multiple groups.

Image segmentation locates objects and boundaries within an image and labels each pixel of the image in such a way that every pixel with the same label shares

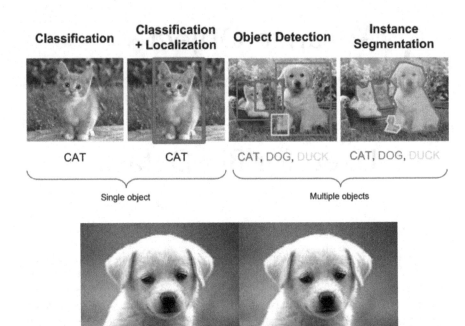

**FIGURE 5.1**    Steps for image detection (https://www.kdnuggets.com/2018/09/object-detection-image-classification-yolo.html)

certain characteristics. Thus, image segmentation is used to convert images into a collection of pixels which are represented by a mask or labeled image. This division of images can be used for processing of some important segments of the image which are of use. There are different approaches, which can be used to detect similarities within regions of images, namely clustering and thresholding. Here in this chapter, we are focusing on the clustering approach.

Clustering uses the same approach as segmentation which divides the data points or population into different groups such that the data points in one group would be similar in characteristics compared to data points in other groups. Thus, clustering is an approach to segregate groups with similar traits and assign them into clusters. Thus, we can say that clustering is one of the popular techniques used in unsupervised learning where grouping of data is done based on the similarity of the data points. A cluster can be formed using the concept that objects with similarities can be grouped together. Similarly, clustering, which is an unsupervised learning method, can be considered as a process that helps the machines to distinguish different objects given in a dataset. Since clustering is an unsupervised learning, no external labels are attached to the given instances and machines find clusters based on the patterns or the trends observed. Various algorithms are used to extract the parameters that can help to group instances into appropriate clusters. Clustering learning mode helps to divide the data into different groups such that each data point is similar to data points in the same group and dissimilar to the data points in the other groups. Clustering is considered to be a useful technique to differentiate groups from the unlabeled datasets.

In order to carry out the clustering technique on the various data objects, it is necessary that the objects have a sufficient number of attributes to help to differentiate them; clusters of different shapes are available. The clustering method can be implemented on the data that are scalable; the input sequence has no effect on the output and has high dimensionality. Clustering is an unsupervised machine learning approach which can be used to improve the accuracy of the supervised machine learning algorithm.

## 5.2 CLUSTERING

Clustering can be classified into two subgroups as hard clustering and soft clustering (Figure 5.2).

In hard clustering, each data point should belong to only one cluster completely, whereas in soft clustering instead of putting each data point into a separate cluster, a probability or likelihood of that data point is assigned in those clusters.

There have been different types of clustering models proposed by different researchers over the past few decades; these models are based on different sets of rules which are used for defining the similarity between data points. Some few basic models used in data science are as follows:

- **Connectivity models:** This model is based on logic that data points which are close in data space are more likely to have similar properties than far data points. In order to achieve this, two approaches can be used. In the first approach, the data points are classified into different clusters and then the aggregation is performed as the distance decreases, whereas in the second approach, all the data points are classified into a single cluster and then the partitioning is done as the distance increases. The distance function choice is subjective and varies with respect to different approaches because it is one of the easiest approaches but lacks in terms of scalability of handling large datasets, for example, hierarchical clustering algorithm.
- **Centroid model:** This is an iterative clustering model which is based on the concept that how close are the data points to the centroid of the clusters. One of the disadvantages with this approach is that we should have prior knowledge of the dataset and also the number of clusters required at the end. One of the popular algorithms used in this approach is the K-means clustering algorithm.

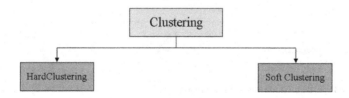

**FIGURE 5.2**  Classification of clustering.

- **Distribution model:** This approach is based on the logic that how probably the data points in a cluster belong to the same distribution as Normal, Gaussian, etc. This model has a disadvantage of overfitting. An example of this approach is the Expectation Maximization algorithm which uses multivariate normal distributions.
- **Density model:** This approach is based on the density of data points in data space. This model uses the approach of separating different density regions and assigning data points within this region in the same cluster. Examples of this approach are Density-Based Spatial Clustering of Applications with Noise (DBSCAN) and Ordering Points to Identify the Clustering Structure (OPTICS).

Clustering can be used in many applications; some of the popular applications are recommendation engines, market segmentation, social network analysis, search result grouping, medical imaging, image segmentation, and anomaly detection.

## 5.3 DIFFERENCES BETWEEN CLUSTERING AND CLASSIFICATION

Classification is the outcome of supervised learning as there are known labels that we want to be generated from system. It can be explained taking example of a fruit classifier who can say that this is an orange and this is an apple based on showing the examples of apples and oranges.

On the other hand, clustering is the outcome of unsupervised learning that does not include labels. Taking the previous example of clustering, clustering includes fruits with soft skin and lots of dimples, fruits with shiny hard skin, and elongated yellow fruits. This classification is based on not merely showing a lot of fruits to the system, but not identifying the names of different types of fruits.

## 5.4 DISTANCE MEASURE

Since clustering utilizes the distance between the data points to differentiate the data points into different groups, thus without the mention and explanation of the distance units, the topic remains incomplete. Some of the distance metrics used in the clustering are as follows (Figure 5.3):

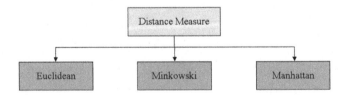

**FIGURE 5.3**   Distance metric used in clustering.

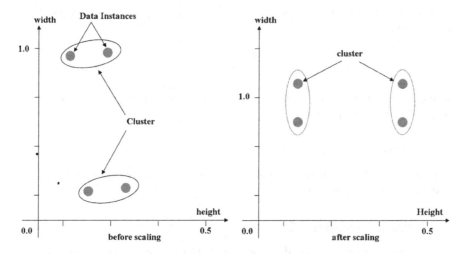

**FIGURE 5.4**   Before and after scaling clusters.

### 5.4.1 EUCLIDEAN DISTANCE

If the distance vectors are all in the same physical units, then the data points can be successfully clustered. However, it might be possible that the decision is to be made as per the relative scaling.

As shown in Figure 5.4, different scaling can lead to different clustering.

### 5.4.2 MINKOWSKI METRIC

For higher dimensional data, a popular measure is the Minkowski metric,

$$d_p\left(x_i, x_j\right) = \left(\sum_{k=1}^{d} \left|x_{i,k} - x_{j,k}\right|\right)^{\frac{1}{p}}$$

where $d$ is the dimensionality of the data.

### 5.4.3 MANHATTAN METRIC

The Manhattan distance is also known as the Taxicab Distance Metric. The Manhattan distance function computes the distance that would be traveled to get from one data point to the other if a grid-like path is followed. The Manhattan distance between two items is the sum of the differences of their corresponding components.

The formula for this distance between a point $X = (X_1, X_2, \ldots)$ and a point $Y = (Y_1, Y_2, \ldots)$ is

$$d = \sum_{i=1}^{n} |x_i - y_i|$$

where $n$ is the number of variables and $X_i$ and $Y_i$ are the values of the $i^{th}$ variable, at points $X$ and $Y$, respectively.

## 5.5 CLUSTERING ALGORITHMS

Taking a view of clustering algorithms, we can divide clustering algorithms into five distinct types as follows (Figure 5.5):

### 5.5.1 PARTITIONING-BASED CLUSTERING

This clustering subdivides the data into subsets of k groups which are predefined in nature. In order to divide the data into clusters, it consists of two requirements:

- Each group should contain at least one point.
- Each point must belong to exactly one group.

The partition-based clustering algorithm is an iterative-based algorithm which minimizes the clustering criteria by relocating data points in an iterative manner between clusters in order to attain optimal partition. An example of this type of clustering is K-means clustering.

### 5.5.1.1 K-Means Clustering

K-means is an unsupervised, iterative, and non-deterministic algorithm. It helps to generate non-hierarchical sets. It generates globular clusters. **K-means** clustering is an unsupervised algorithm that can be used to differentiate the data points from each other. It can help to cluster or partition the given dataset into k-clusters or parts based on the k-centroids. These data are used in the cases where the target class has not been defined. The clusters formed are on the basis of the similar parameters into k groups. The objective of K-means clustering is to minimize the sum of squared distances between all points and the cluster center.

$$J = \sum_{j=1}^{k} \sum_{i=1}^{n} x_i^j - c_j^2$$

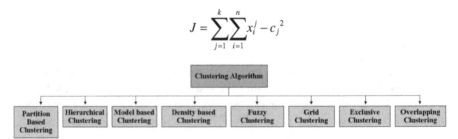

**FIGURE 5.5**   Classification of clustering algorithms.

Here, $J$ represents the objective function, $k$ represents the number of clusters, $n$ represents the number of cases, $xi$ represents the $i^{th}$ case, $c_j$ represents the centroid for cluster $j$, and $\left\| x_i^j - c_j \right\|^2$ represents the distance function.

### Steps in K-means clustering algorithm

1. Decide upon the number of clusters: K.
2. Select centroids in the datasets. Now consider a random K point from the group.
3. Assign the selected data point to the closest centroid.
4. Repeat this procedure for all the data points in the group, thereby creating the clusters. The model for predicting the output of the unlabeled data is ready.

### Choosing the optimal value of K:

Algorithms such as K-means, K-mediods, etc. depend on parameter $K$ which specifies a number of clusters in the dataset. The value of $K$ depends on shape and scale of distribution of points within a dataset. The value of $K$ is chosen such that there should be balance between maximum compression of data using a single cluster and maximum accuracy by means of assigning data points to its own cluster. There are different methods to select the appropriate value of $K$, and one is the Elbow method or silhouette method.

The Elbow method finds the different values of '$K'$ by calculating Within-Cluster-Sum of Squared (WCSS) errors and thus select $K$ where WCSS becomes the first to start to diminish. Thus, this approach can be divided into three parts as in first part it predicts the center of cluster by finding the squared error for each point by means of squaring the distance of point from its representation. Then in the second step, the WSS score is the sum of these squared errors for each point. Finally, the Euclidean distance or the Manhattan distance can be used to find different values of $K$.

The steps for choosing the value of $K$ using the Elbow method can be summarized as follows:

1. Compute K-means clustering for different values of $K$ by varying $K$ from 1 to 10 clusters.
2. For each $K$, calculate the total within-cluster sum of square.
3. Plot the curve of WCSS versus the number of clusters $K$.
4. The location of a bend in the plot indicates an appropriate number of clusters in the datasets.

The Elbow method has an issue of Random Initialization Trap which is based on the random choice of centroids. This issue can be overcome by the initialization procedure for K-means where the initial value of K-means is taken, and a point is considered randomly as the first centroid. After this, the data points are taken based on the probability which depends on the distance of the first point. In this case, we have two centroids, the process is repeated on these two centroids, and probability of each point will be based on its distance to the closest centroid to that point.

The silhouette method finds a value which measures that how similar a point to its own cluster (cohesion) than to other cluster (separation). This method has values ranging from −1 to +1. A greater value represents that the point is placed in the correct cluster. More negative silhouette values represent that cluster creation is either few less or in excess.

The elbow method is based on decision rule, whereas silhouette is a metric which is used for validation while clustering. Thus, we can say that Elbow and silhouette are not alternatives of each other, rather they can be used in combination.

**Different approaches to K-means algorithm:**

There are many researchers who had worked long way back on the K-means algorithm in order to optimize the solution in best possible manner. Long back from 1958, Fisher (1958) investigated the problem of K-Means grouping in one-dimensional cases and named it the grouping problem. Then, later in sixties, seminal procedures of K-means procedures were introduced by Forgy (1965) and MacQueen (1967). The main difference between Forgy and MacQueen algorithms is in their order in which the data points are assigned to clusters and cluster centers are updated. The Forgy method updates the center of clusters after assignment of data points to the closest cluster centers, whereas Mac-Queen K-mean algorithm updates the winning cluster center immediately after every assignment of a data point and all cluster centers one more time after all data points have been assigned to the clusters. Then, in 1982, Lloyd (1982) came up with the quantization algorithm for pulse code modulation of analog signals and termed this algorithm as Lloyd's algorithm. Chen (1977) came up with a similar algorithm for multidimensional case. However, Linde et al. (1980) generalized Lloyd's algorithm to the vector quantization algorithm and named it generalized Lloyd's algorithm.

Later in years, many researchers work on more improvement in the K-means algorithm by proposing different approaches to avoid poor suboptimal solutions by proposing different initialization methods. Zhang (2000) proposed that the K-harmonic means algorithm should run before the K-Means algorithm in order to overcome the problem of slower convergence near solution. Fritzke (1997) proposed the LBG-U method to work on the poor quality minima problem in clustering by presenting the vector quantization method. The LBG-U method repeats the LBG algorithm (Little et al., 1987) until convergence. In this approach, the cluster center with the minimum utility is moved to a new point after each run. The mean vector that possesses the minimum utility is the one that contributes least to the overall sum of squared errors when removed. The new point is chosen close to the mean of the cluster that generates most of the distortion error for clustering. Likas and Verbeek (2003) proposed a global K-mean clustering algorithm which uses a deterministic and incremental global optimization method. It is also independent of any initial parameters and employs the K-means procedure as a local search procedure.

### 5.5.2 Hierarchical Clustering

In hierarchical clustering, objects are categorized into a hierarchical tree-like structure termed as "dendogram." This technique does not require any predefined data as was there in partition-based clustering. Hierarchical clustering works as follows:

1. It calculates the distance between every pair of observation points and stores it in a distance matrix.
2. After the above step, it places each point in its own cluster.
3. Then based on distances from the distance matrix, it merges the closet pair of points. As a result of which, the amount of cluster goes down by 1.
4. Then, it recalculates the distance between new and old clusters and then stores them in a new distance matrix.
5. It repeats steps 2 and 3 until all clusters merge into a single cluster.

Hierarchical clustering can be performed in two ways:

- Bottom-up approach or agglomerative approach
- Top-down approach or divisive Approach

The agglomerative approach starts by observation in a single or distinct cluster and then successfully merges the cluster together until the stopping criteria are fulfilled. On the other hand, the divisive approach begins with the entire pattern in single cluster and then performs splitting until the stopping criteria are fulfilled. The agglomerative approach is bottom-up as in this approach we start with each data point as its own cluster and then combine clusters based on certain similarity measures. The divisive approach is top-down as in this approach all the observations start from one cluster and then the splitting is performed recursively as moving down the hierarchy.

Some of the applications of hierarchical clustering can be described as follows:

1. **Clustering of twitter data:** Comments done by the users in twitter can be one of the criteria to find the mood of any user. Now segregating the words on twitter in a different manner based on the hierarchical cluster-based approach will help us to find the mood of user trending toward anything that can be used for different approaches.
2. **Application in healthcare:** Detection of cancerous cells at the early stage is the need of the hour. Shapes of cancerous cells play a vital role in determining the severity of cancer which is an area of research to propose algorithms for classifying images of cancerous cells through hierarchical clustering. Even the study of SARS virus is confirmed through the hierarchical cluster-based approach.
3. **Relating different species together:** Example of this approach is relating whether pandas are closer to bears or raccoons. The answer to such questions can be found out by applying hierarchical clustering on the DNA similarity between these species.

### 5.5.3 MODEL-BASED CLUSTERING

In this clustering, the data observed arise from a distribution consisting of a mixture of two or more cluster components. Here, each cluster component has a density function having an associated probability or weight in this mixture.

### 5.5.4 DENSITY-BASED CLUSTERING

This clustering is also termed as DBSCAN clustering in machine learning. This clustering works on dense areas in the data space in order to separate them from each other by sparser areas. This clustering is used for evaluating and finding non-linear shape structures based on density. Since the earlier approaches (partition clustering and hierarchical clustering) used for finding a spherical shape cluster or convex cluster and hence the best fit for a compact or well-shaped cluster are also affected by the presence of noise and outliers in data, there is a need for the density-based model to overcome the above disadvantage.

DBSCAN is a density-based clustering algorithm that can help to separate clusters with high-density data points from the data points with low density. DBSCAN can sort the data into clusters of various shapes. However, it may consider some data points as outliers and leave them out in the clustering procedure.

The DBSCAN algorithm uses two parameters for execution of the algorithm:

1. eps: This parameter defines the neighborhood around a data point. Thus, any two points whose distance is lower or equal to eps are considered as neighbor. Thus, eps is a parameter which defines the threshold of the distance between two points. The value of eps is chosen such that it covers maximum points as the lower value of eps will keep more points as outliers. On the other hand, a larger value of eps will merge majority of data points into a single cluster. Thus, different approaches can be used to find the value of eps; one such approach is the $k$-distance graph.

2. MinPts: This parameter defines the minimum number of neighbor or data points which lies within the eps radius. Thus, a large dataset will lead to select the larger value of MinPts. The general formula for finding the value of MinPts is

$$\text{MinPts} \geq (D+1)$$

where $D$ is the dataset, and the minimum value of *MinPts* is 3.

In this algorithm, there are three types of data points as follows:

1. Core Point: A point or data point is considered as the core point if its value is more than the MinPts value within eps.

2. Border Point: A point or data point is considered as the border point if its value is lower than MinPts within eps, but it is in the neighborhood of a core point.

3. Noise or Outlier: These are those points which are neither core point nor border point.

Steps for the DBSCAN algorithm are as follows:

1. In the first step, we have to find all the neighbor points within eps and identify the core points or visited points with more MinPts neighbors.
2. In the second step, we have to create new clusters for all those core points which are not assigned to any cluster.
3. Then, we have to find all density-connected points in a recursive manner and assign them to the same cluster as the core point.
4. Finally, we have to repeat the above steps through all the remaining unvisited points in the dataset and separate those points which do not belong to any dataset as noise or outliers.

The advantage of DBSCAN is that it can handle the outliers within the dataset and is able to separate the clusters of various densities, whereas the disadvantage of DBSCAN is that this algorithm cannot work with clusters of almost similar density or large varying cluster density.

### 5.5.5 Fuzzy Clustering

Fuzzy clustering is used for a dataset with subgrouping of points having indistinct boundaries and overlap between the clusters. Fuzzy clustering segmented the data and defined the cluster by grouping of related attributes in uniquely defined clusters. In this clustering, data points belong to more than one cluster. Here, each component present in cluster has a membership coefficient which corresponds to a degree of being present in that cluster. The fuzzy clustering method is also known as a soft computing of clustering. Examples of some prominent fuzzy clustering algorithms are Fuzzy C-means (FCM), Fuzzy K-means, Gustafson-Kessel (GK) Algorithm, etc.

FCM is an unsupervised clustering algorithm that can be used to analyze multiple features and is more realistic than K-Means clustering. With the development of fuzzy logic, the fuzziness helps to describe a more realistic degree of membership of the data points. A data point is considered to be a member of the class to a certain degree. An image is represented by the feature spaces that can be further classified into the clusters of similar attribute based clustering. The data points are grouped based on the distance of the pixels to the centroids, and these pixels are highly correlated. The spatial relationship of the neighboring pixels can be of great help to image segmentation. The process of image segmentation using the FCM algorithm is to take an input of an image with its size. The centroids are selected, and a possible number of iterations are carried out to minimize the cost function. The data points are implemented with the sigmoid function to decide the degree of the membership with respect to their distance between the centroids and the data points. FCM clustering calculates the cluster centers and assigns points to these centers by using the Euclidian distance formula. Fuzzified membership divides the product obtained by the above process. The center of the cluster is the weighted mean of data, where weights depend on the considered algorithm. The covariance matrix is defined as fuzzy covariance of classic covariance.

FCM proposed by Pham and Prince (1999) can be used in non-supervised image segmentation for voxel classification. FCM determines the set of tissue classes and, as per the attributes, classifies each pixel by its membership values of tissue classes. Each tissue class has a centroid. Thus, FCM helps to compute the membership value in order to minimize the intracluster distance and maximize the intercluster distance.

The GK Algorithm can be used in image processing, classification, and system identification. One of the advantages of the GK clustering algorithm is that it adapts cluster according to the real shape of the cluster. The difference between the FCM and GK clustering algorithms is in terms of measuring the distance; FCM uses an identity matrix to measure the distance, whereas GK uses a parameter based on the covariance matrix of each cluster, allowing the distance norm to adapt to the shape of the sub-clusters to best suit the data.

## 5.5.6 GRID-BASED CLUSTERING

In this clustering, we formulate the data space into a finite number of cells in order to form a grid-like structure. Clustering operation is performed on these grids in a fast and independent manner to the number of data objects.

Some of the grid-based methods are CLIQUE (CLustering in QUEst), STING (Statistical Information Grid), MAFIA (Merging of Adaptive Interval Approach to spatial data mining) Wave Cluster, O-Cluster (Orthogonal portioning Cluster), etc.

CLIQUE uses a density- and grid-based method. It divides the data space into non-overlapping rectangular units termed as grids. These grids are equal in length. The CLIQUE algorithm is used to identify sub-units which contain clusters. Then it merges the dense unit to form a cluster and finally helps in generating the minimal description for clusters.

STING is a grid-based multiresolution technique for clustering which divides the spatial area into rectangular cells using latitude and longitude and employs a hierarchical approach. This technique can be used in GIS systems, image data base exploration, medical imaging, etc.

The MAFIA algorithm is used for fast subspace clustering by using the adaptive grid approach to handle massive datasets and introduces a scalable parallel framework on shared-nothing architecture to handle such big data. This method reduces computation and improves quality of clustering by using the adaptive grid approach which focuses on that data space portion which is dense and has more points and more probability of having clusters. Thus, it adopts the parallelism approach to increase the efficiency of handling large datasets.

Wave Cluster is a multiresolution algorithm which is used to find cluster in a large spatial database. This algorithm quantizes the feature space and then applies discrete wavelet transform to this quantized feature space to create new units. Wave Cluster connects the cluster in two sets of units where they are considered as a cluster. Wave Cluster then labels the units in the feature space that are included in the cluster.

O-cluster is an active sampling technique that uses an axis parallel strategy for identifying continuous areas of high density in input space. This algorithm uses statistical test for validating the quality of the cutting plane which is used to identify good splitting points along data projections. This algorithm also has another advantage that it can be operated on small buffer containing random samples from original datasets. Partition without any ambiguity is "frozen" and associated data points with it are removed from active buffer. It operates in a recursive manner by means of evaluating possible splitting points for all projections within a partition and selecting the "best" one and thus splitting the data into new partitions. It operates by creating a hierarchical tree structure which translates the input stage into rectangular regions. The different stages involved in this algorithm are load buffer stage, followed by compute histogram for active partition, then finding the "best" splitting points for active partition, followed by flagging ambiguous and "frozen" partition, splitting active partition, and finally reloading the buffer. This algorithm normally gives a good result for larger datasets with high record and high dimension.

Adaptive grids are proposed for fast subspace clustering which introduces a scalable parallel framework. On shared-nothing architecture to handle massive datasets, MAFIA proposes adaptive grids for fast subspace clustering and introduces a scalable parallel framework on shared-nothing architecture to handle massive datasets.

### 5.5.7 Exclusive Clustering

In this clustering, the data which are grouped in an exclusive mode are included into a definite cluster and cannot be included in another cluster. The dataset may be clustered into two-dimensional planes. Example: K-Means can be used to classify the data points into different classes.

### 5.5.8 Overlapping Clustering

In this clustering, the fuzzy functions are implemented on the data to cluster into different groups, and each data point can belong to two or more clusters with different degrees of membership rather than belonging to single class. Each data point is given an appropriate membership value.

Examples of these clustering techniques are K-means algorithm, overlapping K-mean (OKM), weighted overlapping K-mean (WOKM), overlapping partition cluster (OPC), and multicluster overlapping K-means extension (MCOKE).

The overlapping K-mean (OKM) algorithm [Cleuziou, 2008] and weighted overlapping K-mean (WOKM) [Cleuziou, 2009] algorithms are extensions of the overlapping case of the K-mean algorithm which is used for building partition. WOKM is an extension to the OKM algorithm, which uses weighted as a parameter. It assigns each object to the nearest cluster and then updates the cluster representatives and set of cluster weights.

Chen and Hu (2006) proposed the OPC algorithm which considers the similarity or dissimilarity between the cluster center and thus kept the cluster center distinct to each other. This algorithm also maximizes the average number of objects in a cluster. This algorithm sets a threshold value which is set a priori, and a minimum value is set such that if objects meet the threshold value then it belongs to the cluster and thus an object can belong to more than one cluster. Any object which does not meet any cluster will result in non-exhausting clustering. This algorithm is best to handle noise as the distance between centroid of clusters is far.

The MCOKE algorithm proposed by Baadel et al. (2015) minimizes the distance between objects and cluster centroid by using the standard K-mean clustering approach where the value of $k$ is predefined which iterates through data objects to attain distinct partitioning of data points. This algorithm also creates a membership table which is used to compare the matrix that is generated after initial K-means run to "maxdist" where maxdist is a variable which gives the value of maximum distance of an object to a centroid that an object was allowed to belong to any cluster. Thus, the maxdist variable is used to mark as a threshold which allows objects to belong to multiple clusters.

## Other Clustering Methods

### Expectation Maximization Algorithm Based on a Mixture of Gaussians

Expectation Maximization (EM) is an unsupervised probabilistic clustering algorithm which is used for estimation of density of data points. This algorithm depends on similarity of parameters. This algorithm performs the Expectation (E) and Maximization (M) process in an iterative manner until we receive the optimal solution.

The Expectation (E) step is used for the calculation of expected similarity of data points by means of inclusion of latent variables, whereas the maximization (M) step is used for computation of maximum similarity estimates of parameters by means of maximizing the expected likelihood found on the last E step. The Expectation Maximization clustering algorithm is used for estimating the probability densities of classes by means of using this algorithm. There is an inverse proportion between the constraint and flexibility of the model. Lesser is the strictness, more is the flexibility in model. This model works with two steps in the following manner: in the first step, estimation of probability distribution of variables is performed; in the second step, log likelihood function increases. These steps are explained as follows:

- E-step: Based on the current hypothesis for the distribution of the class parameters, it performs probabilistic assignments of each data point to some class.
- M-step: Based on the new data assignments, update the hypothesis h for the distributional class parameters.

The EM algorithm is more useful when there are sufficient statistics, and it has a linear function to be maximized. The results of the EM algorithm can be improved by implementing a Kalman filter which is used for the online estimation or for batch-based estimation. The EM algorithm can be used for solving the parameter estimation problems.

### Variants of the EM Algorithm

Some of the variants of the EM algorithm are Parameter-Expanded Expectation Maximization, Expectation Conditional Maximization, or Expectation Conditional Maximization Either Algorithm.

The Parameter-Expanded Expectation Maximization algorithm provides a covariance adjustment to correct the analysis of the M step, whereas the Expectation

Conditional Maximization (ECM) replaces each M step with a sequence of conditional maximization steps in which each parameter $\theta$ is maximized individually, conditionally on the other parameters remaining fixed.

The example of this algorithm is implemented by Shanwen Zhang et al. (2017) with paper title, 'Plant disease leaf image segmentation based on superpixel clustering and EM algorithm' where the author divides the complete color leaf image into a number of compact and uniform superpixels by superpixel clustering, which are quickly and accurately segmented from each superpixel by using the EM algorithm.

### Single-Linkage Clustering: The Algorithm

The single-linkage clustering algorithm is a type of agglomerative scheme which erases rows and columns from the proximity matrix as old clusters are merged into new ones. The proximity cluster is an $N \times N$ matrix, and the cluster with sequence number $m$ and proximity between clusters $(r)$ and $(s)$ can be described as $d[(r),(s)]$.

**The algorithm is composed of the following steps:**

1. Disjoint cluster is observed with the level $L(0) = 0$ and sequence $m = 0$.
2. Find the least Dissimilar pair of clusters, thus $d[(r),(r)] = minimum\ d[(i)\ (j)]$
3. The value of $m$ is increased by one. The clusters are merged into a single cluster to find the clustering of the next level.
4. Update the proximity matrix, by deleting the previous rows and columns and adding one of the newly formed clusters.
5. The process stops when the number of clusters remains 1.

The example of this algorithm is discussed by Daniel Gómez (2015) in his paper entitled "Image segmentation based upon hierarchical clustering" where the authors provide an algorithm to build fuzzy boundaries based on the existing relations between the fuzzy boundary set problem and the (crisp) hierarchical image segmentation problem.

### Self-organizing Maps

The self-organizing map is a clustering unsupervised algorithm that is used to map a multidimensional dataset into a two-dimensional surface. Self-organizing maps have visualization and cluster analysis. Visualization can be implemented for high-dimensional data, because it helps to reveal a lot of information on the data.

### Jarvis-Patrick Clustering

The Jarvis-Patrick clustering algorithm is based on similarity between neighbors which can be determined by using a distance metric. We have to take one or more neighbors for judging the membership of cluster of the objects which are under study. The functions used are deterministic and non-iterative in nature. The algorithm has the following properties:

1. Algorithm chooses the number of clusters.
2. Each cluster should contain at least one item under it.

3. The algorithm is used to partition the inputs into non-hierarchical clusters.
4. The clusters formed should not be overlapped.
5. If two different items from the same input dataset share enough mutual nearest neighbors, then those two items should be in the same cluster.

The parameters used in this algorithm are as follows:

1. The number of Neighbors to Examine
2. The minimum required number of Neighbors in Common

The first parameter Neighbors to Examine is used to specify how many neighboring items should be considered while counting the number of mutual neighbors shared with another item. The minimum value of this should be at least 2. Lower values help the algorithm to finish faster, but the final set of clusters will have many small clusters. Higher values can cause the algorithm to take longer to finish, which may result in fewer clusters and clusters that form longer chains. While the second parameter, Neighbors in Common, is used to specify the minimum number of mutual nearest neighbors where the two items must be in the same cluster. The minimum value of this should be 1, and it should not exceed the value of the Neighbors to Examine parameter. Here, the lower values result in clusters that are compact. Higher values result in clusters that are more dispersed.

The basic procedure for this algorithm is as follows:

1. For each object, find its J-nearest neighbors where 'J' corresponds to the Neighbors to Examine parameter on the Partitioned Clustering dialog.
2. If two items are in each other's list of J-nearest neighbors and $K$ of their J-nearest neighbors are in common, then they can be clustered together, where the value of $K$ corresponds to the neighbors in the common parameter on the partitioned cluster dialog.

Various inputs used in the algorithm are as follows:

1. The dataset
2. A distance metric
3. The number of nearest Neighbors to Examine
4. The number of nearest neighbors two data points must share to be in the same cluster (Neighbors in Common).

This algorithm can be used when we have to work with non-global clusters or tight clusters in large loose clusters or deterministic partitional clusters or in the case when clustering speed is an issue as this algorithm is not iterative in nature.

### Color Clustering Algorithms

The color clustering algorithm can be used for detection of colors and edges in an image during the image segmentation phase. Celenks (1990) discussed about color clustering. In this approach, he first detected the cluster using the 1D histogram and then isolated the cluster and performed the region extraction using the Fisher linear discriminant function. After this, he used the feature extraction algorithm, where he partitioned the remaining part of the test image into its atomic regions of maximally four connected pixels of similar color. Thus, he proposes a histogram-based clustering approach which is applied to several low-contrast color images of skyline.

**Application of clustering:** Clustering can be used in different fields apart from image processing. We will discuss the application of clustering in image processing, but firstly we are going to discuss the application of image processing in other fields as follows:

- **Marketing:** Clustering can be used in the marketing field in order to characterize and discover the demand and need pattern of the customer which can be used for marketing purpose.
- **Biology:** Clustering can be used in biology in order to classify among different species of plants and animals to treat them accordingly.
- **Libraries:** In this, clustering can be used to differentiate the books based on their topics and information.
- **City Planning:** In this, the clustering approach can be used for grouping the houses so that their values can be graded based on their geographical areas, locations, and other factors.
- **Earthquake studies:** Here, clustering can be used to determine the dangerous zones by means of learning the pattern of earthquake affected areas and segregating them accordingly.
- **Pattern recognition in Images:** Clustering can be used for automatic detection on infected fruits or blood cell segmentation for detection of leukemia using image processing.

**Challenges of using Clustering:** Some of the challenges that we have found in the clustering approach are as follows:

1. Current clustering technique cannot address time series easily.
2. Large dimensions can cause issues.
3. The effectiveness of clustering is dependent on the distance metric.
4. Output of clustering can be in different formats.

**Image Processing using Clustering:** In today's scenario, images are considered to be most popular media and are used for various purposes. Images can be converted into pixels, and pixels can be divided into different groups. A set of regions or a set of contours are extracted from the image. In order to divide the input image into meaningful regions or contours, we use a priori knowledge to estimate the parameter for the local texture. Clustering is the search for distinct parameters in the feature space. Image segmentation is the process of converting an image into various regions where each region is homogeneous.

Various unsupervised techniques used for image segmentation can be K-means, FCM, hierarchical clustering, Expectation Maximization, or self-organizing maps.

# REFERENCES

Baadel, S., Thabtah, F., and Lu, J. (2015). Multi-cluster overlapping K-means extension algorithm. In *Proceedings of the XIII International Conference on Machine Learning and Computing, ICMLC'2015*, 2015.

Celenks, M. (1990). A color clustering technique for image segmentation. *Computer Vision, Graphics, and Image Processing* 52: 145–170. 10.1016/0734-189X(90)90052-W.

Chen, D. (1977). On two or more dimensional optimum quantizers. In *Proceedings of IEEE International Conference on Acoustics, Speech, and Signal Processing, ICASSP '77*, Vol. 2, Telecommunication Training Institute, Taiwan, Republic of China, May 1977, pp. 640–643.

Chen, Y. and Hu, H. (2006). An overlapping Cluster algorithm to provide non-exhaustive clustering. *European Journal of Operational Research* 2006: 762–780.

Cleuziou, G. (2008). An extended version of the k-means method for overlapping clustering. In *International Conference on Pattern Recognition ICPR*, pp. 1–4.

Cleuziou, G. (2009). Two variants of the OKM for overlapping clustering. In *Advances in Knowledge Discovery and Management*, pp. 149–166.

Fisher, W. D. (1958). On grouping for maximum homogeneity. *Journal of the American Statistical Association* 53, 789–798.

Forgy, E. (1965). Cluster analysis of multivariate data: Efficiency versus interpretability of classifications. *Biometrics* 21, 768–769. Abstracts in Biometrics.

Fritzke, B. (1997). The LBG-U method for vector quantization an improvement over LBG inspired from neural networks. *Neural Processing Letters* 5, 35–45.

Gómez, D., Guada, C., Rodríguez, J., Montero, J., and Zarrazola, E. (2015). Fuzzy image segmentation based upon hierarchical clustering. *Knowledge-Based Systems*, 87. 10.1016/j.knosys.2015.07.017.

Likas, N. V. and Verbeek, J. J. (2003). The global k-means clustering algorithm. *Pattern Recognition* 36, 451–461.

Linde, Y., Buzo, A., and Gray, R. (1980). An algorithm for vector quantizer design. *IEEE Transactions on Communications* 28, 84–95.

Lloyd, S.P. (1982). Least squares quantization in PCM. *IEEE Transactions on Information Theory* 28, 129–136.

Macqueen, J. (1967). Some methods for classification and analysis of multivariate observations. In *Proc. of the Fifth Berkeley Symposium on Mathematical Statistics and Probability*, 1967, pp. 281–297.

Pham, D. L. and Prince, J. L. (1999). An adaptive fuzzy C-means algorithm for image segmentation in the presence of intensity inhomogeneities. *Pattern Recognition Letters* 20(1), 57–68. https://doi.org/10.1016/S0167-8655(98)00121-4.

Zhang, B. (2000). *Generalized k-harmonic means – boosting in unsupervised learning*. Tech. Report 137, Hewlett Packard, October 2000.

Zhang, S., You, Z., and Wu, X. (2017). Plant disease leaf image segmentation based on super-pixel clustering and EM algorithm. *Neural Computing and Applications* 31. 10.1007/s00521-017-3067-8.

# 6 Advanced Image Compression Techniques Used for Big Data

## 6.1 INTRODUCTION

Image compression is a valuable approach for putting away the huge volume of structured or unstructured data in every field of application of image processing and data innovation technology. It assists with expanding, upgrades operational efficiencies, enables reduction of cost, and manages the risk for business operations. The growth rate of databases is expanding with high quantity and quality as well. This is called big data and these data require data compression for storage and retrieval processes. The main objective of this chapter is to cover advanced image compression techniques utilized in big data management. As we all are aware, the database such as images plays an imperative role in image-based data mining for the association to provide an advanced output. Data with huge volume or complex images consistently lead to an issue. In this manner, image data compression is frantically required by all the organization for smooth, dependable, and ideal retrieval of the data. There are various image-based data compression algorithms created by analysts to compress the data and image documents that apply in different fields, for example, biomedical, space/satellite, agriculture, military operations, and so on. The data are put away in the buffer area of the computer storage unit. A buffer is a consecutive segment of computer memory that holds more than one occurrence of a similar data type. The overflow condition of a buffer happens when a program endeavors to read or write beyond a limit of allocated memory or when a program endeavors to place information in a memory area preceding a buffer. The buffer overwhelm issue can be avoided by industries frantically needing data compression to store the data inside the specified space of the buffer area.

The imaged data compression technique has been one of the empowering advances for the on-going computerized transformation for quite a long time which brought about renowned algorithms such as Huffman Encoding, LZ77, Gzip, RLE, JPEG, and so on. Many researchers have investigated the character/word-based ways to deal with image compression missing out a great opportunity, the bigger part of mining of patterns from huge databases. Our attention to cover research studies focuses around compression perceptions of data mining as recommended by Naren Ramakrishnan et al. wherein there are effective renditions of original algorithms of compression techniques for images that utilize different Frequent Pattern Mining/Clustering procedures.

Image-based data compression is the general term for various procedures and projects created to address this issue. A compression technique is utilized to change over information from a simple-to-utilize introduction to one upgraded for minimization. Similarly, an uncompressed technique restores the data to its original structure. This procedure is utilized on huge information substances in the consistent and physical database. In the physical database, the information is put away in bit shapes as information stream, while on the coherent database, the specific information is put away as information substance types in the output stream, and they trade shared information substances with a little bit of programming code. The logical technique is compressing the data in the database.

## 6.2 AN OVERVIEW OF THE COMPRESSION PROCESS

Currently, image processing is generally utilized for the computer vision framework and for different applications, for example, medical areas, military operations for object detection or tracking, satellite image operations, and so on. Satellite imaging is a significant and urgent field of research. Satellite images are utilized for climate checking, space data investigation, and location detection and tracking operations. Additionally, medical imaging, for example, magnetic resonance imaging (MRI), computed tomography (CT), and ultrasound, serves as an antecedent for deciding a patient's undertaking toward therapeutics or medical surgery. The rising inescapability of interminable sicknesses worldwide has brought about an extraordinary increment in the number of analytical imaging strategies being executed yearly. This, thus, has offered to ascend to further develop imaging advancements and programming to assist in precise determination. For the motivations behind the patient clinical history, these images are put away for extremely significant stretches. Likewise, future research and clinical advancements render such records exceptionally sensitive, emphasizing their requirement to be stored. Storage, be that as it may, represents an incredible test since there is restricted capacity ability to save these ever-developing clinical images. Any technology that improves satellite images and clinical image compression is welcome. The lossy compression is utilized broadly in space frameworks or multimedia applications for at least one target such as lessening transmission time, decreasing transmission bandwidth utilization, and diminishing the information rate. Satellite imaging is an incredible methodology for specialists to contemplate the space data, geoscience, and space data investigation. Image compression is used to diminish the size of the data with a particular ultimate objective to decrease memory space for data storage, which in turn reduces information move limiting necessities for continuous transmission. Image decompression is to give back the first image with no adversity. Image compression and decompression assume a significant role in information transmission. Image compression is one of the key innovations for imaging instruments, and it is the procedure to evacuate the excess and insignificant data from the image with the goal that lone basic data can be spoken to utilizing fewer bits to lessen the capacity size, transmission bandwidth, and transmission time prerequisites. Image decompression is to translate and to remake the first image. It is an application to improve the image in terms of quality or size. Telemedicine is the procedure to give better humane services to the patients at remote locations. Patients who are living in a remote zone can get clinical consideration from specialists far or experts far away as opposed to visiting them straightforwardly. Classes associated with telemedicine are store and forward, remote checking, and real-time instructiveness. Developing advances in this field are video communication and wellbeing data innovation. This kind of clinical consideration is given to creating nation where patients in remote zones are more. Specialist care conveyance manages telecardiology, teletransmission, telepsychiatry, teleradiology, telepathology, teledermatology, teledentistry, teleradiology, and teleophthalmology. A progressed and exploratory help manages telesurgery. In telesurgery, work focuses around the image compression/decompression algorithms for the quick transmission of images. The effective image compression/decompression algorithm decreases the capacity size of the specific image for quick transmission. Lossless compression plays a significant role in clinical image transmission. Image compression/decompression is a significant prerequisite of imaging payloads on telemedicine applications.

### 6.2.1 CONCEPT OF IMAGE COMPRESSION

The basic concept of image compression is listed as follows:

- It is the replacement of frequently occurring data or symbols, with short codes that require fewer bits of capacity than the original image.
- Saves space, yet expects time to save and extract.
- Success changes with the sort of information.
- Works best on information with low spatial changeability and restricted potential qualities.
- Work is inadequately with high spatial changeability information or continuous surfaces.
- Exploits inherent redundancy and superfluity by changing an information record into a little one (Figure 6.1).

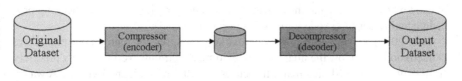

**FIGURE 6.1**   Block diagram of image compression concept.

## 6.3 RELATED WORK OF IMAGE COMPRESSION METHODS

Hagag et al. (2017) introduced a satellite multispectral image compression technique. This technique depends on expelling subbands to diminish the capacity size of multispectral images with high-resolution pixels. Here, discrete wavelet change with an entropy coder is adjusted to perform the compression procedure. By utilizing this strategy, image quality obtained was 3–11 DB. Improved Thematic Mapper in addition to satellite multispectral images is utilized to obtain approval for the above pressure procedure.

Huang et al. (2017) presented a hybrid technique for binary tree coding with adaptive (BTCA) scanning demand. This strategy is a suitable algorithm to give compression low unpredictability. BTCA gives huge memory space; however, it does not give random access memory (RAM). Be that as it may, in this paper, another coding strategy BTCA with ideal truncation is utilized. As per BTCA, images are partitioned into a few obstructs that are encoded separately. It will choose the legitimate truncation focuses for each square to enhance the proportion of twisting at a high compression ratio (CR) with low memory necessity and RAM is acquired. Remote detecting image information is huge in size so it requires pressure with a low-multifaceted nature calculation that can be utilized for space-borne hardware. This strategy is basic and quick which is reasonable for space borne equipment. It improves the peak signal-to-noise ratio (PSNR) just as image visual quality.

Haddad et al. (2017) utilized a wavelet change followed by an adaptive scanning technique. This compression technique is favored for a remote detecting image that is appropriate for board-available compression. Wavelet change is utilized to lessen the capacity size, and the versatile filtering technique focuses on securing the surface data of a specific image. This mix of methods improves coding execution. Here, entropy coding or some other convoluted segments are not utilized.

Jiang et al. (2017) utilized the FPGA-based correspondence stack technique for compacting the information. It is utilized on nano-satellite space missions. This technique allows the satellite administrator to cooperate with the satellite utilizing a CCSDS consistent RF joins for proficient correspondence. It is utilized for both space ground and locally available interchanges. Here, the nano-satellite is fused with ground-station arrangements. Here, the technique is built with less apparatus use so it redirects a large portion of the constrained utilization assets toward tries.

Nasr and Martini (2017) took a shot at introduction based on adaptive lifting DWT with an adjusted SPIHT algorithm. Generally, DWT is embraced for quick computation and low memory necessities. Be that as it may, it does not focus on local data. It gives both geometric and spatial data, which focus on surface data. However, new method introduction was based on versatile lifting DWT, which focuses more on image texture features, and the altered SPIHT algorithm improves the checking procedure and lessens the code bit length and run time.

Hsu (2017) dealt with a joint watermarking compression plan. In this plan, there is likelihood to shadow the images or to legitimize their unwavering quality precisely from their compressed bit stream. It focuses on installed limit and twisting. A watermarked image does not vary from their unique visual which offers a huge ability to offer help for different security administrations. This plan is additionally reached out for checking image integrity and credibility.

Shi et al. (2016) presented different transmission improvement compression strategies. Most of these are utilized in the telehealth application that is particularly embraced for medical images. They are capable of examines to monitor the concerned object for self-satisfaction based on various medical images and then transmitted to a portable telehealth framework for further processes like health-related decision making, etc. In various transmission optimization techniques, images are sorted based on the optics' similarities in the pixels because images are connected with the pixel goals. Subsequently, there are various ways to advance transmission optimization strategies with image recreating techniques under this technique image is recreated at the client site for representation.

Selčan et al. (2015) presented the visual quality assessment technique. For telemedicine applications, this is an on-going method of assessing image quality and video quality. It examines the quality of seeing a diminished size logo typified in an inert segment of the clinical ultrasound outline. This strategy focuses on three distinct measurements, top sign to noise proportion, structure-likeness record metric, and differential mean feeling score, and it need not bother with the underlying stage to assess the viewpoint; it procures immense correspondence for the various measurements utilized. It likewise improves the quality between the inferred logo and the first casing. It brings about packed logo information with its overhead assurance.

Hsu (2015) took a shot at the crusting-based compression technique. It is received for the telemedicine applications and to improve the transference rate, arcade degree, and contact among therapeutic group and outpatients. This strategy incorporates a serious Hopfield neural system and Modified square truncation coding. A serious Hopfield neural system is to bring out better grouping precision and to beat the deformities in swaying fundamental paces of bunching. Changed square truncation coding is to investigate the bunching areas with differentiate pressure proportions and to make sure of significant image goodness information if there should be an occurrence of little size images. This strategy is likewise suggested with the end goal of remote future obligation coupled to cloud databases.

Bouslimi et al. (2015) chips away at a novel division-based pressure conspire. It is utilized for media transmission in telemedicine applications. The primary target of this technique is to overhaul information relocation and discussion among patients and therapeutic laborers. This strategy incorporates an improved watershed change and altered vector quantization.

Improved watershed change is to divide a clinical image into various areas to oversee significant estimation and assignment. Adjusted vector quantization is to review the cut areas with unmistakable compression rates permitting supporting important lineaments and discouraging the image size.

Sandhu and Kaur (2015) proposed that the Genetically Modified Compression Algorithm demonstrated better outcomes by keeping both the PSNR and pressure size in balance. The execution time of the calculation is likewise sensible to run it over the cloud to pack images and consequently spare the extra room. The nature of the image is saved after pressure. The current research work is done on alternate kinds of image information so in future work can be stretched out to sound and video information.

## 6.4 IMAGE COMPRESSION TECHNIQUES

Image compression techniques are divided into two categories as follows (Figure 6.2):
The fundamental description of lossless compression techniques is provided in Chapter 1. This section covers the survey of practical approaches of these compression techniques as follows.

### 6.4.1 LOSSLESS COMPRESSION

Juliet et al. (2016) talked about a novel philosophy, which incorporates Ripplet change to give a decent quality of the images and accomplishes a high compression rate. In this work, to achieve a higher compression rate the images are spoken to at various scales and headings. Cyriac and Chellamuthu (2012) proposed a Visually Lossless Run Length Encoder/Decoder to take care of the development issue of the customary Run Length Encoder/Decoder. In this paper, the proposed strategy can sufficiently pack the image and furthermore helps in the quicker equipment usage of continuous applications. Brahimi et al. (2017) portrayed a novel compression method wherein the sign and the image both get together packed with a solitary codec. The fundamental focal point of this methodology is to insert the wavelet-disintegrated signal into the decayed image, and the resultant image is utilized for the compression. Arif et al. (2015) proposed a productive strategy for the compression of the fluoroscopic images with no misfortune. In this work, the separated region of interest (ROI) is packed with a mix of Run Length and Huffman coding. In this paper, final results express that the proposed procedure gives a compression proportion of 400% in contrast to other regular methods. Das and Kundu (2013) revealed a lossless clinical image watermarking strategy which depends on the idea of the ROI. The principle point of this work is to give answers for the various issues with respect to clinical information conveyance such as security, content confirmation, safe chronicling, and safe recovery and move of information. In this paper, seven distinct modalities are

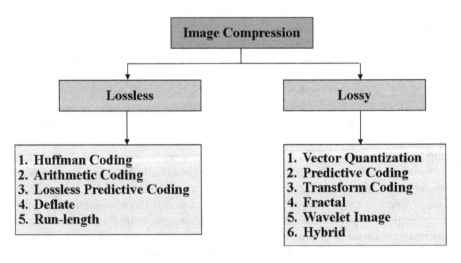

**FIGURE 6.2**   Image compression techniques.

utilized to portray and contrast the outcomes which show that the proposed procedure is basic and apparent in giving security to the clinical database. Lucas et al. (2017) introduced a novel lossless compression method for three-dimensional (3-D) least rate indicators (MRPs) for volumetric arrangements of clinical images. The introduced strategy depends on the instrument of MRPs. In this paper, it is presumed that the introduced method can improve the mistake likelihood of the MRP calculation, and it achieves high compression effectiveness over the high-effectiveness video coding (HEVC) and another standard for profundity clinical signs. Špelič and Žalik (2012) proposed a novel a calculation begat as a fragmented voxel compression calculation to pack 3-D CT images and for successful transmission of graphical information obtained from a CT scanner. This paper portrays that initially Hounsfield scale is utilized to fragment the clinical information and afterward compression is applied. In this work, a model machine is utilized to assess the productivity of the proposed calculation. Anusuya et al. (2014) presented a novel lossless codec utilizing an entropy coder to pack the 3-D mind images. In this work, MRI methodology was utilized to break down the proficiency of the proposed calculation, and this work centers around diminishing the calculation time with the utilization of equal processing. Xiao et al. (2016) acquainted Integer Discrete Tchebichef Transform with an assortment of images with no loss of information. In this work, the proposed strategy is introduced based on factorization of $N \times N$ Discrete Tchebichef Transform into $N + 1$ single line basic reversible frameworks with least adjusting mistakes. The proposed procedure accomplished whole number-to-whole number mapping for powerful lossless compression. In this paper, the clinical modalities alluded to are CT and MRI to assess the outcomes, and it is inferred that the proposed algorithm can accomplish a higher compression proportion than iDCT. Amri et al. (2017) introduced two lossless compression techniques instituted as a repro: TIFF (watermarked Reduction/Expansion Protocol combined with TIFF arrangement) and wREPro.JLS (wREPro combined with JPEG-LS format). In this work, the introduced methods are utilized to diminish the image size and encoding calculations for lossless compression. It is seen that the proposed receptive protects the image quality for high compression rates, and it additionally gives different upgrades over regular JPEG image compression standard. Ramesh and Shanmugam (2010) portrayed the Wavelet Decomposition Prediction Method for lossless compression of clinical images. In this methodology, the forecast condition of each sub-band depends on the connection investigation. It is seen from the trial results that the proposed approach gives a higher compression rate when contrasted with SPHIT and JPEG2000 standard. Ibraheem et al. (2016) introduced two new lossless compression methods which depend on the logarithmic algorithm. The proposed approaches can give improved image quality in contrast to regular DWT. Avramović and Banjac (2012) presented a novel lossless compression method where a basic setting-based entropy coder is utilized. The proposed approach depends on the idea of expectation to evacuate the spatial repetition in images and successfully pack the images with no loss of information. It is reasoned that the proposed approach can accomplish a similar exhibition for great images as the other normalized calculations. Bairagi (2015) revealed the idea of balance for the compression of the clinical images. Here, the introduced approach is lossless and ready to expel the repetitive information from the image successfully and effectively. In this work, the announced idea is teamed up with the current methods to close the outcomes. Zuo et al. (2015) introduced an improved clinical image compression approach IMIC-ROI to adequately and effectively pack the clinical images. The proposed procedure depends on the idea of ROI and non-ROI districts. It is seen that the introduced receptive accomplishes a higher compression proportion and great estimations of GSM and structural similarity index (SSIM) in contrast to other customary procedures. Srinivasan et al. (2011) portrayed a coder for the powerful compression of the electroencephalograph signal grid. The instrument portrayed comprises two phases, initially lossy coding layer (SPHIT) and leftover coding layer (number juggling coding). It is presumed that the two-phase compression conspire is powerful and the idea of preprocessing ready to give 6% improvement and 2 phase yields 3% further improvement in the compression. Taquet and Labit (2012) announced a hierarchical oriented prediction approach for the goals of the adaptable lossless and close lossless compression of the clinical images. It is seen that the proposed approach is best utilized for the close lossless compression since it can give a somewhat better or equivalent PSNR for a high piece rate in contrast to the JPEG 2000 norm.

### 6.4.2 LOSSY COMPRESSION TECHNIQUES

Bruylants et al. (2015) introduced a novel Wavelet-based system that bolsters JPEG 2000 with its volumetric expansion. The introduced approach upgrades the exhibition of the JPEG2000 for volumetric clinical image compression. In this work, the conventional codec system, directional wavelet changes, and nonexclusive intraband forecast mode tried for the wide scope of compression settings for the volumetric compression. In this paper, three clinical modalities (CT, MRI, and US) are considered to figure out the productivity of the proposed approach. Ayoobkhan et al. (2017) introduced a novel compression strategy PE-VQ for the lossy compression of clinical images. In this methodology, to build codebook the fake honey bee province and hereditary calculations are utilized to figure out the ideal outcomes, and expectation mistake and vector quantization ideas are included for the compelling compression of the images. It is seen that the proposed procedure can accomplish a higher PSNR for a given compression proportion in contrast to different calculations. Rufai et al. (2013) depicted a novel lossy compression procedure for clinical image compression. The detailed methodology contains Singular Value Decomposition and Huffman coding. It is seen from the results of simulation that the announced methodology can give better quantitative and visual outcomes in contrast to the other ordinary strategies such as Huffman coding and JPEG2000. Selvi and Nadarajan (2017) proposed a two-dimensional (2-D) lossy compression strategy for the compression of the MRI and CT images. The proposed approach depends on the Wavelet-Based Contourlet Transform and Binary Array Technique. It is presumed that the proposed approach requires less preparation time and produce exact yield brings about the correlation with the current wavelet-based set apportioning in various leveled and inserted square coders. Sriraam and Shyamsunder (2011) presented a 3-D wavelet encoder way to deal with the pack of 3-D clinical images. Here, the revealed approach work is two phases, right off the bat the encoding should be possible with four wavelet changes named Daubechies 4, Daubechies 6, Cohen-Daubechies-Feauveau 9/7, and Cohen-Daubechies-Feauveau 5/3 and at later stage 3-D SPHIT, 3-D SPECK, and 3-D BISK. Hosseini and Naghsh-Nilchi (2012) depicted logical vector quantization for clinical image compression. Here, the clinical methodology ultrasound is utilized to mimic the examination and finish up the outcomes. It is demonstrated that the proposed approach can accomplish a higher compression proportion and PSNR in contrast to the other customary calculations (JPEG, JPEG2K, and SPHIT). Bairagi et al. (2013) detailed a text-based way to deal with the pack of clinical images viably. The detailed component manages visual quality instead of the pixel-wise constancy. Prabhu et al. (2013) introduced 3-D Warped Discrete Cosine Transformation (WDCT) for the compression of the MRI images viably. The introduced approach depends on the idea of 2-D WDCT and in this paper, an image coding plan is utilized for the enormous datasets which depend on the idea of a 3-D WDCT approach.

### 6.4.3 HYBRID COMPRESSION TECHNIQUES

Mofreh et al. (2016) revealed LPC-DWT-Huffman, a novel image compression method to improve the compression rate. This detailed procedure is the blend of the LPC-Huffman and the DWT-Huffman. It is seen that the announced strategy can give a higher compression rate when contrasted with the Huffman and DWT-Huffman. Raza et al. (2012) introduced a half and half-lossless compression strategy for clinical image arrangements. It is seen that the detailed strategy can accomplish an upgraded compression rate when contrasted with other existing strategies. Eben Sophia and Anitha (2017) proposed an improved setting-based compression procedure for the clinical images. The proposed approach depends on the ideas of wavelet change, standardization, and expectation. In this paper, the proposed receptive has to accomplish a decent quality image in contrast to the original image for the chosen logical area. It is seen that the proposed procedure is ready to accomplish better execution quantitatively and subjectively. Parikh et al. (2017) depicted the utilization of HEVC for clinical image compression. In this work, three clinical modalities (MRI, CT, and CR) are utilized to process the test results and contrasted these outcomes and JPEG2000. It is seen that the introduced strategy shows an expansion in compression execution by 54% in contrast to the JPEG2000. Somassoundaram and Subramaniam (2018) revealed a crossbreed approach in which 2-D bi-orthogonal multiwavelet transform and SPECK-Deflate encoder are utilized. The primary reason for this methodology is to lessen the transmitting transfer speed by packing the clinical information. It is seen that the proposed approach can accomplish a higher compression proportion than other regular calculations. Haddad et al. (2017) proposed a novel joint watermarking plan for the clinical images. The proposed method is the blend of JPEG-LS and bit replacement watermarking balance. It is seen that the proposed procedure is ready to furnish the equivalent watermarked images with high-security benefits in contrast to different methods. Perumal and Rajasekaran (2016) introduced a hybrid calculation DWT-BP for clinical image compression. In this paper, the creator thinks about the DWT coding, Back Propagation Neural Network, and a half and half DWTBP to break down the exhibition of the introduced approach. It is presumed that the proposed half-and-half method can give a superior compression proportion and accomplishes a better PSNR. Karthikeyan and Thirumoorthi (2016) portrayed Sparse Fast Fourier Transform, a mixture procedure for clinical image compression. In this work, the creator likewise contrasts the proposed procedure and the other three compression techniques such as Karhunen-Loeve Transforms, Walsh-Hadamard Transform, and Fast Fourier Transform. It is seen that the proposed strategy is ready to give improved and productive outcomes in the entirety of the assessment quantifies in contrast with the writer depicted techniques. Thomas et al. (2014) revealed a crossbreed image compression approach for the clinical images utilizing the lossy and lossless instrument for the telemedicine application. It is seen that the proposed half breed strategy is agreeable to accomplish a higher compression proportion and has less loss of data with the powerful utilization of number-crunching entropy coding. Vaishnav et al. (2017) proposed a novel half breed strategy for the lossy and lossless compression of the clinical images. The proposed approach is the mix of the doubletree wavelet change and the number juggling coding approach. It is seen that the proposed approach is a lot of compelling and productive than the other ordinary calculations such as DWT and SPHIT and ready to accomplish a higher PSNR and compression proportion. Rani et al. (2018) detailed a novel crossbreed strategy for clinical image compression. The announced methodology depends on the Haar Wavelet Transform (HWT) and Particle Swarm Optimization (PSO). It is seen that the proposed approach can accomplish a higher compression proportion and PSNR. Jiang et al. (2012) introduced a half-and-half calculation for clinical image compression. The significant objective of the proposed approach is to pack the indicative-related data with a high-compression proportion. It is seen that the proposed approach can accomplish a great PSNR and compelling running time in contrast to the other portrayed calculations. Sanchez et al. (2010) portrayed another instrument for the compression of the 3-D clinical images with the volume of interest (VOI) coding. It is seen that the proposed receptive accomplishes better recreation quality in contrast to the 3-D JPEG2000 and MAXSHIFT with VOI coding. Hsu (2012) proposed an instrument to isolate the tumor from the mammogram with the assistance of improved watershed change with earlier data. The objective of the proposed component is to proficiently pack the mammogram without trading off the nature of the necessary area. It has appeared from the exploratory outcomes that the proposed instrument reproduces adequately and productively in the use of mammogram compression.

### 6.4.4 Some Advanced Image Compression Techniques

#### 6.4.4.1 Vector Quantization (VQ)

VQ is one of the progressed lossy data compression methods. Vector quantization is a proficient coding method to quantize signal vectors. It has been broadly utilized in sign and image preparation, for example, design acknowledgment and discourse and image coding. A VQ compression technique has two primary advances: codebook preparation (now and then additionally alluded to as codebook age) and coding (i.e., code vector coordinating). In the preparation step, comparative vectors in a preparation arrangement are assembled into bunches, and each group is allowed to a solitary agent vector called a code vector. In the coding step, each information vector is then packed by supplanting it with the closest code vector referenced by a basic group record. The list (or address) of the coordinated code vector in the codebook is then transmitted to the decoder over a channel and is utilized by the decoder to recover a similar code vector from an indistinguishable codebook. This is the remade multiplication of the comparing input vector. The compression is in this manner obtained by transmitting the file of the code vector instead of the whole code vector itself.

A vector quantizes maps $k$-dimensional vectors in the vector space $R_k$ into a finite set of vectors $\{Y = y_i \mid i = 1, 2, 3, \dots \dots, N\}$. Each vector $y_i$ is called a code vector or a codeword and the set of all the codewords is called a codebook (Figure 6.3).

The amount of compression will be described in terms of the rate, which will be measured in bits per sample. Suppose we have a codebook of size k, and the input vector is of dimension L. We need to use $[log_2\ k]$ bits to specify which of the codevectors was selected. The rate for an L-dimensional vector quantizer with a codebook of size K is $\dfrac{\left[\log 2k\right]}{L}$.

**Highlights of Vector quantization:**

- Vector quantization was first proposed by Gray in 1984.
- First, construct codebook which is composed of codevectors.
- For one vector being encoding, find the nearest vector in codebook (determined by the Euclidean distance).
- Replace the vector by the index in the codebook.
- When decoding, find the vector corresponding by the index in the codebook.

**Application of Vector quantization**

The vector quantization technique is efficiently used in various areas of biometric modalities such as fingerprint pattern recognition and face recognition by generating codebooks of desired size.

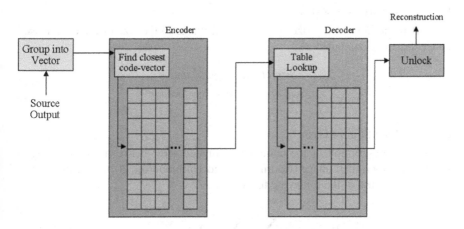

**FIGURE 6.3**   Vector quantization working diagram.

## 6.5 COMPARISON OF VARIOUS COMPRESSION ALGORITHMS

This segment depicts the correlation of different algorithms referenced in the literature study. The fundamental correlation parameters utilized for looking at the lossless satellite image compression calculations are bits per pixel (BPP), compression proportion, blunder flexibility, and multifaceted nature. On account of the lossy algorithm, top sign to commotion proportion and mean square mistake are considered as examination parameters notwithstanding compression proportion and multifaceted nature. Rate contortion bends are utilized to evaluate how much compression can be accomplished by the given lossy algorithm at a specific piece rate. PSNR and mean square error (MSE) values are utilized as bending measures on account of the lossy image compression algorithm. Rate twisting bends are utilized to upgrade the lossy algorithm dependent on the application. The compression proportion is the proportion of the size of the original and the reproduced image. Error versatility is the level of spectral error regulation of the algorithm. Multifaceted nature is the running time of programming usage of the algorithm.

### 6.5.1 PERFORMANCE PARAMETERS OF COMPRESSION TECHNIQUES

The compression techniques use a wide number of performance measures to compute their efficiency and performance. The metrics used to compute the performance are:

#### 6.5.1.1 Peak Signal-to-Noise Ratio

The PSNR is defined as the ratio of the maximum pixel intensity to the mean square error (Abo-Zahhad et al., 2015). The formula used to compute the PSNR is represented as follows:

$$PSNR = 20 \log\left(\frac{2^B - 1}{MSE}\right) dB \qquad (6.1)$$

Here, $B$ is the number of bits and MSE is the mean square error.

#### 6.5.1.2 Compression Ratio

The CR is the ratio of the size of the original image to the size of the compressed image. It can be computed as

$$CR = \frac{Size\ of\ the\ original\ image}{Size\ of\ the\ compressed\ image} \qquad (6.2)$$

#### 6.5.1.3 Mean Square Error

MSE is the description of the cumulative squared error between the compressed image and the original image (Karthikeyan and Thirumoorthi, 2016). It can be computed with the use of the following formula:

$$MSE = \frac{1}{MN} \sum_{j=1}^{M} \sum_{k=1}^{N} \left(X_{j,k} - X'_{j,k}\right)^2 \qquad (6.3)$$

#### 6.5.1.4 Structural Similarity Index

The SSIM is used to measure the tendency of similarity between the original image and the compressed image (Eben Sophia and Anitha, 2017). The formula used to find the SSIM is:

$$SSIM(x,y) = \frac{\left(2\mu_x\mu_y + C_1\right)\left(2\delta_{xy} + C_2\right)}{\left(\mu_x^2 + \mu_x^2 + C_1\right)\left(\delta_x^2 + \delta_x^2 + C_2\right)} \tag{6.4}$$

Here, $x$ is the original image, $y$ is the reconstructed image, C1 and C2 are the constants, $\mu$ is the average gray value, and $\delta$ is the variance

#### 6.5.1.5 Bits per Pixel

BPP is defined as the ratio of the total size of the compressed image to the total number of the pixel in the image (Perumal and Pallikonda Rajasekaran, 2016).

$$BPP = \frac{Size\ of\ the\ compressed\ image}{Total\ no.\ of\ pixel\ in\ the\ image} \tag{6.5a}$$

$$BPP = \frac{16\left(number\ of\ bits\right)}{m \times n}\ size \tag{6.5b}$$

where $m$ and $n$ are image dimensions and size is the dimensions of the compressed image.

#### 6.5.1.6 Signal-to-Noise Ratio

The SNR can be defined as the ratio of the signal power to the noise power. It is measured in dB and can be computed as

$$SNR = 10\log\left\{\frac{\sum_{i=0}^{N-1}\sum_{j=0}^{M-1}\left[f(i,j)^2\right]}{\sum_{i=0}^{N-1}\sum_{j=0}^{M-1}\left[\left|f(i,j)-f^*(i,j)\right|^2\right]}\right\} \tag{6.6a}$$

$$Or \quad SNR = 10\log_{10}\frac{E_X}{E_Y} \tag{6.6b}$$

where $E_X$ and $E_Y$ are the energy of the original image signal and reconstruction error image signal, respectively.

#### 6.5.1.7 Percent Rate of Distortion

It is the measure of the distortion in the reconstructed image. The lesser the value of the PRD, the less distorted the reconstructed image (Selvi et al., 2017). It can be computed with the use of the following formula:

$$PRD = \sqrt{\frac{\sum_{x=1}^{M}\sum_{y=1}^{N}\left[\left|f(x,y)-f'(x,y)\right|^2\right]}{\sum_{x=1}^{M}\sum_{y=1}^{N}\left[f(x,y)^2\right]}} \times 100 \tag{6.7}$$

Here, $M \times N$ represents size of the image, $f(x, y)$ is the original image, and $f'(x, y)$ is the reconstructed image.

### 6.5.1.8 Correlation Coefficient

It is used to describe the existing correlation between the original image and the reconstructed image (Selvi et al., 2017). It can be calculated by,

$$CC = \frac{\sum_{x=1}^{M}\sum_{y=1}^{N} f(x,y) \times f'(x,y)}{\sqrt{\sum_{x=1}^{M}\sum_{y=1}^{N} \left(f(x,y)\right)^2}\sqrt{\sum_{x=1}^{M}\sum_{y=1}^{N} \left(f'(x,y)\right)^2}} \tag{6.8}$$

Here, $M \times N$ represents size of the image, $f(x, y)$ is the original image, and $f'(x, y)$ is the reconstructed image

### 6.5.1.9 Structural Content

It is used to depict the comparison between two images inherited in small patches and to determine the common things images have (Karthikeyan and Thirumoorthi, 2016). The higher the value of SC, the poorer the quality of the image.

$$SC = \frac{\sum_{j=1}^{M}\sum_{k=1}^{N} X_{j,k}^2}{\sum_{j=1}^{M}\sum_{k=1}^{N} X_{j,k}'^2} \tag{6.9}$$

Here, $M$ and $N$ are the dimensions of the image.

## 6.6 APPLICATIONS OF COMPRESSION TECHNIQUES

Some of the application areas of compression techniques are as follows (Figure 6.4):

### 6.6.1 Satellite Images

Satellite images are one of the most impressive and significant apparatuses utilized by the meteorologist. They are basically the eyes in the sky. These images console forecasters to the conduct of the environment as they give a reasonable, brief, and exact portrayal of how situations are developing. Estimating the climate and directing exploration would be amazingly troublesome without satellites. Information taken at stations around the nation is constrained in its portrayals of barometrical

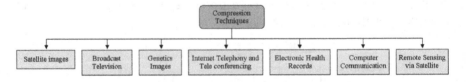

**FIGURE 6.4** Compression techniques.

movement. It is as yet conceivable to carry out a decent investigation from the information, but since the stations are isolated by several miles huge highlights can be missed. Satellite images help in indicating what cannot be estimated or seen. Likewise, the satellite images are seen as truth. There is no possibility of the blunder. Satellite images give information that can be deciphered "direct".

### 6.6.2 BROADCAST TELEVISION

Computerized broadcasting gives superior quality, high-caliber, and better-communicating administration, supplanting conventional simple telecom. The advanced telecom is grouped into satellite-computerized broadcasting and earthbound advanced telecom.

### 6.6.3 GENETIC IMAGES

Imaging genetic qualities is an interesting technique to survey the effect of genetic factors on both the cerebrum structure and capacity. All the more significantly, imaging hereditary qualities manufacture a scaffold to comprehend the social and clinical ramifications of hereditary qualities and neuroimaging. By portraying and evaluating the cerebrum estimates influenced in mental scatters, imaged genetic qualities are adding to distinguishing potential biomarkers for schizophrenia and related issues.

### 6.6.4 INTERNET TELEPHONY AND TELECONFERENCING

Internet telephony or telecommunications offers the opportunity to design a global multimedia communication system that can eventually replace existing telephony infrastructure. It has upper-layer protocol components that are specific to Internet telephony services: real-time transport protocol (RTP) for carrying voice and video data, data streams as required, and Session Initiative Protocol (SIP) for signals. Some complementary protocols, including the Real-Time Streaming Protocol (RTSP) for control of streaming media and the Wide-Area Service Discovery Protocol (WASRV) for the location of telephony gateways.

### 6.6.5 ELECTRONIC HEALTH RECORDS

The electronic health record (EHR) at that point called the electronic medical record (EMR) or computerized patient record. The Electronic Health Record (EHR) is about quality, wellbeing, and proficiency. An EHR is an electronic rendition of a patient's clinical history, that is kept up by the supplier after some time, and may incorporate the entirety of the key managerial clinical information applicable to that people care under a specific supplier, including socioeconomics, progress notes, issues, meds, imperative signs, past clinical history, vaccinations, research center information, and radiology reports. The EHR computerizes access to data and can possibly smooth out the clinician's work process. The EHR likewise can bolster other consideration-related exercises legitimately or by implication through different interfaces, including proof-based choice help, quality administration, and result announcement.

### 6.6.6 COMPUTER COMMUNICATION

Communication is the exchange of information or data between at least two things, for example, individuals, gadgets, governments, associations, or organizations. In advanced correspondence, information is traded between at least two processing gadgets.

### 6.6.7 REMOTE SENSING VIA SATELLITES

Remote sensors gather information by identifying the vitality that is reflected from Earth. These sensors can be on satellites or mounted on airplanes. Remote sensors can be either aloof or dynamic. Inactive sensors react to outside improvements. They record common vitality that is reflected or transmitted from the Earth's surface. The most well-known wellspring of radiation identified by detached sensors is reflected in daylight.

## REFERENCES

Abo-Zahhad, M., Gharieb, R.R., Ahmed, S.M., and Abd-Ellah, M.K. (2015). Huffman image compression incorporating DPCM and DWT. *Journal of Signal and Information Processing* 6(02), 123.

Amri, H., Khalfallah, A., Gargouri, M., Nebhani, N., Lapayre, J.-C., and Bouhlel, M.-S. (2017). Medical image compression approach based on image resizing, digital watermarking and lossless compression. *Journal of Signal Processing Systems* 87(2), 203–214.

Anusuya, V., Srinivasa Raghavan, V., and Kavitha, G. (2014). Lossless compression on MRI images using SWT. *Journal of Digital Imaging* 27(5), 594–600.

Arif, A.S., Mansor, S., Logeswaran, R., and Abdul Karim, H. (2015). Auto-shape lossless compression of pharynx and esophagus fluoroscopic images. *Journal of Medical Systems* 39(2), 5.

Avramović, A. and Banjac, G. (2012). On predictive-based lossless compression of images with higher bit depths. *Telfor Journal* 4(2), 122–127.

Ayoobkhan, M.U.A., Chikkannan, E., and Ramakrishnan, K. (2017). Lossy image compression based on prediction error and vector quantisation. *EURASIP Journal on Image and Video Processing* 1, 35.

Bairagi, V.K. (2015). Symmetry-based biomedical image compression. *Journal of Digital Imaging* 28(6), 718–726.

Bairagi, V.K., Sapkal, A.M., and Tapaswi, A. (2013). Texture-based medical image compression. *Journal of Digital Imaging* 26(1), 65–71.

Bouslimi, D., Coatrieux, G., Quantin, C., Allaërt, F.A., Cozic, M., and Roux, C. (2015). A teleassistance protocol based on joint watermarking–encryption evidence for identification of liabilities in case of litigation. *IRBM* 36(5), 279–286.

Brahimi, T., LarbiBoubchir, R.F., and Naït-Ali, A. (2017). An improved multimodal signal-image compression scheme with application to natural images and biomedical data. *Multimedia Tools and Applications* 76(15), 16783–16805.

Bruylants, T., Munteanu, A., and Schelkens, P. (2015). Wavelet based volumetric medical image compression. *Signal Processing: Image Communication* 31, 112–133.

Cyriac, M. and Chellamuthu, C. (2012). A novel visually lossless spatial domain approach for medical image compression. *European Journal of Scientific Research* 71(3), 347–351

Das, S. and Kundu, M.K. (2013). Effective management of medical information through ROI-lossless fragile image watermarking technique. *Computer Methods and Programs in Biomedicine* 111(3), 662–675.

Eben Sophia, P. and Anitha, J. (2017). Contextual medical image compression using normalized wavelet-transform coefficients and prediction. *IETE Journal of Research* 63(5), 671–683.

Haddad, S., Coatrieux, G., Cozic, M., and Bouslimi, D. (2017). Joint watermarking and lossless JPEG-LS compression for medical image security. *IRBM* 38(4), 198–206.

Hagag, A., Hassan, E.S., Amin, M., El-Samie, F.E.A., and Fan, X. (2017). Satellite multispectral image compression based on removing sub-bands. *Optik* 131, 1023–1035.

Hosseini, S.M. and Naghsh-Nilchi, A.-R. (2012). Medical ultrasound image compression using contextual vector quantization. *Computers in Biology and Medicine* 42(7), 743–750.

Hsu, W.Y. (2015). Segmentation-based compression: New frontiers of telemedicine in telecommunication. *Telematics and Informatics* 32(3), 475–485.

Hsu, W.Y. (2017). Clustering-based compression connected to cloud databases in telemedicine and long-term care applications. *Telematics and Informatics* 34(1), 299–310.

Hsu, W.-Y. (2012). Improved watershed transform for tumor segmentation: application to mammogram image compression. *Expert Systems with Applications* 39(4), 3950–3955.

Huang, K.K., Liu, H., Ren, C.X., Yu, Y.F., and Lai, Z.R. (2017). Remote sensing image compression based on binary tree and optimized truncation. *Digital Signal Processing* 64, 96–106.

Ibraheem, M.S., Zahid Ahmed, S., Hachicha, K., Hochberg, S., and Garda, P. (2016). Medical images compression with clinical diagnostic quality using logarithmic DWT. In *2016 IEEE-EMBS International Conference on Biomedical and Health Informatics (BHI)*, pp. 402–405. IEEE.

Jiang, H., Ma, Z., Hu, Y., Yang, B., and Zhang, L. (2012). Medical image compression based on vector quantization with variable block sizes in wavelet domain. *Computational Intelligence and Neuroscience* 2012, 5.

Jiang, N., Zhuang, Y., and Chiu, D.K. (2017). Multiple transmission optimization of medical images in recourse-constraint mobile telemedicine systems. *Computer Methods and Programs in Biomedicine* 145, 103–113.

Juliet, S., Rajsingh, E.B., and Ezra, K. (2016). A novel medical image compression using Ripplet transform. *Journal of Real-Time Image Processing* 11(2), 401–412.

Karthikeyan T. and Thirumoorthi, C. (2016). A hybrid medical image compression techniques for lung cancer. *Indian Journal of Science and Technology (IJST)* 9(39), 1–6.

Lucas, L.F.R., Rodrigues, N.M.M., da Silva Cruz, L.A., and de Faria, S.M.M. (2017). Lossless compression of medical images using 3-d predictors. *IEEE Transactions on Medical Imaging* 36(11), 2250–2260.

Mofreh, A., Barakat, T.M., and Refaat, A.M. (2016). A new lossless medical image compression technique using hybrid prediction model. *Signal Processing: An International Journal (SPIJ)* 10(3), 20.

Nasr, K.M. and Martini, M.G. (2017). A visual quality evaluation method for telemedicine applications. *Signal Processing: Image Communication* 57, 211–218.

Parikh, S.S., Ruiz, D., Kalva, H., Fernández-Escribano, G., and Adzic, V. (2017). High bit-depth medical image compression with HEVC. *IEEE Journal of Biomedical and Health Informatics* 22(2), 552–560.

Perumal, B. and Pallikonda Rajasekaran, M. (2016). A hybrid discrete wavelet transform with neural network back propagation approach for efficient medical image compression. In *2016 International Conference on Emerging Trends in Engineering, Technology and Science (ICETETS)*, pp. 1–5. IEEE.

Perumal, B. and Rajasekaran, M.P. (2016, February). A hybrid discrete wavelet transform with neural network back propagation approach for efficient medical image compression. In *2016 International Conference on Emerging Trends in Engineering, Technology and Science (ICETETS)* (pp. 1–5). IEEE.

Prabhu, K.M.M., Sridhar, K., Mischi, M., and Bharath H.N. (2013). 3-D warped discrete cosine transform for MRI image compression. *Biomedical Signal Processing and Control* 8(1), 50–58.

Ramesh, S.M. and Shanmugam, A. (2010). *Medical image compression using wavelet decomposition for prediction method.* arXiv preprint arXiv:1002.2418.

Rani, M., Shanthi, M., and Chitra, P. (2018). A hybrid medical image coding method based on Haar wavelet transform and particle swarm optimization technique. *International Journal of Pure and Applied Mathematics* 118(18), 3059–3067.

Raza, M., Adnan, A., Sharif, M., and Waqas Haider, S. (2012). Lossless compression method for medical Image sequences using super-spatial structure prediction and Inter-frame coding. *Journal of Applied Research and Technology* 10(4), 618–628.

Rufai, A.M., Anbarjafari, G., and Demirel, H. (2013). Lossy medical image compression using Huffman coding and singular value decomposition. In *2013 21st Signal Processing and Communications Applications Conference (SIU)*, pp. 1–4. IEEE.

Sanchez, V., Abugharbieh, R., and Nasiopoulos, P. (2010). 3-D scalable medical image compression with optimized volume of interest coding. *IEEE Transactions on Medical Imaging* 29(10), 1808–1820.

Sandhu, A.K. and Kaur, E.A. (2015). *Genetically Modified Compression Approach for Multimedia Data on Cloud Storage.*

Selčan, D., Kirbiš, G., and Kramberger, I. (2015). FPGA-based CCSDS compliant miniaturized satellite communication stack. *IFAC-PapersOnLine* 48(10), 28–33.

Selvi, G.U.V. and Nadarajan, R. (2017). CT and MRI image compression using wavelet-based contourlet transform and binary array technique. *Journal of Real-Time Image Processing* 13(2), 261–272.

Selvi, G., Uma, V., and Nadarajan, R. (2017). CT and MRI image compression using wavelet-based contourlet transform and binary array technique. *Journal of Real-Time Image Processing* 13(2), 261–272.

Shi, C., Zhang, J., and Zhang, Y. (2016). Content-based onboard compression for remote sensing images. *Neurocomputing* 191, 330–340.

Somassoundaram, T. and Subramaniam, N.P. (2018). High performance angiogram sequence compression using 2D bi-orthogonal multi wavelet and hybrid speck-deflate algorithm. *Biomedical Research* (0970-938X).

Špelič, D. and Žalik, B. (2012). Lossless compression of threshold-segmented medical images. *Journal of Medical Systems* 36(4), 2349–2357.

Srinivasan, K., Dauwels, J., and Ramasubba Reddy, M. (2011). A two-dimensional approach for lossless EEG compression. *Biomedical Signal Processing and Control* 6(4), 387–394.

Sriraam, N. and Shyamsunder, R. (2011). 3-D medical image compression using 3-D wavelet coders. *Digital Signal Processing* 21(1), 100–109.

Taquet, J. and Labit, C. (2012). Hierarchical oriented predictions for resolution scalable lossless and near-lossless compression of CT and MRI biomedical images. *IEEE Transactions on Image Processing* 21(5), 2641–2652.

Thomas, D.S., Moorthi, M., and Muthalagu, R. (2014). Medical image compression based on automated ROI selection for telemedicine application. *International Journal of Engineering and Computer Science* 3, 3638–3642.

Vaishnav, M., Kamargaonkar, C., and Sharma, M. (2017). Medical image compression using dual tree complex wavelet transform and arithmetic coding technique. *International Journal of Scientific Research in Computer Science, Engineering and Information Technology* 2(3).

Xiao, B., Lu, G., Zhang, Y., Li, W, and Wang, G. (2016). Lossless image compression based on integer discrete Tchebichef transform. *Neurocomputing* 214, 587–593.

Zuo, Z., Lan, X., Deng, L., Yao, S., and Wang, X. (2015). An improved medical image compression technique with lossless region of interest. *Optik* 126(21), 2825–2831.

# Part III

## Various Application of Image Processing

# 7 Application of Image Processing and Data in Remote Sensing

## 7.1 INTRODUCTION

Remote sensing is one of the important data tools of the Global Information System (GIS) through which we can access the remotely sensed images of satellites in digital form, and thus it helps in the rapid integration of remote sensing data into the GIS and in getting detailed results. Satellites are used for continuous acquisition of data for the entire world with different time frames from couple of weeks to a matter of hours.

GIS is an integration of software and hardware which is used for storing, retrieving, mapping, or analyzing geographical data. It stores the spatial features in coordinate systems with reference to particular space of the Earth. However, these spatial features are associated with descriptive attributes in tabular form. These spatial features along with descriptive attributes in a coordinate system can be used for mapping and analysis of data, scientific investigation, resource management, and development planning.

With advancement in digital technology, the techniques of restoration, enhancement, and interpretation of remotely sensed images are faster and reach a new level of GIS. Remote sensing plays an important role in giving the data input to the GIS, and the integration of remote sensing with image processing systems will help to analyze and interpret the satellite images in a more detailed manner.

## 7.2 REMOTE SENSING

Remote sensing can be defined as a process of gathering information about objects or areas without having contact with them. One of the best examples of remote sensing is our eyes, which use visible light energy for gathering information of our surroundings. Generally, remote sensing is used for the study of data in terms of interaction of the Earth's surface with electromagnetic energy which can be used for GIS application for further processes. Thus, remote sensing can be defined as recording of data from the Earth's surface from a distance without direct inspection or drawing of maps. The idea of remote sensing came from invention of photography and aviation, which enables capturing pictures from balloons, planes, and later from satellites, etc.

For landscape ecology, the information for remotely sensed data comes from different regions of the spectrum, which depends on backscattering properties of various surface materials such as the type of vegetation or soil or areas of water and types of sensors being used. Take an example of green vegetation, where the leaf pigment absorbs a high level of blue and red part from the visible spectrum and a low level of absorption of the green spectral range which is responsible for leaves to appear green in color. The leaf surface disperses a high degree of infrared (IR) radiation which makes this wavelength suitable for distinguishing between different vegetation types. On the other hand, a dry or ill leaf with a damaged structure is recognized as low reflection of IR from the spectrum. There is also high backscattering of shortwave IR due to the low water content which is responsible for the color of dry and ill leaves.

A spectral area consists of visible light, IR, and thermal areas. A human perception lies between 0.4 and 0.7 μm, whereas the remaining wavelength can be used for the recording purpose and by remote sensing devices. Those radiations are reflected by the Earth's surface with widths ranging from 0.1 to 0.2 μm and hence do not take part in the continuous spectrum and can be recorded digitally. Most satellite sensors record in the near infrared (NIR) region in the range of 0.7–0.9 μm, which is a region that can be recorded by color infrared (CIR) aerial pictures. Thermal infrared (TIR) is a result from the characteristic temperature of an object. Optical sensors pick up radiation in spectral ranges emitted from the Earth's surface where there is no absorption of oxygen, ozone, carbon dioxide, methane, steam, or nitrogen oxides, which exists in the range of 0.3–1 μm.

Some of the fundamental parameters used for remote sensing are as follows (Figure 7.1):

**Energy Source:** Energy source for the sensors can be classified into two groups as active and passive. The active sensors provide their own source of energy, whereas passive sensors take energy from the existing source of energy. Most of the sensors fall under the passive group where they use energy from the sun as the major energy source. An example of this approach is photography. Airborne cameras are able to measure and record the reflection of light earth features but most of the remote sensing applications still make use of aerial photography, whereas newer solid-state technologies have extended capabilities for viewing in the visible and NIR wavelengths to include longer-wavelength solar radiation. Most of the sensors make use of solar energy but some also use TIR and passive microwaves which make use of the Earth's energy emissions. Examples of active source of energy are flash cameras which make use of their own source of energy. One of the examples of active energy that is used for environmental and mapping application is the radio detection and ranging sensor (RADAR). RADAR emits energy in the microwave region of the electromagnetic spectrum; the reflection of this energy from the Earth's surface is measured, which is used to produce an image of the area being sensed.

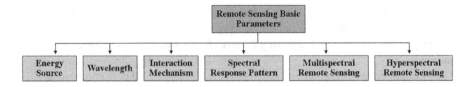

**FIGURE 7.1**    Basic parameters used for remote sensing.

**Wavelength:** As remote sensing makes use of electromagnetic energy and the electromagnetic spectrum is large, all wavelengths are not equally effective for the purpose of remote sensing and also all electromagnetic spectra do not have significant interaction with the Earth's surface that can be used for our purpose. The Earth's atmosphere generally absorbs or scatters shorter wavelengths, such as ultraviolet, and similar is the case with lens glass of many sensors. The IR wavelength is also useful in many geological and monitoring applications such as monitoring of fire to studies of animal distribution to the studies of conditions of soil moisture, etc. Apart from thermal IR wavelength radiations, there are also microwave radiations which can be used for radar imaging because the Earth's surface causes significant interaction with several microwave wavelength regions, and hence it can be used at night and in the region of persistent cloud cover.

**Interaction Mechanism:** The interaction between electromagnetic energy and materials can be of three types: reflection, absorption, or transmission. In case of sensors, mostly we focus on reflection which returns radiations back to sensor systems. The amount of reflection varies from material to material, whereas the electromagnetic spectrum measures this reflection for measurement and characterizes the result as a spectral response pattern.

**Spectral Response Pattern:** The spectral response pattern is a type of signature which is used for describing the degree of energy being reflected in different regions of the spectrum. An example of such a spectrum is the human eye which is a type of multispectral sensor for understanding the concept of color.

**Multispectral Remote Sensing:** Remotely sensed images are visually interpreted by means of a variety of image characteristics such as color, texture, pattern, shape, size, context, etc. Computer-aided interpretation mostly uses color as an image characteristic, which is termed as a spectral response pattern, and hence, the stress is mostly on multispectral response sensors. An example of satellites which provide multispectral imaging is LANDSAT which uses a thermal mapper (TM) system which provides multispectral imaging in seven spectral bands from 30-meter resolution.

Analytical techniques such as principal component analysis can be used to show that bands carrying the greatest amount of information about the natural environment are the NIR and red wavelength bands. Infrared wavelength strongly absorbed the water and hence is highly distinctive in that region. In case of plant species, red color is of utmost importance as it is the primary region which absorbs chlorophyll energy for the process of photosynthesis, and hence this band can be used for differentiating between vegetation and non-vegetation surfaces. The combination of red, green, and blue can be used for interpretation of cultural landscape as well as natural and vegetated surfaces. Satellites such as the LANDSAT TM system with band 5 can be used to determine the difference of moisture between soil and leaves by placing it between two water absorption bands, whereas the LANDSAT TM system with band 7 can be used for detection of hydrothermal alteration zones in bare rock surfaces. The advanced very high-resolution radiometer (AVHRR) system on the national oceanic and atmospheric administration (NOAA) series satellites uses a thermal channel for sensing of cloud temperature characteristics.

**Hyperspectral Remote Sensing:** Apart from multispectral imaging, there are many systems such as AVIRIS and MODIS which can be used for hyperspectral remote sensing which is used for capturing hyperspectral data. These systems cover a similar wavelength range to multispectral systems, but in much narrower bands which increases the number of bands available for image classification. Hyperspectral signature libraries have been created under laboratory conditions and contain hundreds of signatures for different types of land covers, including many minerals and other earth materials. Thus, it should be possible to match signatures to surface materials with great precision. Classification procedures have not been developed for hyperspectral data to the degree they have been for multispectral imagery. As a consequence, multispectral imagery still represents the major tool of remote sensing today.

**Sensors and Platform Systems:** Sensors are being modified day by day; there are a variety of platforms available for capturing remotely sensed data. Some of the sensors or platform combinations available to the GIS community can be divided as follows:

1. Airplane systems/aerial photography: Airplane systems are further subdivided as follows:
   a. Large-scale photography
   b. Small-scale photography
   c. Color photography
2. Aerial videography
   a. Satellite-based scanning systems
   b. Photographic imagery
   c. Digital scanner data

**Aeroplane System/Aerial Photography:** This is one of the oldest and widely used methods for remote sensing. In this photography, cameras are mounted on light aircraft flying from a range of 200–1500 meters used for capturing a quantity of detailed information. Aerial photos provide an instant visual inventory of a portion of the Earth's surface and can be used to create detailed maps. Aerial photographs commonly are taken by commercial aerial photography firms which have and operate specially modified aircraft equipped with large format (23 cm × 23 cm) mapping quality cameras. Aerial photos can also be taken using small format cameras (35 mm and 70 mm), hand-held or mounted, in unmodified light aircraft.

We can group the configuration of cameras and platform as oblique and vertical, where the oblique aerial photograph is taken at an angle to cover the area of the ground, where the resulting images give a view as if the observer is looking out of an airplane window. These images are easier to interpret than vertical photographs, but it is difficult to locate and measure features on them for mapping purposes.

Vertical aerial photography is taken with a camera pointed straightly downward. This technique forms images which depict ground features in the plan form and are easily compared with maps. This technique is generally being used for surveying the resources in areas where there are no maps available. Hence, aerial photography can be used for depiction of field pattern, vegetation, etc. which are often omitted from the maps. This photography contains subtle displacements due to relief, tip and tilt of the aircraft, and lens distortion. Vertical images may be taken with overlap, typically about 60% along the flight line and at least 20% between lines. Overlapping images can be viewed with a stereoscope to create a three-dimensional view, called a stereo model.

**Large Format Photography:** In this photography, light single or twin engine aircraft is used which is equipped with large-format mapping cameras such as Wild RC-10, Eastman Kodak, etc. which use a 23 cm × 23 cm film which is available in rolls. In this photography, a negative film is used where prints are the desired product, while a positive film is used where transparencies are required. However, a print film is allowed for detailed enlargements such as large wall-sized prints. A print film is also used where multiple prints are to be distributed and used in the field.

**Small Format Photography:** This photography uses small-format cameras in aircraft which is an inexpensive alternative to large-format photography which uses a camera of 35 × 70 *mm*. This photography has disadvantages as it uses light unpressurized aircraft and these aircrafts are typically limited to altitudes below 4000 m. Furthermore, due to the small size of film, the resolution or area covered per frame is not very fine. The small format photography suffers from distortion in camera systems due to which this technique is not fit for precise mapping. Furthermore, the presentation-quality wall-size prints cannot be made from small negative. However, small format photography can be used for reconnaissance surveys and can be used as point samples.

**Color Photography:** This photography consists of three film layers with intervening filters that act to isolate, in effect, red, green, and blue wavelengths separately to the different film layers. With the CIR film, these wavelengths are shifted to longer wavelengths to produce a composite that has isolated reflectances from the green, red, and NIR wavelength regions. We can also use a group of several cameras on a single aircraft mount, each with black and white film and a filter designed to isolate a specific wavelength range as a substitute to this photography. The advantage of this arrangement is that the bands are independently accessible and can be photographically enhanced. If a color composite is desired, it is possible to create it from the individual bands at a later time.

The photographs created are not a format that can be used immediately for digital analysis. These photographs are scanned digitally using a scanner in order to create multispectral datasets by scanning individual band images and color images or separating the bands. Aerial photography geometry is difficult to use directly; however, it needs to be processed by special photogrammetric software in order to rectify the images and remove differential parallax effects.

**Aerial Videography:** Aerial videography uses inexpensive video cameras and recorders mounted on aircraft which are used to capture videos as output. Several cameras with filters are used simultaneously to isolate a specific wavelength range which make possible to isolate multispectral image bands that can be used individually or in combination in the form of a color composite. The frames are freeze from continuous videos by means of frame grabber which convert these images in TIF or TARGA format. This technique is not suitable for detailed mapping but can be used for reconnaissance surveys and can be used in conjunction with ground point sampling.

**Satellite-Based Scanning System:** The development of satellite platforms is needed for the development of solid-state scanners as major format used for capturing remotely sensed data. Scanning system uses instantaneous field of view (IFOV) which sweeps the view of small field in west to east direction; at the same time, the satellite moves from north to south direction. Together, this movement provides a means of composing a composite raster image of environment. The scanning technique uses a rotating mirror that is used to sweep field of view in a consistent manner from east to west direction. The captured field of view is then intercepted using prism which is used to spread energy contained within IFOV into spectral components. Then, in the path of this spectrum, photoelectric detectors are used which provide electrical measurements of energy detected in various parts of the electromagnetic spectrum. Because the scanner moves from west to east, detectors are polled to detect a set of readings along the east-west scan. Satellite movement from north to south positions the system such that it detects the next row which is used for the production of a set of raster images as a record of reflectance over a range of spectral bands.

Different satellite systems are used for different applications which have different ranges and applications. These satellite data have specific characteristics which make them appropriate for particular applications.

Two characteristics which help in guiding the choice of satellite data are as follows:

1. Spatial resolution
2. Spectral resolution

Spectral resolution is used to find the size of an area of the ground which is summarized by one data value in the imagery, which is termed as IFOV, whereas spectral resolution is used to find the number and width of spectral bands detected by satellite sensors.

**Sensors:** Sensors used in remote sensing can be classified into two groups based on the source of energy as active sensors and passive sensors.

1. Active sensors
2. Passive sensors

Active sensors are those sensors which provide their own energy to illuminate the objects observed. Thus, active sensors emit radiation to the target of investigation. These sensors measure the reflected or backscattered radiations from the target. Active sensors operate in the microwave portion of the electromagnetic spectrum, which makes them able to penetrate the atmosphere under most conditions. An active technique views the target from either end of a baseline of known length. The change in the apparent view direction (parallax) is related to the absolute distance between the instrument and target.

On the other hand, passive sensors use natural energy (sunlight) or radiations emitted or reflected by the object. These sensors include different types of radiometers and spectrometers. These sensors operate in visible, IR, microwave, or TIR regions of the electromagnetic spectrum.

Some of the examples of active sensors are as follows:

1. RADAR: The active RADAR uses its own source of electromagnetic energy which emits microwave radiations in a series of pulses from an antenna. It uses the backscattered or reflected radiations from the target source for determining the distance or range of the target. Thus, by measuring range and magnitude of the energy reflected from all targets as the system passes, we can achieve a two-dimensional image of the surface.

2. LIDAR: The light detection and ranging sensor (LIDAR) uses laser radar for transmitting light pulses and receiving backscattered or reflected light using sensitive detectors. They are used for determining the distance by means of recording the time from transmission to backscattered pulses with respect to speed of light.

3. Laser altimeters: These sensors are used to measure the height of a platform such as aircraft or spacecraft above the Earth's surface which can be used for determining the topography of the underlying surface.

4. Ranging instruments: They are used for measuring the distance between the instrument and target object using transmitted waves as light or microwave and time taken by that wave to reach back to source.

5. Scatterometers: These are high-frequency microwave radars which are used in ocean surfaces and measure backscattered radiations. They use a microwave spectral region for deriving maps of surface wind speed and directions.

6. Sounders: These are instruments that measure vertical distribution of atmospheric parameters such as temperature, humidity, cloud composition, precipitation, etc.

7. Radar sensors: Radar sensors are active sensors which carry source of radiations and have defined wavelength and radiate active radar waves. The ground resolution for these sensors is from 18 to 30 meters which makes it suitable for collecting data of landscape ecology. They deliver the information of the three-dimensional structure of the surface. The data are interpreted using mathematical processes.

Whereas examples of passive sensors are as follows:

1. Radiometer: A radiometer is a device that measures the intensity of electromagnetic radiation in some bands within the spectrum.

2. Imaging radiometer: These radiometers have the scanning capability which is used to provide a two-dimensional array of pixels which is used to form an image. Scanning can be performed mechanically or electronically by using an array of detectors.

3. Hyperspectral radiometer: It is an advanced multispectral sensor which is used to detect hundreds of very narrow spectral bands throughout the visible, NIR, and mid-infrared portions of the electromagnetic spectrum. The sensors used in this device are of high spectral resolution, and hence they provide fine discrimination among different target objects based on their spectral response in each of the narrow bands.

4. Accelerometer: This device is used to measure acceleration or change in velocity per unit time. They are of two types, where one measures translational accelerations (changes in linear motions in one or more dimensions), and the other measures angular accelerations (changes in rotation rate per unit time).
5. Sounder: This device is used to measure vertical distribution of atmospheric parameters such as temperature, pressure, and composition from multispectral information.
6. Spectrometer: This device detects, measures, and analyzes the spectral content of incident electromagnetic radiation.
7. Spectroradiometer: This device measures the intensity of radiation in multiple wavelength bands.

Broader classification of sensors used for data collections is as follows:

1. Image plane scanning sensors
2. Object plane scanning sensors

Image plane scanning sensors are a combination of passive, scanning, and imaging. The examples of these cameras are TV cameras and solid-state scanners, whereas object plane scanning sensors are multispectral scanners (MSSs) or optical mechanical sensors and scanning microwave radiometers.

**Remote Sensing and Digital Image Processing**

A digital image processing involves the use of a number of statistical and image manipulation functions. There are basically two types of images namely analog and digital. Analog images are the images captured by the photographic sensors on the paper or transparent media. The analog images can be identified by the variations in the image brightness. Digital images are captured by the electro-optical sensor that consists of tiny pixels arranged in a rectangular array. In digital images, each pixel represents an area on the Earth. A pixel can consist of the intensity value and a location address. The intensity value describes the average value for the ground covered by the pixel. It is recorded as a digital number. The address of a pixel is denoted by the row and column coordinates in the two-dimensional image. Geographical coordinates such as longitude and latitude are represented by its row and column indices.

Satellite images obtained may be in multispectral and panchromatic mode. Remote sensing satellites capture the information in the form of digital data. These data are stored in formats of Band Sequential, Band Interleaved by Lines, and Band Interleaved by Pixels. Each of the formats of the satellite images has a header and trailer apart from the information such as date of acquisition, altitude of satellite, and sun angle. All the stated details help to correctly find the data geometrically. In the Band Sequential format, all the data for a single band covering the complete image of a scenario are stored in one single file. Each band is saved as a separate image sequentially for a multiband image. In order to extract information from five band images, five files have to be read, whereas in the Band Interleaved by Lines format, the images of the different bands are stored in the computer memory line by line, where each line is represented in all the bands before recording the next line. This makes the lines inseparable, and if the format is required to be analyzed, then all the lines are required to be analyzed. In the Band Interleaved by Pixels, the image information is stored pixel by pixel where the brightness of the image is stored in the pixels. GeoTIFF is the format that stores geographical and cartographic data. It is a metadata format that also provides coordinates given by the satellites.

Some of the most popular satellites used for image purposes are as follows:

1. LANDSAT
2. SPOT
3. IRS
4. IKONOS
5. NOAA-AVHRR
6. MODIS
7. RADARSAT
8. ERS
9. JERS

**LANDSAT:** It is system of remote processing which is operated by United States Geological Survey. It provides images available on a variety of distribution media, as well as photographic products of MSS and TM scenes in false color and black and white. The first LANDSAT satellite was launched in 1972. Multiple LANDSAT satellites have been launched out of which LANDSAT 6 was lost during launching, whereas LANDSAT 5 is operational today also and LANDSAT 7 was launched in April, 1999.

The LANDSAT satellite consists of two sensors, namely, MSS and TM. The MSS is used for acquiring images in four spectral bands, namely, blue, green, red, and NIR, whereas the TM collects seven bands, namely, blue, green, red, NIR, two mid-infrared, and one TIR. MSS has a spatial resolution of 80 meters, whereas TM has a spatial resolution of 30 meters. Both sensors image a 185-km wide swath, passing over each day at 09:45 local time and returning every 16 days.

**SPOT:** Système Pour L'Observation de la Terre (SPOT) was launched and operated by French consortium from 1985. It carries two high-resolution visible pushbroom sensors which operate in multispectral or panchromatic mode. The multispectral image of SPOT has a 20-meter spatial resolution, whereas panchromatic images have a 10-meter resolution. There are multiple SPOT satellites being launched where SPOT 1-3 provides three multispectral bands, namely, green, red, and infrared, whereas SPOT 4 was launched in 1998 and provides three bands as SPOT 1-3 and also a shortwave IR band. The panchromatic band for SPOT 1-3 is 0.51–0.73 μm while that of SPOT 4 is 0.61–0.68 μm. The covering capacity of SPOT is of 60 kilometer, where the sensors of SPOT point to image along adjacent paths, which allows the instrument to capture repeated images of an area 12 times during its 26-day orbital period. SPOT satellites can also be used for stereo satellite imagery due to its pointing capabilities.

**IRS:** Indian Space Research organization has also launched multiple satellites in IRS systems, with at least seven planned by 2004. IRS-1C and IRS-1D satellites jointly provide continuous global coverage through sensors like IRS-pan (5.8 m panchromatic), IRS-LISSS3 (23.5 m multispectral in the following bands: green

(0.52–0.59), red (0.62–0.68), near-infrared (0.77–0.86), shortwave infrared (1.55–1.7)), and IRS-WiFS (180 m multispectral in the following bands: red (0.62–0.68) and near-infrared (0.77–0.86)).

**IKONOS:** IKONOS satellites were first launched on 24 September 1999, from USA. It is a high-resolution satellite with a capturing capability of 3.2 m multispectral, Near-Infrared (NIR) 0.82 m panchromatic resolution. It can be used for mapping of natural vegetation, natural disaster, tax mapping, analysis of agriculture and forestry mining, engineering, construction, and change detection in urban and rural areas.

**NOAA-AVHRR:** The AVHRR is a series of satellites that has been carried by U.S. NOAA and hence named NOAA-AVHRR. This satellite has capacity of acquiring data along a 2400-km-wide swath each day. It collects images from five bands as red, NIR, and three TIR. The spatial resolution of this satellite is 1.1 km where the data collected are termed as local area coverage. For studying very large areas, a resampled version with a resolution of about 4 km is also available and is termed as global area coverage.

This satellite provides "high" spatial resolution for meteorological applications but the images portray only broad patterns and little detail for terrestrial studies. This satellite finds its use for famine prediction and early warning activities.

**MODIS:** MODIS uses the EOS AM-1 platform which was launched in 1999 that was an extension of the AVHRR satellite which provides 36 bands of medium-to-coarse resolution imagery with a high temporal repeat cycle, here 1 and 2 bands provide 250-m resolution images in the red and NIR regions, whereas 3–7 bands provide 500-m resolution multispectral images in the visible and IR regions and 8–36 bands provide hyperspectral coverage in the visible, reflected IR, and TIR regions, with a 1-km resolution.

**RADARSAT:** It is an earth observation satellite launched by Canadian space agency in November 1995. It provides the spatial resolution of the C-band SAR imagery ranging from 8 to 100 meters per pixel, and the ground coverage repeat interval is of 24 days. It collects stereo RADAR imagery by means of pointing sensors at specified locations. The RADAR signals used by this satellite can also penetrate clouds cover making accessing areas invisible to other remote sensing systems. However, the returning RADAR signals are more affected by electrical and physical characteristics in the target than by its reflection and spectral pattern, therefore requiring special interpretation and spatial georegistration techniques.

**ERS:** European Remote Sensing Satellite (ERS) was developed by European Space Agency which provides a variety of C-band RADAR imagery output formats. It can be used for GIS application where the main output of interest is the side-looking airborne RADAR (SAR) output that provides 100-km wide swaths with a 30-m resolution. This satellite can be used for study of vegetation and mapping projects where cloud penetration is one of the issues.

**JERS:** Japanese Earth Resource Satellite (JERS) was developed by Japan which provides a resolution of 18-m L-band side-looking RADAR imagery. It provides a longer-wavelength band than the typical C-band used in earth resource applications. The L-band radar used in this satellite can penetrate vegetation as well as unconsolidated sand. This satellite founds its applications in geologic, topographic, and coastal mapping.

Different Image processing techniques used in remote sensing are as follows:

1. Image Enhancement
2. Image Filtering
3. Image transformation
4. Image Classification
5. Image Analysis

**Image Enhancement:** Image enhancement is essential for the satellite data because the information being processed is very raw and at times the details require extraction which cannot be done. The image enhancement process can be carried out either permanently or temporarily. There are three types of image enhancements as shown in Figure 7.2.

**Point Operations:** Point operations are the modifications of the brightness of each pixel recorded for image data independently. This method helps in highlighting the contrast of the image such as radiometric enhancement.

**Local Operations:** Local operations are the modification of the pixel value which is based on the values of the neighboring pixels such as spatial enhancement.

**Multi-Band operations:** Multi-band operations are carried out on the images by modifying the values of each pixel on the different bands such as spectral enhancement.

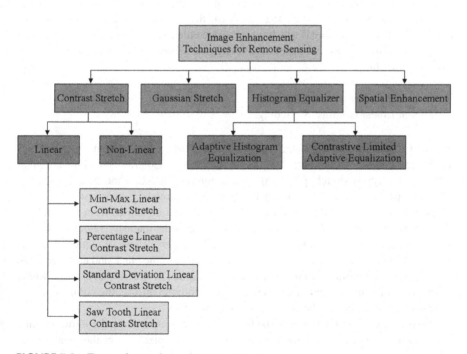

**FIGURE 7.2**   Types of operations of image enhancement.

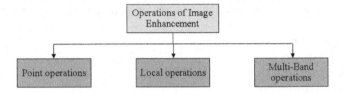

**FIGURE 7.3**    Different image enhancement techniques.

Different image enhancement techniques used are as follows (Figure 7.3):

1. Contrast Stretch
2. Histogram Equalizations
3. Gaussian Stretch
4. Spatial Enhancement

**Contrast Stretch:** Visual clarity is known as contrast. Higher contrast sometimes helps to interpret the images with better clarity. Contrast stretching is a type of point operation or zero operation that works only on the pixels of the image. Contrast is considered to be the difference between the average gray levels of the object and its surroundings. The contrast ratio is the ratio of the luminance of the brightest color white to that of the dark color black that the system can produce. It can also be defined as the ratio of the maximum intensity to the minimum intensity of an image. It is easier to interpret images with higher contrast than the lower contrast ratios.

If an image has a low or average contrast, then it becomes difficult to identify objects. Contrast stretching is a technique used to enhance the differentiation between the objects. The contrast is improved pixel by pixel. There are basically two types of contrast stretching:

1. Linear Contrast Stretching
2. Non Linear Contrast Stretching.

*Linear Contrast Stretching* is the type of stretching where the input and output values are linear in nature. Different techniques used for Linear Contrast Stretching are min–max linear contrast stretch, percentage linear contrast stretch, standard deviation linear contrast stretch, and saw tooth linear contrast stretch. Linear contrast stretch linearly expands the digital values of the raw image data obtained from the satellites into a new distribution. It helps to stretch the range of the intensity values it contains to span a desired range of values. An object that has a lower range of number from the threshold of the image mean is assigned 0 that is an extreme black and an object with a higher range of number from the threshold is assigned 1, which is an extreme white.

**Min–Max Linear Contrast Stretch:** This technique utilizes the complete available brightness values of the spectrum, that is, 0–255.

**Percentage Linear Contrast Stretch:** This technique utilizes the minimum and maximum values that lie in the certain percentage of pixels from the mean of the histogram.

**Standard Deviation Linear Contrast Stretch:** This method utilizes the specified minimum and maximum values that lie outside a certain standard deviation of pixels from the mean of the histogram. A standard deviation from the mean is often used to push the tails of the histogram.

**Saw Tooth Linear Contrast Stretch:** Continuous data are divided into the interval data.

**Nonlinear Contrast Stretch:** Both input and output data values follow a nonlinear transformation. Input and output can be related to transformation functions and the contrast is increased or decreased in the different regions of the histogram. The nonlinear enhancement makes use of the three types of transfer functions:

1. Mathematical Functions: Mathematical functions such as logarithmic, inverse log, exponential
2. Statistical Functions: Statistical functions such as histogram equalizations and Gaussian stretch
3. Trigonometric Functions: Trigonometric functions such as arc tangents

**Histogram:** Histogram equalization is a computer image processing technique that is used to improve contrast in images. It stretches out the intensity range of the image, thereby allowing areas of lower local contrast to gain a higher contrast. There are two types of Histogram Equalizations:

1. Adaptive Histogram Equalization: Adaptive Histogram Equalization computes many histograms where each histogram corresponds to a distinct part of the image, thereby making it suitable for enhancing the definitions of the edges in each region of an image.
2. Contrastive Limited Adaptive Equalization: Contrastive Limited Adaptive Equalization has a transformation function derived from the contrast limiting procedure applied to each neighboring pixel of an image.

**Gaussian Stretch:** It stretches the normal available histogram into the Gaussian form curve. It is capable of highlighting certain gray-level ranges. It forces a skewed histogram of the input image to a normal or non-skewed histogram. This stretch is useful if distributions are skewed in such a way that features could become abnormally light or dark when stretched linearly. The Gaussian stretch prevents saturation while enhancing overall scene contrast.

**Spatial Enhancement:** The features of spatial enhancement are as follows:

- Spatial Enhancement is implemented on the image texture.
- Smooth areas of an image have low spatial frequencies with gradual change in the gray values.
- Rough areas of an image have high spatial frequencies with sudden and broken gray-colored pixels.

**Image Filtering:** Filters can be applied to the images to enhance the images. Digital filters are applied to the image to operate on the neighboring values by carrying out the visual enhancement and noise removal. There are basically two types of filters used for visual enhancement of the satellite images, namely, high-pass filters and low-pass filters. High-pass filters are used to enhance information of high frequencies (local extremes, lines and edges), whereas low-pass filters can be used for smoothing of images (postclassification correction).

**High-Pass Filters:** They enhance the differences between the values of the neighboring pixels, and the change of the values is represented using edges and the lines. High-pass filters are used to enhance objects with a width smaller than a half of the filter window, and the wider objects than the filter window are suppressed. These filters are used for sharpening of images, edges, and line detection in order to increase the difference between pixels. High-pass filters make use of edges and lines.

- Edge is a border between two types of the forest with no width.
- Lines are used to represent rivers, streams, and roads

**Low-Pass Filters:** These filters use a filter window to enhance the digital images. In the case of low-pass filters, the rate of smoothing depends on the size of the filter window which can help in denoising and postclass correction. There are basically two types of filters used, and they are mean filter and median filter.

- The mean filter utilizes the same weight within all the filter window fields, and the resulting value for the central pixels is the total of the digital number (DN) of the original image which is then divided by the total number of fields available in the filter window.
- The median filter utilizes the median after arranging the DNs from the lowest value to the highest value and then finding the middle value as the central pixel for the filtering purpose.

**Image Transformation:** Image data are transformed into either the spectral or spatial domains for the purpose of the extraction or filtering. Sometimes, the images are transformed to be able to carry out operations such as smoothing, edge detection, or enhancement. An image transformation can involve various operations on the multiple bands of the data which can be multispectral or multitemporal. Thus, image transformations generate new images from multiple sources that help to highlight particular features better from the original images. The basic image transformations that apply simple arithmetic operations are as follows:

1. Image subtraction
2. Image division
3. Normalized difference vegetation index

In the image data, image subtraction helps to find the difference between the images that have been stored on different days. When all pixel brightness is subtracted from the target image, then the subtracted image is obtained.

Image division is also known as the spectral rationing, and it helps to highlight the hidden parts of various surface covers when required. By rationing the data from two different spectral bands, the resultant image enhances variations in the slopes of the spectral reflectance curves between the two different spectral ranges that may otherwise be masked by the pixel brightness variations in each of the bands. It is highly possible to better identify areas of unhealthy or stressed vegetation, which show low NIR reflectance, as the ratios would be lower than for healthy green vegetation. It also further reduces the topographic effects in the image because only ratios of the brightness values instead of absolute values are considered.

One widely used image transform is the **normalized difference vegetation index (NDVI)** which has been used to monitor vegetation conditions on continental and global scales using the AVHRR sensor onboard the NOAA series of satellites.

Different bands of multispectral data are often highly correlated. Image transformation techniques based on complex processing of the statistical characteristics of multiband datasets can be used to reduce data redundancy and correlation between bands. One such transform is called **principal component analysis**. The objective of this transformation is to reduce the dimensionality number of bands and compress the maximum information into fewer bands. The "new" bands that result from this statistical procedure are called components. This process attempts to maximize (statistically) the amount of information (or variance) from the original data into the least number of new components.

**Image Classification:** Image classification is the process of assigning land cover classes to pixels. For example, classes include water, urban, forest, agriculture, and grassland.

The three main image classification techniques in remote sensing are as follows:

- Unsupervised image classification
- Supervised image classification
- Object-based image analysis

Unsupervised and supervised image classifications are the two most common approaches. However, object-based classification has gained more popularity because it is useful for high-resolution data.

**Unsupervised Image Classification:** In unsupervised image classification, it first groups pixels into "clusters" based on their properties. Then, it classifies each cluster with a land cover class. Overall, unsupervised classification is the most basic technique. Samples are not required for unsupervised classification, and hence it is an easy way to segment and understand an image.

The two basic steps for unsupervised classification are as follows:

- Generate clusters
- Assign classes

Thus, clustering is an approach to segregate groups with similar traits and assign them into clusters. Thus, we can say that clustering is one of the popular techniques used in unsupervised learning where grouping of data is done based on the similarity of the data points. Clusters can be formed using the concept that objects with similarities can be grouped together. Similarly, clustering which is an unsupervised learning method can be considered as a process that helps the machines to distinguish different objects given in a dataset. Since clustering is an unsupervised learning, no external labels are attached to the given instances and machines find clusters based on the patterns or the trends observed. Various algorithms are used to extract the parameters that can help to group instances into appropriate clusters. Clustering learning mode helps to divide the data into different groups as classes such that each data point is similar to data points in the same group and dissimilar to the data points in the other groups. Clustering is considered to be a useful technique to differentiate groups from the unlabeled datasets.

Some of the common image clustering algorithms are as follows:

- K-means
- ISODATA

K-Means: K-Means is an unsupervised, iterative, and nondeterministic algorithm. It helps to generate the nonhierarchical sets. It generates globular clusters. **K-Means** clustering is an unsupervised algorithm that can be used to differentiate the data points from each other. It can help to cluster or partition the given dataset into the k-clusters or parts based on the k-centroids. These data are used in the cases where the target class has not been defined. The clusters formed are on the basis of the similar parameters into k groups. The objective of K-Means clustering is to minimize the sum of squared distances between all points and the cluster center.

**Steps in the K-Means algorithm:**

1. Decide upon the number of clusters: K.
2. Select centroids in the datasets. Now consider a random K point from the group.
3. Assign the selected data point to the closest centroid.
4. Repeat this procedure for all the data points in the group, thereby creating the clusters.
5. Model for predicting the output of the unlabeled data is ready.

After picking a clustering algorithm, you identify the number of groups you want to generate. For example, you can create 8, 20, or 42 clusters. Fewer clusters have more resembling pixels within groups. However, more clusters increase the variability within groups. To be clear, these are unclassified clusters. The next step is to manually assign land cover classes to each cluster. For example, if you want to classify vegetation and non-vegetation, you can select those clusters that represent them best.

The ISODATA algorithm works by splitting and merging the clusters where the merging of clusters is done when the number of members or pixels is less than the certain threshold or if centers of two clusters are closer enough than the specified threshold. In this algorithm, a cluster is divided into two different subclusters in case if cluster standard deviation exceeds a certain predefined value and the number of members or pixels is twice the threshold for the minimum number of members. Thus, we can say that the ISODATA algorithm is more or less similar to the K-mean algorithm but with a difference that the ISODATA algorithm allows for different numbers of clusters whereas in K-mean the number of clusters is known in advance.

**Supervised Image Classification:** Representative samples for each training site are used by this algorithm and are applied then to the entire image. There are three basic steps for the supervised classification, and they are as follows:

- Selecting training areas
- Generating signature file
- Classification of the images

In this method, we have to first select the training area where classification needs to be done by marking areas in images and then adding training site representatives in the entire image.

Sometimes training samples are created for the supervised classification when we mark the urban areas in the images. For different classes of the land, training samples are created that could be provided to the algorithms for the training of the spectral information. The signature file is then used for the classification, and supervised algorithms popularly used for the remote sensing images are maximum likelihood, minimum distance, principal component analysis, support vector machines, and Iso cluster.

In maximum likelihood classification, pixels with maximum likelihood are classified to specific class. It is expressed by the posterior probability of a pixel belonging to a class (Radhika et al., 2017). In the minimum distance classification scheme, the Euclidean Distance (ED) is calculated between the mean value of class and pixel under consideration and accordingly the pixel is allocated to class which is at minimum ED (Zhu and Nandi, 2014). The principal component analysis technique is used to reduce the dimensionality of datasets which consist of multiple variables correlated with each other. This dimensionality can be done heavily or lightly while retaining variation present in the dataset, up to the maximum extent (Sloby, 2020). In support vector machine analysis, the dataset is classified in best hyperplane which separates data points of one class from another class. The best hyperplane is defined as the one with maximum margin between classes. The support vector machine represents data points which are close to this hyperplane. These points lie within the vicinity of the vector slab (Bui et al., 2016). Iso cluster is a tool which uses an iterative optimization clustering procedure termed as migration means techniques. In this technique, cells are separated into user-specified numbers of distinct unimodal groups in the multidimensional space of input bands (Khaleghi, 2014).

**Object-Based Image Analysis:** Supervised and unsupervised classification is based on the pixels. Each pixel is classified into a class. However, in the object-based image analysis, the pixel groups are classified into the representative vector dependent on their size and geometry. It generates objects with different geometries (Veljanovski et al., 2011).

In object-based image analysis classification, different methods that can be used for classifying the objects are as follows:

- Shape: The buildings can be classified using a rectangular fit. This tests an object's geometry to the shape of a rectangle.
- Texture: Texture is the granularity of an object. Forests are considered to have the shadows and so it has a mixture of green and black. Water is considered to be homogeneous so it has dark blue shade in the images.

- Spectral: Mean value of the spectral properties such as shortwave IR red, green, or blue.
- Geographic Context: Objects have distance and near relationships between the adjacent pixels.

Some of the steps to carry out the object-based image analysis classification can be listed as follows:

1. A multiresolution segmentation is carried out.
2. Training areas are selected.
3. Various statistics relevant to the images are carried out.
4. Classification of objects is done for image extraction.

In this approach, firstly, a multiresolution segmentation of the image is performed and then, the training area where image classification needs to be done is selected from the segmented area. Then, the various statistics of the image need classification which is selected from the training area, and finally the classification of object is done to extract the image.

Two most common segmentation algorithms used in the multiresolution are as follows:

- Multiresolution segmentation in ECognition
- Segment mean shift

The multiresolution segmentation method for echocardiographic images was proposed by Yu et al. (2006) which begins the algorithm by presegmentation at a low-resolution level and transmits the result to optimally segmentalize on a higher resolution scale. At the low resolution, a region-based Gaussian noise model is applied to analyze the echocardiographic images and combined with a geodesic contour model for the presegmentation, while the combinative model is competent to accurately and automatically extract the boundary. A fast mathematical morphology-based approach is developed to transmit the presegmentation result where interpolation becomes unnecessary. At the high resolution, a local active contour optimization model and a new intensity-based objective function are proposed.

The segment mean shift approach is used to identify features or segments in images by grouping pixels of similar spectral characteristics together which is used to control the amount of spatial and spectral smoothing in order to help derive features of interest (Jin and Hans, 2017).

Nearest Neighbor Classification: Nearest Neighbor classification is a supervised classification. This algorithm classifies objects based on their similarities to the objects of the training sites and the statistics defined.

**Selection of Image Classification Techniques**

With the development of improved sensors and powerful computation techniques, high-spatial-resolution remote sensing data have been easily acquired and widely applied. For example, to classify water through a high-spatial-resolution image, the selection of pixels plays an important role. Let us consider a real-time situation, during the process, if fewer NDVI pixels are selected then it can mislead the process through misconfiguring the object. This provides the salt and pepper look in the supervised and unsupervised classification that leads to the technique of multifunctional segmentation of a group of homogeneous pixels in objects. Spatial resolution is an important factor while selecting image classification techniques. When it is a low spatial resolution, then pixel-based and object-based classification techniques perform well; however, it is the reverse situation in the high spatial resolution (Lesti and Spiegel, 2016).

In comparison between unsupervised versus supervised versus object-based classification, object-based image classification uses both spectral and contextual information; thus it has higher accuracy.

Major digital image processing software used for satellite-based image processing are as follows:

- ENVI
- MATLAB
- PCI Geomatica
- IDRISI, etc.

ENVI is image analysis software which is used for image processing and analysis in order to extract the meaningful information from images. It can be deployed in desktop, cloud, or mobile devices and can be customized as per requirements using APIs. MATLAB is short form for matrix laboratory which consists of software used in the field of digital image processing. PCI Geomatica is used for remote sensing desktop software package used for processing of earth observation data. It can be used for loading of satellite and aerial imaginary data with advanced analysis features. IDRISI is a GIS analytical tool used for GIS-based application for finding remote sensing data. Some of the open source software packages that are available for remote sensing applications are ILWIS, Opticks, GRASS, OSSIN, Multispec, etc.

**Errors in Remote Image Sensing:** In remote sensing images, there are basically two categories of errors:

1. Radiometric Errors
2. Geometric Errors

**Radiometric Errors:** Any undesirable temporal or spatial variations caused in the image brightness are referred as noise. These variations are not associated with the variations in the image surface. They are caused either due to the detector imbalances or atmospheric deficiencies. Radiometric corrections are also known as cosmetic corrections that help to improve the visual appearance of the image. Most of the commonly induced radiometric errors include line or column dropouts, line or column stripping, random bad pixels, and partial line or column dropouts. Radiometric errors are generally associated with the change in the DN value.

**Geometric Errors:** Geometric Errors occur depending on the way the data are acquired for the remotely sensed images. Such errors form an integral part of the errors. Geometric Errors can be classified into symmetric and nonsymmetric errors. Symmetric errors can be corrected using the data from platform and internal sensor distortion knowledge, whereas nonsymmetric errors cannot be corrected with an acceptable accuracy without a sufficient number of ground control points. Geometric errors change the position of a DN value. Geometric corrections can be done using the given procedures. The image to map the rectification process involves transformation of remotely sensed images in a manner that they have the scale and projection of a map.

**Resampling Techniques**: Changing the pixel dimensions of an image is called resampling. Resampling also affects the display size of an image. Resampling to smaller dimensions reduces the file size and sharpens the appearance. Resampling techniques involve three steps:

1. To create an output grid
2. To back transform map to an image
3. Resample to fill the output grid

**Major techniques for creating the output grid are as follows:**

1. Nearest neighbor
2. Bilinear Interpolation Method
3. Cubic Convolution

**Nearest Neighbor:** It is easy to compute and the output values match with the original input values. Since the original data are retained, this method is considered to be most favorable for the classification.

The output image may have a chopping stair stepped effect with a rough appearance which is relative to the original unrectified data. There is a possibility that the data values may be lost while some may be redundant costing us space complexity.

**Bilinear Interpolation Method:** It utilizes the weighted average of the possible nearest four pixels to the output pixel. The output image achieved by this method appears to be smooth. It reduces the original amount of contrast by making all the adjacent pixels to be of the same texture and color.

**Cubic Convolution Method:** It utilizes the weighted average of the nearest 16 pixels to the output pixel. Here, the output is similar to that derived in the above method of bilinear interpolation. The smoothing effect caused by this method is more smooth and better in visual representation. However, the computational complexity is increasing compared to the nearest neighbor and bilinear interpolation methods.

## REFERENCES

Jin, X. and Han, J. (2017). *Mean shift*. 10.1007/978-1-4899-7687-1_532.

Khaleghi, M. (2014). Spectral angle mapping, spectral information divergence and principal component analysis of the ASTER SWIR data for exploration of porphyry copper mineralization in the Sarduiyeh area, Kerman Province, Iran. *Applied Geomatics* 6, 49–58.

Lesti, G. and Spiegel, S.. (2016). *Fast nearest neighbour classification*. 10.13140/RG.2.1.3431.8963.

Radhika, K. and Sourirajan, V. (2017). *Satellite image classification of different resolution images using cluster ensemble techniques*. 1–6. 10.1109/ICAMMAET.2017.8186672.

Sloby, C. (2020). *Principal components analysis*. 10.1002/9783527809080.cataz13551.

Tien Bui, Dieu Tuan, Tran Hoang, Nhat-Duc Thanh, Nguyen Nguyen, Duy Liem, Ngo, and Pradhan, Biswajeet. (2016). Spatial prediction of rainfall-induced landslides for the Lao Cai area (Vietnam) using a novel hybrid intelligent approach of least squares support vector machines inference model and artificial bee colony optimization. *Landslides* 14. 10.1007/s10346-016-0711-9.

Veljanovski, T., Kanjir, U., and Oštir, K. (2011). Object-based image analysis of remote sensing data. *Geodetski vestnik* 55, 641–664. 10.15292/geodetski-vestnik.2011.04.641-664.

Yu, G., Li, P., Miao, Y., and Bian, Z. (2006). *Multi-resolution segmentation model for echocardiographic image*. 40, 432–436.

Zhu, Z. and Nandi, A. (2014). Blind digital modulation classification using minimum distance centroid estimator and non-parametric likelihood function. *Wireless Communications, IEEE Transactions on* 13, 4483–4494. 10.1109/TWC.2014.2320724.

# 8 Application of Image Processing and Data Science in Medical Science

## 8.1 INTRODUCTION

In today's technological era, data science has touched all aspects of human life. The last few years have also seen a huge contribution of data science in the field of healthcare and medical science. Most doctors in this technological world are using a variety of advanced medical devices, which generate a large amount of health data. Health care data production includes hospital records arising from various sources such as doctor expertise, medical records of patients, results of medical tests, and so forth. Biomedical research plays a very important role in generating an important piece of data relevant to public health service. According to the World Health Organization, approximately 1.2 billion clinical documents are produced in the United States every year, about 80% of which is unstructured data, in which doctors' drug prescriptions and images of various organs of the patient and so forth are considered. These types of data require proper management and analysis to obtain meaningful information. Otherwise, searching for a solution by analyzing the data in a way becomes comparable to finding a needle in the sea. Hence, data analysis plays an important role in handling these types of unstructured data (which are generated from image processing). This can only be achieved using a high-quality computing solution for data analysis.

From the data perspective, biomedical images are an original source in the medical science and healthcare industries. These biomedical images are characterized as human body images. These biomedical images play an important role in understanding the nature of the human biological system. The most widely used biomedical imaging techniques to assess the current state of any organ or tissue are X-rays, CT (computed tomography) scans, sound (ultrasound), magnetism (MRI), radioactive pharmaceuticals (nuclear medicine: SPECT and PET), or light (endoscopy and OCT). Image processing embedded with data analysis can process and examine human healthy using these biomedical images which can be of great use for the health industry. Computer vision software based on learning algorithms in the healthcare industry is already making things simpler and more comfortable. Such software is increasingly making an automated analysis possible with higher efficiency and more accurate results. Most hospitals have not yet started using such automated analysis techniques. When these techniques are used appropriately, these techniques based on medical imaging data science help us reduce our dependence on manual analysis. These can be used to obtain advanced and accurate diagnostic procedures, including molecular imaging, from macroscopic to microscopic. Image processing can play an important role in detecting various diseases such as glioma, AIDS, dementia, Alzheimer's disease, cancer metastasis, tumor diagnosis, and so on.

In order to provide relevant solutions for improving public health, the appropriate infrastructure must be fully equipped to generate and systematically analyze the data of all healthcare providers in a completely systematic way. Efficient management, accurate analysis, and fine interpretation of all data can change the game of the biomedical industrial world by opening new avenues for modern healthcare. This is why various industries, including the healthcare industry, are taking vigorous steps to transform image-processing-based data science capability into better services and financial benefits. With a strong integration of biomedical and healthcare data, the modern healthcare organization is probably poised to bring a revolution in medical treatment and personalized medicine. This chapter covers the sources of medical data, the role of data analysis, and the handling tools and techniques of biomedical image processing with advanced social analytical tools.

## 8.2 IDEAL DATASET OF MEDICAL IMAGING FOR DATA ANALYSIS

An ideal medical image dataset must have sufficient data volume, annotation, truth, and reusability during a data analysis application in medical science. On this basis, each medical imaging dataset object contains data elements, metadata, and variables (identifiers). This type of combination represents the imaging examination. It is mandatory to have sufficient imaging examinations in a collection of data objects or datasets for hypothetical analysis. In order to make the algorithm fully efficient, both the dataset itself and each imaging exam must be correctly described and labeled. For ground reality, each imaging exam must be fully labeled and as accurate and reproducible as possible (Figure 8.1). In addition, an ideal dataset must be of Findable, Accessible, Interoperable, and Reusable nature (Wilkinson et al., 2016)

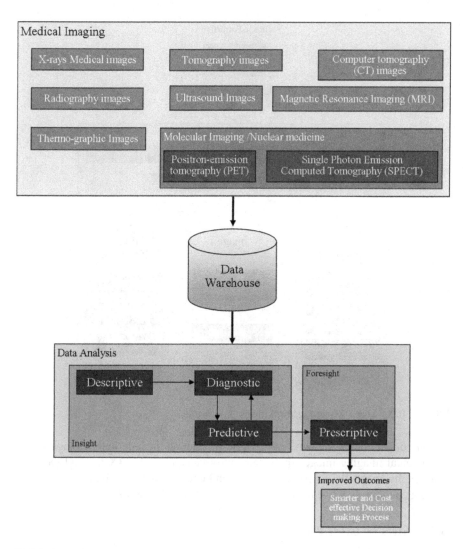

**FIGURE 8.1**   Workflow of data analytics to obtain a smarter healthcare option based on the medical imaging dataset.

## 8.3 FUNDAMENTALS OF MEDICAL IMAGE PROCESSING

Medical image processing produces visual images of the internal structures of the body for scientific and pharmacological study and treatment, as well as visualization of the function of internal tissues. This type of process pursues the identification and management of the disorder in the patient's body. In this process, a data bank of regular structure is created which makes it easy to detect anomalies in the functioning of

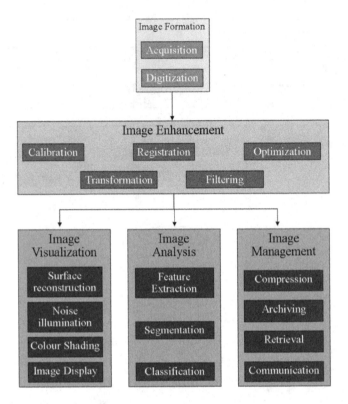

**FIGURE 8.2**    Major steps of medical image processing.

various organs of the human body. These procedures include both biological and radiological imaging images that use electromagnetic energy (X-ray and gamma), sonography, magnetic, scope, and thermal and isotope imaging. Medical image processing encompasses five major areas as presented in Figure 8.2.

### 8.3.1 STEPS OF IMAGE PROCESSING

"Biomedical image processing", commonly used in the biomedical field, refers to the provision of digital image processing for biomedical science. Secondly, data science comes to light due to the increasing use of image processing in the field of medical science to make biomedical decisions. In general, biomedical image processing involves five major areas:

1. **Image Formation:** This step of image processing covers all the steps from capturing the image to making the digital image a matrix form.
2. **Image Enhancement:** Digital images are adjusted simultaneously at this step of image processing to make the results more suitable for display or further image analysis. For example, this step is capable of removing, sharpening, or brightening a layer from an image. This makes it easy to identify the key features of the image.

3. **Image Visualization:** This step of image processing refers to all types of manipulation of the image matrix form, which results in a customized output of the image.
4. **Image Analysis:** This step of image processing involves all stages of image processing, which are also used for abstract interpretations of biomedical images along with quantitative measurements. These steps require a piece of prior knowledge to understand the nature and content of the images, which are integrated into the algorithm at a high level of abstraction. Thus, the process of image analysis is very specific, and rarely this developed algorithm can be directly transferred to other application domains.
5. **Image management:** All techniques are presented on this step of image processing which provides efficient storage, communication, transmission, collection, and access (retrieval) of image data. Thus, a part of image management can also be demonstrated through the method of telemedicine.

An image analysis is often also referred to as high-level image processing. On the other hand, low-level processing refers to manual or automated techniques that can be realized without a priori knowledge on the specific content of the images. This type of automatic algorithm has similar effects regardless of the position of the images. This can usually be seen on any holiday photograph. This is why low-level processing methods are usually available with programs to enhance the image.

## 8.4 PROBLEMS WITH MEDICAL IMAGES

With the definition and use of the field of biomedical science, a particular type of problem naturally becomes apparent in the high-level processing of medical images. As a result of its natural complexity, it is extremely difficult to make medicine a priori knowledge, so that it can be directly and easily integrated with the aid of image processing algorithms for the diagnosis of diseases in humans. In the literature, this is known as the semantic difference, which means there is discrepancy between the cognitive interpretation of the clinical image by the clinician (higher level) and the simple structure of discrete pixels, used in computer programs to represent an image. There are many factors that affect the accuracy of computer-based systems of analysis and interpretation in medical image processing (Figure 8.3).

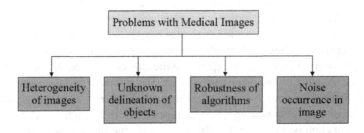

**FIGURE 8.3** Factors affecting the accuracy of computer-based medical image processing.

### 8.4.1 Heterogeneity of Images

Medical images are helpful in displaying living tissue, organs, or body parts of the human body. All these medical images have a variety of differences, whether these images are captured in the same manner or using the same standardized acquisition protocol. Apart from this, there are notable differences in the shape, size, and internal structure of these images among patients. Many variations have been found in the same patient even with the change in time. In other words, biological structures are subject to both interim and individual variability. Thus, creating a primordial knowledge universally is impossible in biomedical science.

### 8.4.2 Unknown Delineation of Objects

In most biomedical sciences, biological structures cannot be distinguished from their backgrounds. The entire image of this is to be represented as diagnostically or clinically relevant objects. Even if a certain object is seen in biomedical images, their segmentation is problematic. The reason for this is to represent their shape or borderline themselves or only partially. This is why medically related objects are often more and more abstract at the level of texture.

### 8.4.3 Robustness of Algorithms

Insufficient properties of medical images, which confound their critical level of processing, special prerequisites of reliability, and robustness of diagnostic algorithms. When the diagnostic algorithm is implemented in the framework, image processing algorithms run in parallel and also play a similar diagnostic role in the field as requested. Generally, automated program analysis of images in medicine should not give miscalculation. This means that drawings, which cannot be prepared effectively, should consequently be delegated, rejected, and pulled back from further handling. Thus, all photographs that have not been rejected must be evaluated effectively. Furthermore, the volume of the dismissed image is not allowed to be too large, as most clinical imaging methods are unsupervised and cannot be redone as a result of image preparation blunders.

### 8.4.4 Noise Occurrence in Image

One of the most significant difficulties is the presence of noise in medical/clinical images. There are various procedures for clinical imaging, for example, CT scan, ultrasound, advanced digital radiography, magnetic resonance imaging (MRI), spectroscopy, and so forth. The imaging strategies have been utilized as progressive techniques in analytic radiology. The clinical images which are utilized by doctors in their examination are inclined to experience the side effects from noise. Under these conditions, the location precision may endure. The computer proposes utilizing suitable calculations for noise evacuation. Mostly, the brightness of an image is considered uniform except at what point it changes to form the image. The variety in brightness or contrast value is normally irregular and has no specific pattern. This can decrease the quality of the image and is particularly huge when the items being imaged are little and have low differentiation. This irregular variety in image brightness or low differentiation is known as commotion.

Noise in digital images is an unwanted signal that corrupts original images. Different sources might contribute to the noise, for example, blunders in the image acquisition process that may bring about pixel esteems not mirroring the genuine idea of the scene. During securing, transmission, storage, and recovery forms, the commotion might be blended in with a unique image. A digital image that is transferred electronically contaminates noise sources. Noise can be caused in images by irregular vacillations in the image signal. The commotion signal present in the clinical image represents an extraordinary test in programmed clinical image examination. A portion of the significant focuses identified with noise in clinical images are:

• Some type of noise contained in all medical images.
• The noise might be different kinds such as grainy, snowy appearance, textured, and so forth.
• Various sources may contribute noise in an image.
• No imaging technique is liberated from noise.
• Image de-noising turns into a fundamental advance in all CAD frameworks.
• High noise found in nuclear images.
• Noise makes more trouble in MRI, CT, and ultrasound imaging when contrasted with other imaging modalities.
• Minimum noise is present in images produced by radiography.
• The process of removing noise is called filtering and denoising.
• Noise additionally diminishes the deceivability of specific highlights inside the picture.
• The loss of deceivability is particularly critical for low-differentiated pictures.
• The primary point of picture handling is to extricate clear data from the image debased by noise.

Huan et al. (2010) talked about three significant kinds of noise signals: (1) impulse noise, (2) multiplicative noise, and (3) additive noise. Noise found in digital images is seen as an added substance in nature with uniform power in the whole data transfer capacity with Gaussian likelihood conveyance. This kind of noise is called Additive White Gaussian Noise. This noise is a multiplicative commotion, and an undesirable irregular sign gets duplicated into some important sign during carrying out transmission or another image processing technique. A significant case of noise in clinical images is the spot commotion that could be ordinarily seen in radar imaging methodology. Scarcely any models are shadows because of undulations on the outside of the imaged objects, shadows cast by complex articles such as foliage, dull spots brought about by dust in the focal point or picture sensor, and varieties in the addition of individual components of the image sensor. Multiplicative commotion shows up in different image processing applications, for example, manufactured gap radar, ultrasound imaging, molecule outflow registered tomography, and positron emanation tomography. Hence, the expulsion of multiplicative commotion is extremely basic in imaging frameworks and image-preparing applications. Because the spot commotion is for the most part found in clinical images, this is quickly examined here.

### 8.4.4.1 Speckle Noise

The speckle naturally found in digital images is basically a grainy "noise". This degrades the quality of noise-activated radar and Synthetic Aperture Radar (SAR) images. Some of the salient features of this macular noise are:

- Speckle noise arises from random fluctuations in the return signal of an object in conventional radars. It is no larger than a single image-processing element.
- Speckle noise increases the average gray level of a local area.
- This noise found in SAR images is very severe due to which there are many difficulties in image interpretation.
- Speckle noise arises due to the coherent processing of backscattered signals from multiple distributed targets.
- It is also caused by the signals of the primary skater and the waves containing cells of gravity.
- There are many different methods available in the literature to remove speckle noise from medical images.
- All these methods are based on different types of mathematical models.
- Non-adaptive filters are used to eliminate noise.
- Adaptive speckle filtering is one of the better techniques to preserve edges and expand into areas of high texture.
- A nonadaptive filtering process is a better option to meet the simplicity and less computational time requirement.
- Such adaptive speckle filtering is divided into two types.
- There are several forms of adaptive spec filtering involving frost filters.
- Speckle noise in SAR images is a qualitative noise as in where the noise is present in direct proportion to the local gray level.
- In some cases, speckle noise can also be used to represent useful information, for example, laser speckle where the change of the speckle pattern is only a measure of surface activity.

Figure 8.4 shows the speckle noise as particle noise in a digital image.

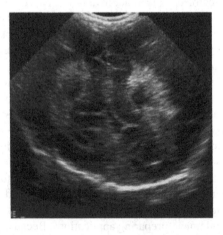

**FIGURE 8.4**    Speckle noise as granular noise reduction in ultrasound images.

## 8.5 CATEGORIES OF MEDICAL IMAGE DATA FORMATION

Since 1895 when the disclosure of X-rays by Wilhelm Conrad Röntgen, the clinical image has become an important part of diagnostics, systems of treatment, and strategies and follow-up examinations in the field of medical science. Moreover, clinical pictures are utilized for training, documentation, and research portraying morphology just as physical and natural capacities in one-dimensional, two-dimensional (2D), three-dimensional (3D), and four-dimensional (4D) image data, for example, cardiovascular MRI, where up to eight volumes are procured during a solitary heart cycle. Today, a vast assortment of imaging modalities has been established, which depends on the transmission, reflection or refraction of light, radiation, temperature, sound, or bend.

### 8.5.1 IMAGE ACQUISITION

In present-day medication, clinical imaging has experienced significant advancement. Today, this capacity to accomplish data about the human body has numerous helpful clinical applications. The route toward making a visual portrayal of within fragments or inside bits of a body for clinical examination, therapeutic intercession, and visual portrayal of the capacity of a couple of organs or tissues is called Medical imaging. These visual portrayals are handled productively, assessed with a particular target, and made accessible and imparted to numerous spots with the assistance of correspondence systems and conventions specifically Picture Archiving and Communication Systems (PACS) and Digital Imaging and Communications in Medicine (DICOM). Computerized imaging methods made it workable for doctors to handily determine infections to have the assistance of advanced picture handling strategies in the clinical field (Figure 8.5).

A set of images data from multiple acquisitions of images (known as volume or three dimensional images), a single tomographic, or a volume image over time to produce a dynamic series of acquisitions (known as 4D imaging). Typically, a medical image data formation consists of one or more images. All these images represent the projection of physical volume onto the image plane (projection or plane imaging). A series of images representing thin slices are formed through a volume (tomographic or multisailis to two-dimensional imaging). A set of data from multiple acquisitions of volume (volume or three dimensional imaging), or the same tomographic or volume image overtime, is useful to produce a dynamic series of acquisitions (4D imaging). Clinical images are the portrayal of the interior structure or capacity of an anatomic district as a variety of image components called pixels or voxels. It is a discrete portrayal coming about because of a testing/reproduction process that maps numerical qualities to places of the space. The quantity of pixels used to portray the field-of-perspective on a specific procurement methodology is a statement of the detail with which the life systems or capacity can be delineated. What the numerical estimation of the pixel communicates relies upon the imaging methodology, the securing convention, the remaking, and in the end, the post-handling.

Clinical imaging can be utilized for both finding and restorative purposes, making it one of our most impressive assets accessible to adequately think about our patients. Throughout the years, various sorts of clinical imaging have been developed, each

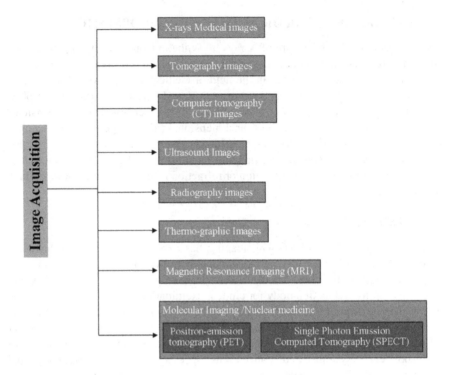

**FIGURE 8.5** Various kinds of medical images considered under the image acquisition process.

with their own points of interest and disservices. As far as diagnosis is concerned, regular imaging types include the following:

### 8.5.1.1 X-ray Medical Images

X-rays are produced to radiate electromagnetic waves. X-ray images are used to expose the internal parts of the body radiation, in which different parts of the body are taken. This is because the amount of radiation absorbed in different tissues of the body varies. The amount of calcium present in the bones of the human body absorbs a large number of X-rays, so the bones appear white in the images. The same body fat and other soft tissue absorb X-rays in very small amounts, causing them to appear gray in images. Absorption of X-rays by air is extremely low, so radiation-enhancing lungs appear black in images. The most important use of X-ray images is detecting broken bones. For example, pneumonia is detected in human chest X-rays and using mammograms for breast cancer. Figure 8.6 shows an example of an X-ray image.

X-ray testing is an easy and proficient test that produces pictures of structures inside the body, especially bones in the human body. Rays go through the body, retaining differing sums relying upon the thickness of the material they go through. Now and again, iodine or barium is acquainted with the body by giving more details on X-ray pictures.

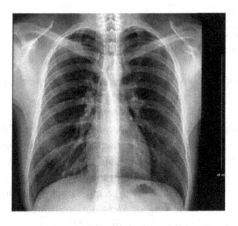

**FIGURE 8.6**    Human chest X-ray images.

X-rays are utilized to identify the following:

- Breaks and contaminations in bones and teeth.
- Joint inflammation and dental caries.
- Osteoporosis with bone thickness.
- Lung malignant growth and bone disease.
- Breast cancer growth identification utilizing mammography which is an exceptional kind of X-ray image.
- Swallowed articles can be recognized by utilizing X-rays.

**Advantages**

- Easy, fast, and noninvasive
- It can help in diagnosing different ailments and wounds, including broken bones, a few malignant growths, and diseases.

**Disadvantages**

- The small expanded danger of cancer growth later on from presentation to ionizing radiation (X-rays).
- Risk is more prominent for children.

### 8.5.1.2 Tomography Images

Tomography is the strategy for clinical imaging that creates a slice of an object.
There are different sorts of tomography as follows:

- Straight tomography is the essential type of tomography where the X-ray tube is moved starting with one point then onto the next. The supports are set to the territory of intrigue, and the focuses above and underneath the central plane are blurred out.

- Polytomography is a perplexing type of tomography.
- Zonography is a variation of direct tomography, where a restricted circular segment of development is utilized.

An example of tomography images is presented in Figure 8.7.

### 8.5.1.3 CT Images

CT is likewise alluded to as Computed Axial Tomography (CAT) which is helical tomography, and the 2D image of the structures in a slim segment of the body is delivered. CT examination utilizes X-rays and has a more noteworthy ionizing radiation portion trouble than projection radiography. For the most part, CT depends on indistinguishable standards from X-ray projections yet on account of CT the patient is encased in an encompassing ring of identifiers relegated with 500–1000 sparkle finders. A CT scan image is presented in Figure 8.8.

These images utilize X-rays to deliver cross-sectional pictures of the body and have a more prominent ionizing radiation portion trouble than projection radiography. For the most part, CT depends on indistinguishable standards from X-Ray

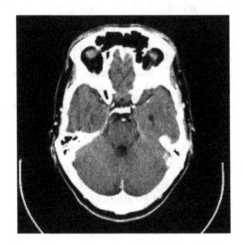

**FIGURE 8.7**   Tomography image.

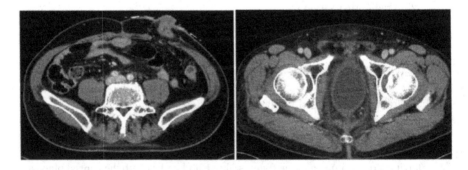

**FIGURE 8.8**   CT images of an abdominal-pelvic.

projections yet on account of CT the patient is encased in an encompassing ring of finders appointed with 500–1000 glimmer identifiers. Figure 8.8 shows a case of a CT scan image. The CT scanner has a huge roundabout opening for the patient to lie on a mechanized table. The X-ray source and a finder at that point pivot around the patient delivering tight "fan-shaped" X-rays beams that go through an area of the patient's body to make a preview.

These depictions are then ordered into one or various pictures of the inside organs and tissues. CT scans give more prominent lucidity than traditional X-rays with increasing point by point pictures of the inside organs, bones, delicate tissue, and veins inside the body.

Some remarkable highlights about CT scan are as follows:

- CT is a unique sort of X-ray imaging utilizing X-ray hardware to create cross-sectional photos of the body.
- It is also called CAT images which is an alternate type of imaging known as cross-sectional imaging.
- The starting point of "tomography" is from the Greek word "tomos" signifying "cut" or "area" and "graph" signifying "drawing."
- CT filters are utilized to recognize broken bones, tumors, blood clusters, inside dying, and so forth.
- Positron discharge tomography (PET) is utilized related to processed tomography and known as PET-CT.

**Advantages**

- Easy, quick, and effortless.
- It can help analyze and control treatment for a more extensive scope of conditions than plain X-beams.
- It can distinguish or prohibit the nearness of increasingly major issues.
- It can be utilized to check if a formerly treated infection has repeated.

**Disadvantages**

- Small expanded danger of disease later on from presentation to ionizing radiation (X-rays). Hazard is more prominent for children.
- Uses higher dosages of radiation than plain X-rays, so the dangers (while still little) are commonly more noteworthy than for other imaging types.
- Injection of a different medium (color) can mess up kidneys or bring about hypersensitive or infusion site responses in certain individuals.
- Some strategies require sedation.

## 8.5.1.4 Radiography Images

Radiography is a universally useful term utilized additionally as X-rays. Essentially, two types of radiographic images are used in clinical imaging: (1) projection radiography and (2) fluoroscopy. This imaging methodology utilizes a wide light x-ray for

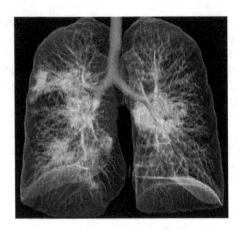

**FIGURE 8.9**    Radiographic image describing coronavirus.

image securing and is the main imaging procedure accessible in present-day medication. Fluoroscopy creates on-going pictures of inner structures of the body along these lines to radiography. However, this methodology utilizes a steady contribution of X-rays, at a lower portion rate. Complexity media, for example, barium, iodine, and air, are utilized to image inner organs as they work. An image receptor changes over the radiation into an image after it goes through the zone of intrigue. Projection radiographs, otherwise called X-rays, are utilized to decide the sort and degree of a crack just as for distinguishing neurotic changes in the lungs. The example of radiographic images is presented in Figure 8.9.

Fluoroscopy delivers continuous images of inward structures of the body along these lines to radiography. Be that as it may, this methodology utilizes a consistent contribution of X-rays, at a lower portion rate. Differentiation media, for example, barium, iodine, and air, are utilized to image inside organs as they work. An image receptor changes over the radiation into an image after it goes through the region of intrigue. Projection radiographs, otherwise called X-rays, are utilized to decide the sort and degree of a break just as for identifying obsessive changes in the lungs.

### 8.5.1.5 MRI

An MRI methodology is generally utilized in the detection of human brain tumors. An MRI instrument likewise is known as a MRI scanner or a nuclear magnetic resonance imaging scanner is utilized and ground-breaking magnets Polaris and energize hydrogen cores in water particles in human tissue which creates a perceivable sign which is spatially encoded, bringing about pictures of the body.

Radio frequency pulses are transmitted which ties to hydrogen, and the instrument sends the beat to the zone of the body to be inspected. The pulses cause the protons around there to retain the vitality expected to make them turn an alternate way. Remarkable highlights of MRI methodology are accounted for as follows:

- Like CT, MRI makes a 2D picture of a dainty "cut" of the body.
- MRI is considered as a topographic imaging strategy.

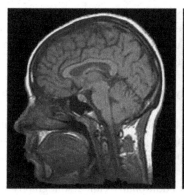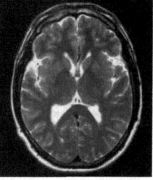

**FIGURE 8.10**   MRI images.

- MRI instruments can deliver images as blocks of 3D, which might be viewed as a speculation of the single-cut.
- CT and MRI are touchy to various tissue properties and the presence of the pictures obtained with the two methods varies.
- Any core with a net atomic turn can be utilized; the proton of the hydrogen molecule remains the most broadly utilized, particularly in the clinical setting.
- MRI utilizes a huge amount of magnetic and radio waves to take a gander at organs and structures inside the human body.
- Physicians use MRI sweeps to analyze an assortment of infection conditions, from torn tendons to tumors.
- MRI images are extremely helpful for analyzing the mind and spinal line issues.
- MRI examination is easy, and the machine makes a great deal of commotion.
- The physician asks while examining if the patient is pregnant and has bits of metal in the body then have metal or electronic devices in the patient body, for example, a heart pacemaker or a metal fake joint.

An example of an MRI image is shown in Figure 8.10.

### 8.5.1.6 Ultrasound Images

Medical imaging utilizes high-frequency broadband sound waves in the range of Megahertz (MHz), which are reflected by tissue to shifting degrees to deliver clinical pictures. This methodology is usually utilized in imaging the embryo in pregnant ladies. Other significant utilizations of ultrasound pictures are in the imaging of stomach organs, heart, bosom, muscles, courses, and veins. Remarkable highlights of this methodology are given as follows:

- This gives less anatomical subtleties when contrasted with that of CT or MRI yet has a few points of interest, for example, it gives checking of moving structures in the body; it does not have ionizing radiation and so forth.
- Ultrasound is utilized as a significant apparatus for catching crude information that could be utilized in tissue portrayal.
- This methodology is very easy to use.

- The ultrasound images are carefully gained and broke down by the radiologists.
- The hatchling status could be resolved, and the age of the embryo can likewise be resolved with the assistance of ultrasound images.
- The commotion present in the image could make issues in deciding the status of the baby.
- Ultrasound imaging is additionally utilized in the location of variations from the norm in the pancreas.
- Ultrasound scanners can be used for basically sick patients in escalated care units with no dangers while moving the patient.
- Doppler abilities of the scanners permit the bloodstream in supply routes and veins to be surveyed.
- Diagnostic ultrasound imaging is additionally called sonography which utilizes high-frequency sound waves to create pictures of structures inside the human body.
- Ultrasound might be utilized for a few purposes, for example, appraisal of the embryo, determination of gallbladder illness, assessment of bosom bump, disease location, and so on.

An example of an ultrasound image is shown in Figure 8.11.

**Advantages**

- Normally, it is an effortless and noninvasive methodology.
- It uses no ionizing radiation.
- It can help analyze and enable direct treatment for a wide scope of conditions.
- It can give comparative data to CT in certain kinds of examinations.

**Disadvantages**

- It can be an extensive and uproarious methodology.
- Its slight development can demolish the picture, requiring retesting.
- It can cause a few people to feel claustrophobic.
- Its sedation or sedation might be required for little youngsters or other people who cannot stay still.

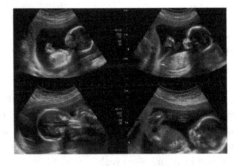

**FIGURE 8.11**    Third-month pregnancy ultrasound images.

- Infusion of a differentiation medium (color) if necessary can mess up kidneys or bring about unfavorably susceptible or infusion site responses in certain individuals.
- It cannot be attempted in certain circumstances (e.g., when a heart pacemaker is available).

### 8.5.1.7 Thermo Graphic Images

This is utilized in breast cancer growth location and imaging of breast images. This methodology is of three types: (1) tele-thermography, (2) contact thermography, and (3) dynamic angiothermography. Few striking highlights of thermo-realistic imaging are as follows:

The methodology is essentially an infrared imaging procedure,

- This deals with the idea of metabolic movement and vascular dissemination in both pre-harmful tissue and the encompassing region.
- Cancerous tumors need more supplements and this is met by expanding dissemination to their cells by holding open existing veins and opening lethargic vessels. This can be found in thermograms.
- Tele-thermography and contact thermography bring about an expansion in provincial surface temperatures of breast.
- Thermography is considered as an exact method for distinguishing breast tumors.
- Warnings are given against thermography in not many nations.
- Dynamic angiothermography misuses warm imaging.
- This imaging can be utilized in mix with different methods for the finding of bosom malignant growth.
- The strategy is a minimal effort as contrasted and different procedures.

An example of thermo-graphic pictures is introduced in Figure 8.12.

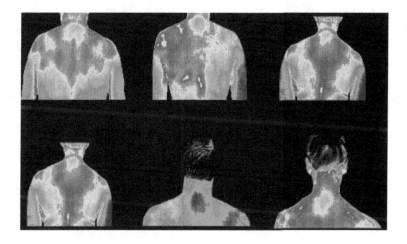

**FIGURE 8.12**   Thermographic image.

## 8.5.1.8 Molecular Imaging or Nuclear Medicine

A molecular image is a moderately new control that permits the organic procedures occurring in the body to be seen at a cellular and sub-atomic level. This advancement empowers specialists to recognize infection in its most punctual stages, frequently a long time before they would be seen on CT and MR pictures and would some way or another require intrusive medical procedure or biopsy—the evacuation of tissue for assessment under the magnifying instrument, that is, microscope.

Molecular imaging strategies are utilized for the following:

- This is to analyze and deal with the treatment of cerebrum and bone issue.
- This is to analyze and deal with the treatment of malignant growth and gastro-intestinal clutters.
- This is to analyze and deal with the treatment of heart and kidney sicknesses.
- This is to analyze and deal with the treatment of lung and thyroid issue.

The biochemical action of the cells changes when illness occurs and, as it advances, this irregular movement begins to influence the body and makes changes bones and tissue that probably won't be seen utilizing regular CT or MRI examines. Malignant growth cells, for instance, start by duplicating at an expanding rate and afterward structure a mass or tumor. By recognizing these progressions sooner, specialists can make a therapeutic move at a lot prior to the phase of the ailment than they could beforehand.

Most of the molecular imaging techniques are carried out with PET or single photon emission computed tomography (SPECT) imaging devices. An extremely limited quantity of a radioactive substance, called a radiopharmaceutical, is normally infused into the patient's circulatory system preceding the output. Contingent upon the piece of the body is focused on, various radiopharmaceuticals are utilized. These radiopharmaceuticals append themselves to the objective organ or explicit cells and are identified by the imaging device, which shows how they are dispersed in the body. This dissemination design assists specialists in seeing how well the organs and tissues are working.

### 8.5.1.8.1 PET

A PET filter is an imaging strategy that uses a radioactive substance known as a tracer to look for illness in the body. A PET output features the working of organs and tissues. The notable highlights of PET imaging are as follows:

- This is not the same as MRI and CT filter imaging, which really shows the structure of lymphatic tissue and bloodstream.
- PET is an exceptionally valuable methodology in the identification of the life systems of different structures of the body.
- PET is additionally utilized in blend with CT and MRI and alluded to as PET-CT and PET-MRI individually.
- The PET output is used for catching cerebrum, bosom, heart, and lungs in the body.
- PET is an atomic medication utilized as a practical imaging method.
- PET creates a 3D picture of practical procedures in the body.

A case of the PET output picture is shown in Figure 8.13.

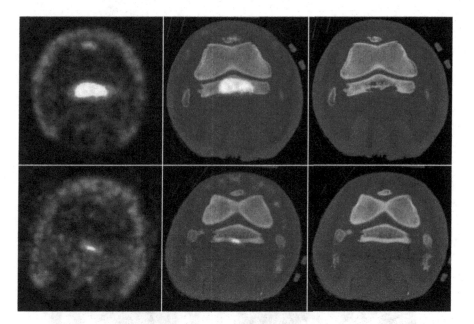

**FIGURE 8.13**   PET scan images.

*8.5.1.8.2 SPECT*

SPECT is broadly utilized as a method for imaging the conveyance of regulated radiotracers that have a single-photon outflow. The most broadly utilized SPECT frameworks depend on the Anger gamma camera, typically including double indicators that pivot around the patient. A few components influence the nature of SPECT pictures (e.g., goals and commotion) and the capacity to perform total measurement (e.g., constriction, dissipate, movement, and goals). The remarkable highlights of SPECT imaging are as follows:

- Imaging modalities in preclinical models is exceptionally significant as it has an incredible breadth for noninvasively examining dynamic organic procedures at the atomic and cell levels.
- The nonintrusive nature of imaging gives focal points in examining the beginning and the movement of the illness, surveying the organic impacts of medication applicants, and aiding the advancement of ailment biomarkers and observing the helpful viability of new treatment or potentially pharmaceuticals.
- Give crossing over seat investigations of illness demonstrated in vitro to their usage in clinically important creature models of indicative or therapeutics for their interpretation into the centers.
- Indeed, the usage of imaging in rodents has incredible significance due to the far-reaching utilization of hereditarily altered mice in biomedical research and the need to describe the in vivo anatomical and practical phenotypes of creature malady models.

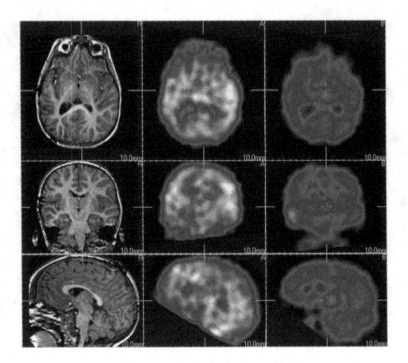

**FIGURE 8.14**    SPECT images.

- Imaging modalities produced for little creatures is that the innovation can moderately be made a straightforward interpretation for application in clinical practice (Figure 8.14).

Molecular imaging systems are nonintrusive. The measure of ionizing radiation utilized in these methods is little, with respect to the advantages of an exact determination and treatment specialists, and makers, for example, Siemens, are cooperating to limit the radiation portion and further decrease the hazard in question. In any case, ladies ought to consistently inform their doctor or X-ray technologist if there is any likelihood that they are pregnant.

**Advantages**

- Normally it is an easy, effortless process.
- It can help to analyze, treat, or anticipate the result for a wide scope of conditions.
- Not at all like most other imaging types can show how various pieces of the body are working and can identify issues a lot prior.
- It can check how far malignant growth has spread and how well treatment is functioning.

**Disadvantages**

- Disadvantages include exposure to ionizing radiation (for example, gamma rays).

- Radioactive material may cause hypersensitive or infusion site responses in certain individuals.
- PET scanners cause a few people to feel claustrophobic, which may mean sedation is required.

## 8.5.2 IMAGE DIGITALIZATION

Two phases considered in the image digitization procedure:

1. Spatial sampling: Spatial domain
2. Quantization: Gray level

Computerized picture handling infers the discrete idea of the images. Whether or not a film-based radiograph is digitized optionally with a scanner, or the gadget principally conveys a computerized pixel (voxel) grid, digitization impacts adjust the picture. Digitization applies to both the definition (inspecting) and the worth range (quantization).

### 8.5.2.1 Quantization

Quantization alludes to the digitization of the worth range. We have to decide the maximal number of gray scales for each image. Typically, 8 bits and 24 bits are picked for grayscale and full-shading pictures, separately, permitting 256 unique qualities in each band. In medication, radiography or CT for the most part conveys 12 bits = 4,096 unique qualities. On the off chance that we expect a persistent brilliance, quantization consistently compounds the picture quality. The change can be displayed as added substance noise, and the signal-to-noise ratio of our computerized picture is improved by an expanded number of gray scales.

### 8.5.2.2 Spatial Sampling

Image sampling is the way toward gathering perceptions in a 2D system. It alludes to the digitization of the definition extent. As per the straight framework hypothesis, a simple sign can be unambiguously spoken to with a discrete arrangement of tests if the inspecting rate surpasses multiple times the most elevated recurrence happening in the image (Nyquist hypothesis). Cautious consideration is paid to

1. The amount of the considered samples directed the correct financial conditions.
2. The area of the considering samples.

An inspecting plan is commonly intended to augment the likelihood of catching the spatial variation of the variable under examination. When starting examples have been gathered and their variety archived, extra estimations can be taken in different areas.

## 8.5.3 IMAGE ENHANCEMENT

Low-level techniques for imaging handling, that is, systems and algorithms that are performed without from the earlier information about the particular substance of an image, are for the most part applied to pre-or post-preparing of clinical image. Subsequently, the fundamental strategies for histogram changes, convolution, and (morphological) separation are for the most part dismissed except if required for additional understanding of the picture improvement. As a unique pre-preparing strategy for clinical pictures, strategies for adjustment and registration are quickly presented.

### 8.5.3.1 Histogram Transforms

Transformation of pixel depends on the image histogram. Adjusting the pixel esteems, all pixels are changed freely from their situations in the picture and their prompt neighborhood. Thus, this kind of change is likewise alluded to as point activity.

The histogram shows the recurrence conveyance of pixel esteems (e.g., gray-scales) ignoring certain positions where the dark scales occur in the picture. Basic pixel changes can be characterized by utilizing a histogram. For instance, through the extending of dim scales, the complexity of an image is improved. In the wake of deciding the histogram, upper and lower limits are found, and a straight change is applied that maps the lower bound to zero and the upper bound to the maximal gray-scale (i.e., 255 for 8-bit of image). On the off chance that the histogram of the underlying picture does not contain all conceivable dark scales, the grayscale separation between neighbored pixels is augmented, which brings about an improved complexity (Figure 8.15).

For the purposes of quantitative estimations from an image, a cautious adjustment of the imaging methodology is required. Both geometry (spatial area) and color shading or brightness force (esteem space) must be adjusted to the methodology.

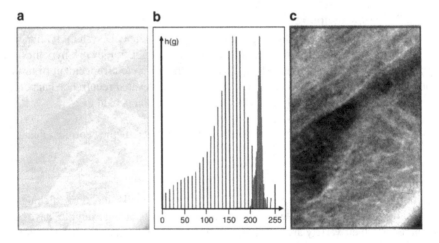

**FIGURE 8.15**   Histogram extension. A region of interest is taken in the zone of the temporo-mandibular joint from an intra-oral radiograph. (a) Outcomes because of under-introduction; the springy bone structure is shown ineffectively. (b) The related histogram is just thin involved (red). By extending the histogram, the sections are straight pulled separated (blue) and the complexity of the changed radiograph is expanded. (c) Calibration process.

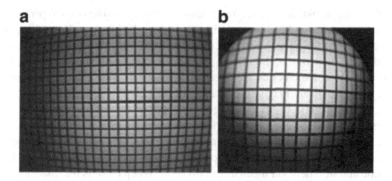

**FIGURE 8.16**   Geometric twisting and brighten variety. By endoscopic assessments, barrel twists are regularly created, which must be rectified before the picture can be investigated quantitatively. Likewise, the limit zones in the video seem darker and obscured. (a) The image is produced with an unbending laryngoscope, which is utilized for the assessment of the larynx. (b) The image is taken with an adaptable endoscope for nasal laryngoscopy. The two endoscopes are utilized in clinical everyday practice. Microscopy and other optical techniques may create comparable antiquities.

Alignment is device explicit yet dismisses the natural substance caught, and in this way, it is a piece of low-level handling strategies. While perusing a radiograph, alignment is made unknowingly by the radiologist.

Be that as it may, it must be expressly executed for automated image examination and estimations.

Geometric variations (contortions) have the outcome that significant structures of a similar size are shown relying upon the situation inside the image. In the biomedical sciences, the situating of the imaging devices must not influence any estimation. For instance in endoscopy, coming about because of the optical gadgets being used, alleged barrel mutilations are begun. Indeed, even in basic planar radiography, the articles, which are far away from the image plane, seem bigger than those, which are found near the imaging devices. This must be remembered at whatever point geometric estimations in advanced X-beams are taken and shown to the doctors: point removes in computerized images can be changed over into length estimations just if a fixed scale is expected, which is regularly not satisfied (Figure 8.16).

Similarly, the outright task of the pixel esteems to physical estimations ordinarily is hazardous. For instance in X-ray imaging, the straight correspondence of brilliance esteems to the gathered ingestion coefficient of the imaged structure is conceivable, if an aluminum (step) wedge with known X-rays retention properties is put next to the item. In advanced video recording, white adjusting must be performed to such an extent that the shading esteem compares with the real world. In any case, unique light of a similar scene may even now change the caught hues.

### 8.5.3.2  Phase of Registration

The image registration process is especially significant for arranging careful and radiation treatment, following changes in tissue morphology related to ailment movement or reaction to treatment, and relating anatomic data to changes in useful qualities, for example, glucose take-up, blood stream, and cell digestion. The need to perform such enlistment is settled and has been read generally for the instance of enrolling inflexible items. The procedures that have been accounted for shift in detail however can be ordered dependent on the highlights that are being coordinated. Such highlights incorporate outer markers that are fixed on the patient, inside anatomic markers that are recognizable on all images, the focal point of gravity for at least one object in the image, peak lines of items in the images, or slopes of force. One may likewise limit the separation between comparing surface purposes of a predefined object.

The identification of comparable structures in pictures is essential for some image registration procedures. In certain endeavors, this has been accomplished as a manual technique and in others via mechanized division. When there is the chance of tissue disfigurement between assessments, just like the case with delicate tissue structures in the midsection or pelvis, flexible twisting is required to change one informational collection into the other. The trouble lies in characterizing enough normal highlights in the pictures to empower indicating suitable nearby misshapenness. Specifically noteworthy, for instance, is an investigation of divider movement in the heart, which requires relating places of specific areas as a component of time so as to gauge the varieties in anxiety related with various pathologies.

### 8.5.4 Image Data Visualization

As biomedical imaging propels regarding the refinement of information securing methods, the need to create improved apparatuses for picture handling and representation has become a significant bottleneck. This need is especially intense for the consolidated translation of 3D anatomic and physiologic or metabolic information. The test owes not exclusively to the enormous size of the accessible informational collections yet in addition to the complexities of the connections through various data. One way to deal with this issue is information decrease or combination of parametric image, as has been depicted in past segments. Different methodologies incorporate the utilization of shading overlays of physiologic parameters onto anatomic structures. Such methodologies are valuable for making anatomic connections and however have restricted extension for giving a quantitative translation of the connections among various parameters.

Representation strategies at present being explored in computerized designs investigated and being applied for the examination of biomedical information incorporate surface rendered anatomical showcases with pivot and concealing, volume-rendered patterns with an upgraded accentuation of specific items, straightforward surfaces inside surfaces with shading concealing and revolution, and projection methods utilizing different weightings of pixels of premium, for example, greatest pixel force projection and profundity weighting. A model that is as of now in routine use is the MRI angiogram, which is imagined in three measurements by projecting at various edges to shape a grouping of pictures that can be played back in the '"cine" mode to re-enact the pivot of the vessels. The structure and assessment of strategies for speaking to biomedical picture information comprise a most encouraging region for examination, requiring close cooperation between computerized researchers and the clinicians who will eventually decipher the information.

## 8.5.5 Image Data Analysis

### 8.5.5.1 Feature Extraction

Extraction of features is characterized as the main phase of canny (elevated level) image examination. It is trailed by division and characterization, which regularly do not happen in the image itself, that is, the information or pixel level, however, is performed at higher deliberation levels. Along these lines, the undertaking of highlight extraction is to underscore picture data on the specific level, where the resulting calculations work. A stage of highlight extraction comprises various sub-steps that depend on the territorial level are as per the following.

#### 8.5.5.1.1 Data Level

Information put together highlights depends on the joint data everything being equal. In this way, all changes controlling the entire network of an image without a moment's delay can be considered for information highlight extraction. The most renowned case of an information highlight change is the Fourier change, which depicts a 2D image as far as frequencies, as indicated by their plentiful nature and stage. These strategies are not in the focal point of research in biomedical image handling. Truth be told, these methodologies are fairly adjusted from specialized regions into clinical applications.

#### 8.5.5.1.2 Pixel Level

Because pixel-put together highlights depend on the estimations of individual pixels, all point activities can be viewed as highlight extraction on the pixel level. The deduction of reference and review image after fitting registration in both spatial and worth reaches authorize nearby changes in the image as trademark pixels.

#### 8.5.5.1.3 Edge Level

Edge-based features are characterized as neighborhood differentiate, that is, a solid contrast of (grayscale or shading) estimations of contiguous pixels. In this manner, the discrete convolution can be utilized with fitting layouts for edge extraction. All covers for high-pass sifting enhance edges in a picture. The layouts of the alleged Sobel administrator are especially appropriate for edge extraction. Anisotropic Sobel-based edge imaging is accomplished, for example, by a direct or greatest blend of the eight sub-images.

#### 8.5.5.1.4 Texture Level

Features like textural have been utilized in medication for quite a while. In course readings on pathology, one can peruse numerous similitudes to depict the surface, for example, a cobblestone-formed mucosal alleviation, onion-like separation of sub intima, or honeycomb-organized lung tissue. As natural as these representations are for individuals, as troublesome is their computational surface handling, and an assortment of strategies and approaches have been created. Surface investigation endeavors to evaluate equitably the homogeneity in a heterogeneous yet at any rate abstractly intermittent structure. All in all, we can recognize:

- Structural methodologies that depend on surface natives (content one, surface component, and texel) and their standards of blends and
- Statistical methodologies that depict surface by a set of exact parameters.

*8.5.5.1.5 Region Level*

Regional features are utilized basically for object classification and recognizable proof. They are typically determined for each section after the division procedure. The most significant parameters to be referenced here are:

- Localization: Descriptive estimations, for example, size, position, and direction of the significant hub.
- Delineation: Descriptive estimates, for example, shape, convexity, and length of the outskirt.

Since the level of deliberation on the provincial level is fairly high when contrasted with the past levels, the earlier information has just been to a great extent incorporated into the image preparing chain. Along these lines, general models cannot be determined. Actually, the meaning of provincial component extraction is emphatically reliant on the particular application.

## 8.5.5.2 Image Segmentation

Segmentation alludes to a subclass of upgrade strategies by which a specific article, organ, or image trademark is separated from the image information for reasons for perception and estimation. Division includes partnering a pixel with a specific article class dependent on the nearby force, spatial position, neighboring pixels, or earlier data about the shape qualities of the item class. The focal point of investigation into division is to decide rationale or techniques that achieve acceptably precise division with as meager intuitive examination as could be expected under the circumstances. Segmentation is a focal issue of image investigation because it is essential for most of the examination strategies, including image enlistment, shape examination, movement recognition, and volume and territory estimation.

Lamentably, there is no regular strategy or class of techniques pertinent to even most of the images. The vast majority of the division strategies being applied to clinical images depend on the supposition that the objects of intrigue have the power or edge qualities that permit them to be isolated from the foundation and commotion, just as from one another. At the point when the scopes of pixel forces related to various physiologic highlights are noncovering or almost thus, complete thresholding (emphasizing or erasing all pixels above or beneath a separating limit of power) might be adequate to give the characterization required. For instance, bone is somewhat handily portioned from x-ray images as a result of the wide partition of dark scale levels between the high-signal-force bone and different tissues; the power levels of the pixels fall into two territories, and pixels in each can be controlled to highlight the distinction. Complete thresholding is not satisfactory, be that as it may, for separating heart muscle from chest tissues or recognizing cerebral dim and white issue. Grouping of articles dependent on pixel power can likewise be executed by the utilization of preparing focuses, neural systems, histograms, fluffy rationale, or bunch investigation. In spite of an extensive assemblage of writing here, generally hardly any reports have shown dependable division dependence on the power attributes of a solitary three-dimensional image.

Edge recognition is basically executed by tasks that scan for changes in power inclinations; notwithstanding, this is confused in light of the fact that powers in biomedical images regularly increase or decrease from the structure important to the encompassing structure(s) from which division is to be affected. Indeed, even factual edge-discovering methods flop in most clinical imaging applications where the grayscale levels and surfaces of the objective organ and encompassing tissues are comparable—which is the standard case. Progression and network are solid measures for isolating clamor from objects and have been abused generally, either legitimately by the rationale rules utilized in area growing or by applying post-preparing disintegration and enlargement to isolate little islands of commotion or spatially particular articles with comparative powers.

A modern and fruitful way to deal with division depends on the otherworldly qualities of every pixel. LANDSAT image investigation utilizes the force compared to various frequencies to separate districts of changing soil or vegetation content from each other. Comparative methodologies have been applied to MRI, wherein diverse heartbeat arrangements bring out various qualities of the attractive reverberation properties of tissues, so bunch examination would then be able to be utilized to section tissues with comparable properties. This methodology is extremely incredible yet requires the procurement of different images.

The normal standard for approving or contrasting division strategies is with analyzing hand-drawn shapes on progressive sectional outputs, for the most part with some guide from district developing and thresholding. The objective of division strategies is to computerize this dull system, and one technique is, in any case, some model of the item. This model goes about as a bound or manual for the procedures, to help dispense with some uncertainty about power, nearby pixel esteems, or edges. Using from the earlier information about the potential states of object has not been executed in an effective division framework for organs, yet this is a productive territory for division investigation.

### 8.5.5.3 Image Classification

Image classification is a huge and significant methodology in the region of clinical image information examination, and it has been recharged because of promising applications, for example, information mining, money related determining, association, and recovery of media and bioinformatics. Previously, a few order calculations have been proposed, including a closest neighbor, decision tree acceptance, error back propagation, lazy learning, and rule-based learning and the general new expansion is measurable learning. Strangely, these order techniques are getting tremendous and continually expanding. In the interim, these are headways in clinical imaging to be specific: image division, computer supported finding frameworks, and substance-based image recovery image annotation. Along these lines, the significance of clinical picture characterization is obvious to everybody. In addition, the tremendous measure of clinical image information available to the overall population calls for growing new instruments and characterization techniques to adequately analyze, breaks down, and group clinical information.

Because soft computing gives distinctive arrangement strategies that are general in nature, it can be applied to a collection of information. In this way, the subject of whom characterization strategy may be reasonable for a particular report is not anything but difficult to reply. Notwithstanding, grouping techniques that are specific to specific applications can regularly accomplish better execution as far as precision and unpredictability time by considering different components and earlier information. Ali and Smith made a point-by-point examination and correlations of eight distinctive grouping calculations with a hundred diverse arrangement issues (Han and Kamber, 2006). The relative weight execution measures show that there was no single-order calculation to tackle each of the hundred arrangement issues with the best execution over the distinctive trial arrangements. Moreover, the engendering of huge datasets inside numerous areas presents remarkable difficulties to information mining. There have been numerous correlations of various grouping techniques; notwithstanding, no single characterization strategy has been seen as better over all datasets. Accordingly, the issue stays an examination theme.

However, the primary target of all the proposed characterization calculations, regardless of whether it depends on describing surface to its measurements or demonstrating the clinical image, plans to gain from how curiously observe clinical pictures to inevitably create "knowledge" computerized frameworks (Han and Kamber, 2006; Smitha et al., 2011).

### 8.5.6 Image Management

Initially, we have added with the expression "image management" all images control methods, which serve as the powerful chronicling (short and long terms), transmission (correspondence), and the entrance (recovery) of information. For every one of the three focuses, the points of interest in clinical applications and human services conditions have prompted explicit arrangements, which are quickly presented in the accompanying segments.

### 8.5.6.1 Archiving

As of now in the seventies, the innovation of CT and its coordination with clinical routine has included the establishment of the primary PACS, whose principle task is the filing of image information. The center issue of filing clinical images is the huge volume of information. Straightforward radiography with 40 × 40 cm (e.g., a chest X-beam) with a goal of five-line sets for every millimeter and 10 bits = 1,024 dark levels for each pixel as of now requires a capacity limit of in excess of 10 MB. Computerized mammography, which is caught with high goals on the two bosoms in two perspectives results in around 250 MB of crude information for every assessment. Ten years back, radiography, CT, and MRI were used in a college clinic to effectively around 2 TB of picture information every year. This gauge can without much of a stretch increment ten times with the goals expanded novel modalities, for example, winding CT and entire body MRI. For example in Germany, as per significant enactments, the information must be kept at any rate for a long time. Consequently, productive capacity, recovery, and correspondence of clinical image have required successful pressure procedures and fast systems. Because of noise in biomedical images, lossless pressure generally has a constrained impact of pressure paces of a few. Just as of late, practical half breed stockpiling ideas have opened up. The capacity of and access to clinical image information is still of high pertinence.

### 8.5.6.2 Communication

With the expanding digitization of demonstrative imaging, the motive for clinical data frameworks, that is, to give "the correct data at the ideal time and the perfect spot," is anticipated to the field of clinical image handling. Consequently, image correspondence is the center of the present PACS. Image information is not just moved electronically inside a division of radiology or the emergency clinic yet in addition between broadly isolated foundations. For this assignment, basic bitmap configurations, for example, the Tagged Image File Format (TIFF) or the Graphics Interchange Format are deficient, in light of the fact that, next to the image, which may have been caught in various measurements, clinical meta-data on patients (e.g., Identifier (ID), name, date of birth, etc.), the methodology (e.g., gadget, parameters, etc.) and association (e.g., examination, study, etc.) should likewise be moved in a normalized manner.

Since 1995, the correspondence depends on the standard. In its present form, DICOM incorporates:

- Structural data about the substance of the information ("object classes"),
- Commands on what ought to befall the information ("administration classes"), and
- Data transmission protocols.

DICOM depends on the customer server worldview and permits the coupling of PACS in the Radiology Information System or Hospital Information Systems. DICOM fuses existing norms for correspondence: the International Organization for Standardization Open System Interconnection model, the Transmission Control Protocol Internet Protocol, and the Health Level 7 (HL7) standard. Full DICOM consistence for imaging gadgets and picture preparing applications is accomplished with just a couple of bolstered articles or administration classes, because other DICOM objects, which are not significant for the present gadget, essentially are given over to the following framework in the DICOM organization. The synchronization between the customer and server is regularized by conformance claims, which are additionally indicated as a major aspect of the DICOM standard. Be that as it may, the subtleties of the execution of individual administrations are not indicated in the norm, thus by and by, merchant explicit DICOM tongues have been created, which can prompt contradictions when building PACS. Lately, Integrating Healthcare Enterprises activity got significant targets managing the utilization of DICOM and different principles to such an extent that total interoperability is accomplished.

### 8.5.6.3 Retrieval

In the present-day DICOM archives, images can be recovered deliberately, just if the patient's name with date of birth or the inner framework ID is known. All things considered, the recovery depends on alphanumerical qualities, which are put away along the image information. Clearly demonstrative execution of PACS is amplified altogether if images would be legitimately accessible from comparative substances of given model images. Giving the Query by Example worldview is a significant errand of future frameworks for Contend-Based Image Retrieval (CBIR). Once more, this field of biomedical research requires thoughtfully various techniques as it is requested in business CBIR frameworks for other application regions, on account of the assorted and complex structure of demonstrative data that is caught in biomedical images.

Figure 8.17 shows the framework design of the IRMA system. This design mirrors the chain of preparing that we have talked about in this part, that is, registration, extraction of features, segmentation, and order of picture objects toward the tip of the pyramid, which is the representative translation individual scene investigation.

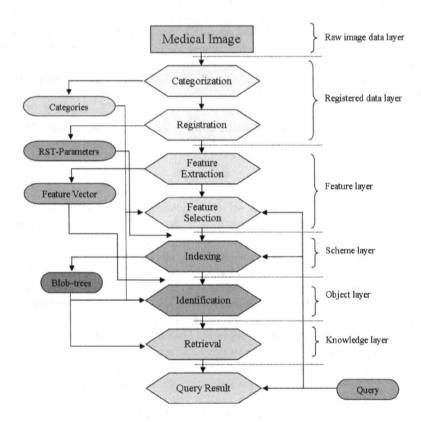

**FIGURE 8.17** System engineering of the Image Retrieval in Medical Applications (IRMA) structure. The preparing steps in IRMA appear in the center section. Order depends on features considered globally and arranges images as far as imaging methodology; see heading, anatomic district, and body framework. As indicated by its class, the images geometry and complexity are enlisted to a reference. The deliberation depends on nearby highlights, which are chosen explicitly to setting and inquiry. The recovery itself is performed effectively on preoccupied and consequently data diminished levels. This design follows the worldview of picture examination. The middle of portrayals as introduced on the left depicts the picture progressively theoretical. The degrees of reflection are named on the right side.

In IRMA, the picture data that are significant for recovery are bit by bit consolidated and disconnected. The image bitmap is emblematically spoken to by a semantic system (progressive tree structure). The hubs contain trademark data to the spoke to regions (portions) of the image. Its topology depicts the spatial and additionally fleeting state of each item. With this innovation, radiologists and specialists are upheld also in persistent consideration, research, and education.

## REFERENCES

Ali, S. and Smith, K.A. (2006). On learning algorithms selection for classification. *Applied Soft Computing* 6, 119–138.

Han, J. and Kamber, M. (2006). *Data Mining: Concepts and Techniques*, Second Edition, Morgan Kaufmann.

Smitha, P., Shaji, L., and Mini, M.G. (2011). *A review of medical image classification technique*, International Conference on VLSI, Communication & Instrumentation.

Wilkinson, M.D., Dumontier, M., Aalbersberg, I.J. et al. (2016). The FAIR guiding principles for scientific data management and stewardship. *Sci Data*. doi: 10.1038/sdata.2016.18.

# 9 Application of Image Processing in Traffic Management and Analysis

## 9.1 INTRODUCTION

Every city has lifeline as roads that help people to go from one place to another. Traffic Control Management is the plan of the traffic control at various locations that can be flagging, detours, full closure divergent, pedestrian lanes, and traffic movement plans. Traffic management systems can be categorized as air traffic management systems, freight and cargo systems, rail management systems, and road traffic management systems.

Traffic management systems of air, freight and cargo, and railways have been utilizing the technologies to solve the various issues in the management of traffic. However, road traffic management systems have been for a long time used by the manual traffic policemen to handle road traffic. In the present scenario, road traffic management systems are utilizing technology to handle traffic issues, and the term used to define is known as the smart traffic management systems.

Taking the traffic management system of past decades, even before the invention of the automobiles, traffic jams were a problem like for horse-drawn carriages, civilians crowding the road, etc. Earlier there were no such technologies to monitor traffic for the speed limitation guidelines for automobiles, so the roads were even more prone to accidents. Even broad highways were considered very unsafe as for the smaller vehicles because people do rash driving which later result in crashes. Now moving and visualizing the current status of traffic management, it has been determined that there are frequent traffic jams on the road, which sometimes lead to accidents and even deaths in certain cases. It has been a very persistent issue now. People generally do speed on the roads due to lack of proper surveillance and their mindset to some extent.

Now, let us study the example of the very first traffic management system, that is, traffic lights. We can see that traffic signals are located on the intersection of most roads in many towns and cities in numerous countries. The first traffic signal that was installed was believed to be installed on November 9, 1868, at the intersection of bridge Street and great George Street in the London borough. However, it failed miserably as it worked on gas, and it required a police officer to be stationed at and operate the signal. Unfortunately, a police officer was injured due to gas leak, and then they decided to abolish this idea.

After nearly four decades of the accident, in the early 1900s, the automobile sector grew drastically, and there again a need of a traffic system was felt, so in 1910, an American inventor named Ernest Sirinne introduced an automatically controlled traffic signal in Chicago, which was arranged in a cross manner indicating the stop and proceed only.

Later in 1912, the first electric traffic light used red and green light, which was invented by Leicester Farnsworth, who was a police officer in Salt Lake City, Utah. According to the research, his model resembled a four-sided birdhouse mounted on a tall pole and got placed at the intersection and was overhead powered by trolley wires, but it also needed a police officer to manually switch the directions of the lights.

Many such models came and went, but in 1923, Garett Morgan (also invented the gas mask) discovered an electric automatic traffic signal who was the first African American to even own a car in Cleveland. His design included a T-shaped pole with three positions. Besides go and stop signals, the system also stops the traffic in all directions to get drivers ready, which is very similar to what we see nowadays, that is, three lights red, yellow, and green indicating stop, get ready, and go, respectively. They gave us the idea about the vacancy instructions like when to stop driving, when to walk through the streets, and when to drive safely and also turn safely.

However, the conventional mode of the traffic management systems is not that efficient in case of the heavy outpour of the traffic, especially with the new economic zones coming all over the world with increased economic and commercial activities. Moreover, the traffic police also needs to be more equipped for taking better decisions about the management of the traffic.

## 9.2 SMART TRAFFIC MANAGEMENT SYSTEMS

As the population keeps increasing, transportation needs to be efficient, which thereby improves the economic productivity and the environment. The smart traffic system comprises the smart lights, sensors, and detectors, which help to regulate the city traffic. It helps to reduce the day-to-day congestion or prioritize the traffic thereby reducing the traffic jams.

Moreover, smart cities are one of the impressive projects of the Government, which utilizes various artificial intelligence (AI) algorithms to carry out various tasks without the need of the human intervention. One of the major parts of the smart cities is to manage the traffic intelligently by observing the previous trends of the traffic. Smart traffic management systems basically mean modulating the traffic in smart ways, that is, with the help of technology rather than human intervention. In very simple words, we can describe any traffic management system as smart if it uses smart technologies such as AI, image processing, sensors, and many more.

The smart traffic management system is the need of the hour as not only the Metropolitan cities have been crowded but the cities that are very much smaller in areas and even less in population have rush on the roads, which is not being managed properly by the human efforts in labor form. Therefore, this concept has to be brought into action.

Since then, a lot of technologies have been developed in the field of signaling systems. The trend of traffic signals has evolved from the fixed time programmed signals to the detector-based real-time traffic signals where technology inputs have improved both on hardware and software sides of signaling systems.

The possibility to utilize the AI for the traffic management system is very high because a lot of research is taking place in this direction. In the near future, when self-driving vehicles become the norm of the day, smart traffic management systems can help to provide a great possibility of directing and controlling such self-driven vehicles. Presently even in India, some of the metro cities are making use of the automated traffic signals, which provides help to the traffic police for analyzing various parameters that can help them to gain insight into the scenario of the traffic and thus manage the traffic. Such traffic management systems have been using high-resolution closed-circuit television (CCTV) cameras to capture the traffic, and automated number place recognition systems can further aid in handling the regular traffic law breakers. The traffic lights in the smart traffic management systems can further analyze themselves that which lane has more traffic and can thus allow that lane to be open for more amount of time.

The advanced road traffic management system is that there is a continuous flow of data from the IoT sensors installed on the roadside, due to which the authorities can take more informed decisions. The three devices used for smart systems are a central control system, smart traffic lights, and cameras and detectors to help the traffic light movement based on the dynamic traffic in real time. Traffic lights and sensors collect information from the sensors and communicate with the vehicles to help the possible congestion. Sensors are placed at major intersections that help to synchronize the vehicles for smooth movement. Sensors can be traced from the control room, and vehicles can also describe the speed in which the drivers can move so that accidents or rash driving can be avoided. A new concept of always a green light also is becoming popular where the drivers are informed regularly about the prediction of the speed that they should maintain to have the green light. Smart traffic lights will further give smart information to the ambulances to be able to reach to the nearest hospitals in reduced timeframe. They also gather data on the pollution expelled by the vehicles to help conserve the environment. For real-time systems, detector sensors are installed on every intersection, which counts the number of vehicles that stop or wait at any intersection side or corner. The inputs from the detector are then processed by controller software, and signals are synchronized in such a way that heavy traffic paths are given longer clearways. A lot of technological improvements have been reported in hardware such as detector types, controllers, connectors, and signals.

It is being researched and implemented through various means such as the use of wireless sensor networks, RFID, applying various concepts of graph theory to find the minimized path and many others. Here, the concept of Intelligent Traffic System (ITS) has been classified into two main broader categories as follows in Figure 9.1:

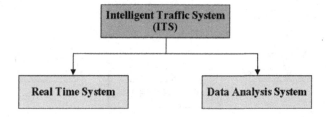

**FIGURE 9.1** Classification of the intelligent traffic system.

## 9.2.1 Real-Time System

In real-time systems, the commuters can get real-time situation of the traffic, road, and other parameters associated with traffic management. It gives more information about the routes to be taken leading to reduced journey time as this information can be about the congestions, accidents, etc. Advanced traffic management systems can also include information about the public transport that can be provided to the public in order to plan their travel in advance. Smart parking systems are useful in the metro as well as any nook and corner of countries because the cities are not planned in view of the current population and vehicle density, causing an acute dearth on the space to park the vehicles. Vehicles are allocated parking spots using various guidance systems and parking spaces in some places are also being allocated online to provide more convenience. Multimodal mobility systems are used to help the traffic management systems apart from the pedestrian management systems.

## 9.2.2 Data Analysis System

The data analysis system is used to analyze the data collected from various sources such as sensors, cameras, etc. which can be used for the purpose of decision making. There are many cases where the prediction of the future number of vehicles in a city can be used for planning the traffic management and road and highway construction based on this analysis. Even the data analysis system can be used for parking and other utilities associated with traffic management to provide efficient and smart traffic management in Figure 9.2.

Sensors installed in the traditional roads can help to detect the location and the speed of a vehicle, which can make the drivers abide by the traffic laws. Further faster information about an accident can reach the control room that can further cause faster movement of help reaching to the location. Especially in fog times, the sensors

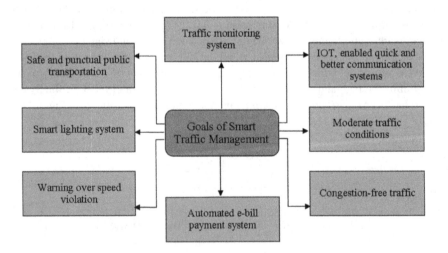

**FIGURE 9.2**    Goals for smart traffic management.

can help the drivers to drive safely by making the predictions and providing a clear view of the roads in spite of the environmental hazards.

The goals of the smart traffic management system can be summarized as follows:

1. Prioritize moderate traffic conditions by analyzing real-time traffic situations.
2. Providing congestion-free traffic.
3. Improvising traditional ticketing with an automated e-bill payment system.
4. Speed sensors to warn commuters over speed violation.
5. Provide a smart lighting system that reserves renewable energy sources.
6. Offer safe and punctual public transportation.
7. Advanced traffic monitoring systems at intersections and narrow road ends to provide the right traffic guidance.
8. Optimizing road networking systems, through building IoT, enabled quick and better communication systems.

The goals for smarter traffic management include all the aspects from construction of bigger and wider roads to parking to speed management to traffic management. These all aspects are the goals which ensure for smarter traffic management. Even the smart lighting system which focuses on renewable energy or conservation of energy is the need for smarter traffic management. Thus, the goals of traffic management defined in Figure 9.1 include points like prioritizing the condition of traffic by means of analyzing the real-time traffic pattern captured by means of various smart sensors and cameras and analyzed these data to provide the real-time situation of traffic in order to help the decision-making bodies to take real-time actions and prevention based on these data. This analysis also helps in providing congestion-free traffic as the data from real-time traffic can be used for future decision-making processes to handle traffic to provide congestion-free traffic. The ticketing system is also the aspect of smart traffic management. Changing the ticketing system to e-ticketing system will enable managing traffic jams at many tolls, etc. Speeding is one of the major issues which need to be addressed for efficient and smarter traffic management. Installation of sensors which can sense the speed of the vehicle from remote locations is performed. These sensors provide the speed of the vehicle on real-time basis and based on this will get the information of those vehicles which are over speeding. Lighting is another feature which needs to be addressed in smart traffic management. There are smart traffic lighting systems adopted in smart cities in many countries which provide a real-time lighting intensity based on the number of vehicles in the road across the lightening. These lights glow bright when the number of traffic across the road is more while diminishes as the number of traffic goes low, and thus reduces the energy by means of managing the intensity of light on real-time basis based on intensity of traffic across the road. Based on demand of energy, we should also focus on relying more on green energy. So, the dependency of lightening systems on green and natural energy is also implemented and in action in many smart traffic management projects. Safety and punctuality are also some of the major factors which contribute for smart traffic management. Safety is ensured by means of providing the real-time data of the traffic and vehicles plying on the road for smart traffic management. Using technology such as IoT, sensor-based technologies, etc. will help in providing these smart traffic management systems.

## 9.3 REVIEW WORK

Real-time systems of traffic management can be further classified into two categories as in Figure 9.3:

There are various research studies that are being carried out in the area of path optimization and the traffic density. Image processing is one of the research fields that are being extensively used for the advanced traffic management systems. Pukale et al. (2016) in their research on traffic management system used video processing with OpenCV for density-based traffic management systems. They use the blob algorithm for finding the real-time density of the vehicle and by using OpenCV library template matching detect the emergency vehicle to give priority to these emergency vehicles. The proposed approach can also be used for reporting violation of traffic rules.

Hongal et al. (2016) provided an architecture of intelligent traffic control systems. In their research, a vehicle is categorized as a normal mode and emergency mode. By using image processing technique, the density of the traffic is sensed across the road, and based on this real-time information, a system is implemented where vehicles are provided with sensors that can help to implement an automatic brake and make use of the GPS tracker to track stolen vehicles.

Jain et al. (2012) presented in their research that a simple automated mechanisms utilizing image processing steps to detect the congestion levels with the help of the images of the road collected by the CCTV installed at the various traffic signals of Kenya and Brazil. They utilized a local decongestion protocol that coordinates the traffic signal behavior within a small area based on the simple network topologies used to enhance the road potential and reduce the traffic congestion.

The basic causes of the congestion in the traffic can be insufficient capacity, unrestrained demand, and large delays in the traffic lights. In order to make the traffic lights more dynamic and make them act in real time, video monitoring is done with the help of the sensors placed on the roads which help to estimate the traffic density and the vehicle classification. Kanungo et al. (2014) proposed that video feed from the sensors can be segmented by the image processing steps and

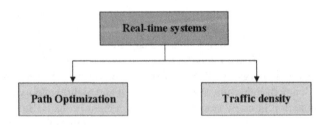

**FIGURE 9.3**    Classification of real-time systems.

it focuses on the algorithm to switch the traffic lights dependent on the density of the traffic available on the roads. It further reduces waiting time and fuel consumption.

Image processing can be used to detect objects, and basic steps for better traffic management involve image analysis, object detection, typed count object, motion detection, and result representation which are used to create a self-adaptive system that can help to manage traffic in such a manner that the free flow traffic can be implemented at the location of the choice by the users. The tracking system will be able to detect the vehicles under various lightning conditions (Nagaraj et al., 2013).

In one of the patents, Slavin et al. (2018) had proposed a lane-level vehicle routing that can perform simulation of the individual vehicles in the traffic, and an optimizer for the traffic was also proposed, which utilized image segmentation processing to evaluate the candidate paths for the user to reach from the source to the destination in the most optimal time.

Gaikwad et al. (2014) proposed that the populations of the present day cities and vehicles are increasing exponentially, due to which it becomes necessary that the traffic should be controlled. The present scenario requires the traffic lights not to be present, but should react as per the need of the hour. The proposed research presents the project to prevent heavy traffic congestion by measuring the number of vehicles on the road using the image processing techniques with the help of the cameras arranged on the vehicles. The proposed algorithm was implemented by the authors in MATLAB®.

Bhaskar and Yong (2014) proposed an optimal method to detect traffic data from the video recorded by the surveillance systems using the Gaussian Mixture model and the blob detection scheme. The difference between the foreground and the background has been counted, and rectangular regions are formed over the detected object as in the case of semantic segmentation that can be further improvised using the Gaussian Mixture mode and blob detection approaches.

Autonomous ITSs utilize the computer vision and image processing. Hu et al. (2004) proposed a probabilistic model for predicting the traffic accidents that uses a three-dimensional model-based vehicle tracking. It can be applied to learn the activity patterns available from the samples which can further predict the accidents. The activity patterns are learned using the fuzzy self-organizing neural network.

Maheshwari (2015) in their paper had proposed a traffic management system that allows using the route information by using the navigation systems installed in the vehicles and alters the route to reach the destination by predicting the traffic congestion ahead on the route in real-time basis.

Rosenbaum et al. (2010) proposed an aircraft borne camera to obtain the traffic data. Based on the image processing techniques for image extraction from the three cameras, the road data were recorded from a height of 1500 meters. The direct georeferencing and orthorectified images can help extract the road data with more precision. Vehicle detection is performed using the combination of Adaboost for pixel-wise classification and clustering carried out by SVM. These experimental implementations were carried by the authors in Munich.

Ozawa (1999) proposed an intelligent transport system where image processing can be helpful for intelligent transport systems, which recently have been used widely. The image seen from the camera located beside or upon the road can be used for vehicle detection, velocity of car, car detection for parking, etc. Moreover, the image seen from the camera located in the vehicle can be used for preceding car detection, obstacle detection, lane detection, etc.

Traffic congestion in the developing countries has been studied by Biswas et al. (2015), and they made a comparative study of the potential research studies in the ITS, and some of the research studies are highlighted and judged and finally a model proposing the use of infrared proximity and a microcontroller that implements the traffic monitoring system.

Hamsaveni (2013) studied the increasing congestion on the highways and the problems that were linked with the vehicle detection technologies. The authors proposed to develop a self-adaptive system that can process the free flowing traffic using various image processing technologies, and the traffic density is calculated using cheaper detectors or sensors. Moreover, the user can also find the traffic density at the location of choice.

Swathy et al. (2017) in their paper found the basic issue of the traffic density for traffic management, and the intelligent transportation detects the moving vehicles from the video of the traffic scenes recorded by the cameras installed at the roads. Vision-based traffic surveillance is one of the emerging fields in the road management schemes and highway monitoring. Many methods and algorithms have been proposed to detect the vehicles on the highways.

Danti et al. (2012) carried out an extensive research on the Indian roads that have various issues such as the faded lanes, irregular potholes apart from the temperature causing tires to burst which has led to various accidents and loss of precious lives. Image processing methods can be very easily used to detect such problems and inform the automatic driver guidance systems about the possible dangers. In their paper, they have made used of the Hough transformation method making color segmentation and shape modeling or k-means clustering techniques for lane detection, faded road sign detection, and pothole detection. The experiments were carried out in real-time datasets, and the results were found to be quite good.

In their studies of the traffic congestion, Ali et al. (2013) found that the traffic congestion is at peak during specific time of the day, and therefore, a dynamic traffic signal light can be proposed which can handle the vehicle flows detecting the flow of the traffic from the previously collected data and based on the obtained pattern of the traffic flow.

Zhang and Forshaw (1997), in their innovative approach, described a method to not only find the speed of the vehicle but also to detect the possible direction of the movement of the vehicle using various image processing techniques. They use the streaming video of CCTV cameras, the pixels are extracted, and these techniques use 35 transputers and an image grabber with a SUN Sparc IPC as the host machine; the software consists of median filtering, feature extraction, spatio-temporal analysis, matching of image features in successive images by neural networks, and aggregation of matched results. This algorithm has been tested using data for a signal-controlled junction aiming to capture an opposed turning traffic movement with promising results. It has also been shown that a real-time system based on the described algorithm is feasible.

Hooda et al. (2016) studied the requirements of the smart traffic management system for the smart cities, and the authors using the existing infrastructure created a traffic light that could dynamically detect the traffic flow from the streaming video of the CCTV cameras and based on this information created the traffic lights to be dynamical in nature, and their paper also focused on the pre-emption system for the emergency vehicle.

In the smart cities, apart from the focus to the traffic management systems, there is a dire need for the management of the pedestrian facilities. Data collection and pedestrian analysis require to be done. The authors have studied and classified the pedestrian into two categories, and they are the microscopic and macroscopic pedestrian analysis. The individual units with speed and interaction were categorized into the microscopic level, whereas pedestrian facilities with the flow, speed, and area modules into the macroscopic level. In a situation of dense activities, Teknomo (2016) took the case studies about the performance of the pedestrians owning to their comfort ability and the delay that can help to reject the linearity of the space and flow in the macroscopic level. The movement of pedestrians needed to be controlled so that the interaction problem is reduced.

Pena-Gonzalez and Nuno (2014) in their paper proposed a vision-based system to detect, track, count, and classify moving vehicles based on the information processing to be carried out on the data acquired on the HD-RGB camera placed on the road. Information processing was carried out using the clustering and classification algorithms. The system obtained an efficiency score over 95% in test cases, as well as, the correct classification of 85% of the test objects. Furthermore, the system achieves 30 fps in image processing with a resolution of $1280 \times 720$.

Some research has also been carried out on the environment of the interior of the vehicles using a camera to determine at least one characteristic of an object in the vehicle. This vehicle can be arranged at some point of the vehicle and depending on the obtained characteristic, the optimal control of a reactive component is coupled to the processor (Breed et al., 2005).

Xie et al. (2014) developed a graphical user interface system using MATLAB Software that can detect the license plates of the vehicles running on the roads. The license plate recognition system had the following phases of image acquisition, image pre-processing, license plate locator, character segmentation, character recognition, output results, etc., and this system was unique because it could detect the Chinese character recognition. The identification procedure could be completed in a small amount of time.

Oh et al. (2000) applied new reinforcement learning on the problem of the vehicle road interaction dynamics, which helps to learn how to keep the vehicles on track based on the patterns observed during the movement of the vehicle around the high-curvature roads. The experiments provided results with good efficiency even for different lightning conditions and noisy data. The experiments also provided promising results for handling the uncertainties in non-ideal road conditions.

Traffic rules are the informal rules generally developed and implemented to keep some discipline on the roads. Road signs can help the users for various data. Various research studies have been carried out on these issues too on the Indian scenario using image processing techniques (Rajagopal, 2020).

Rotake and Karmore (2012) suggested a system which utilized an AVR 32 micro-controller with various sensors and memory; these sensors sense the fire brigades and ambulances and control the traffic lights to only allow the movement of these emergency vehicles. Furthermore, Krishna et al. (2014) proposed a priority-based traffic light controller making use of the sigmoid function of the fuzzy logic and wireless sensor network to define the direction of any emergency vehicle which is further handled by the central monitoring system.

## 9.4 WORKING OF REAL-TIME TRAFFIC MANAGEMENT

The management of traffic in real-time basis is the need of the hour. Managing and monitoring the traffic in real-time will provide an efficient traffic management. The real-time traffic management can be performed by multiple methods but discussing working of some methods over here as follows.

Real-time systems in case of traffic managing systems take the input of the current situation through video surveillance or WSNs and deal with the situation. The traffic signals are controlled according to the presence of vehicles and are operated automatically in real time. A real-time optimization model was used by Dotolie who investigated the issue of traffic control in urban areas. The model took into considerations the traffic scenarios which also include civilians. This technique was applied for analyzing real case studies. Here, the time that a vehicle requires to reach the intersection from a particular point, dynamically, is calculated by the use of sensors. By this, data were subjected to various calculations to find the green light length. This technique uses real-time data to monitor current traffic flows in a junction so that the traffic could be controlled in a convenient way. Reliable short-term forecasting videos captured in a recorder play an important role in monitoring the traffic management system. The data required can be easily provided by the CCTV cameras that can be beside the roads as per requirement. Other ways can be by means of visualizing the use of transportation incident management explorer for calculating real-time data.

There are other methods proposing a distributed wireless network of vehicular sensors to get a view of the actual scenario, and they are used in various sectors to lower the congestion but not for taking decisions in real time. The use of two types of sensor networks was proposed, vehicular sensor network and wireless sensor network, and the combination of these two permits the monitoring as well as managing of the traffic.

Video surveillance for realizing the real-time scenario can also be used. It deals with decreasing response time of the emergency cars by establishing communication between emergency cars and traffic lights. The data collected in real time can be used to determine the traffic density and also based on the traffic present. To implement connected vehicle technology with multiple traffic light systems to communicate directly with the car and improve safety and efficiency, this process works as communications are sent from over 40 traffic lights to cars in vehicles equipped with the technology of this thing to receive the basic safety messages on the rear view mirror or in dash computer screens.

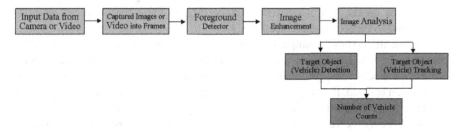

**FIGURE 9.4**     Working procedure of real-time traffic management using the frame difference method.

Here are some of the methods that are being used as a part of smart traffic management systems around the globe. Because hardware methods have been very tedious and they involved a large number of hardware which was also costly and was very labor consuming work, therefore there have been discoveries in the field of image processing and image enhancement.

One more method is FRAME DIFFERENCE METHOD as presented in Figure 9.4; in this method, when the cameras are installed somewhere and live video is recorded, then the video is divided into certain frames and it is taken as the input frames. It is known as the matching technique in which the subtraction is done between the previous image and the current image, and according to the difference, we will get the percentage of traffic on the road.

Another popular technique used is the background subtraction and it is the process that separates the foreground objects from the background in a sequence of the frames or images. Varying complexities are used for the background subtraction, and they are low-complexity, medium-complexity, and high-complexity approaches. The low-complexity approach makes use of the frame difference method. The medium-complexity approach uses an approximate median method, whereas the high-complexity approach makes use of the Gaussian methods.

The working of this algorithm involves steps as follows:

1. Convert the incoming frame to grayscale.
2. Subtract the current frame from the background model.
3. For each pixel, if the difference between the current frame and background is greater than a threshold, then the pixel is considered part of the foreground.

This technique used a foreground detector. The foreground detector basically filters and detects the ground. It also changes the image type from RGB to Gray and then into the binary and then applies filtering at different levels. Then, image enhancement is performed with frames. Image enhancement is that it adjusts the digital images so that the results are more suitable to show for further analysis like it can eliminate noise in the picture which will make it easy to detect the object or identify the object. After the images from frames are enhanced, there is the vehicle detection method. Vehicle detection can be performed using simple Haar cascading methods, and thus vehicles are counted and will be able to easily find the congestions on the road successfully. According to the research, these methods have sound to be around 90% accurate.

Another method or technique used in the process is to place a camera at a certain place on a highway, and vehicle detection techniques were used to detect the vehicles until a distance is reached and if the number of vehicles counted is greater than the limit which is listed, then it will display that there is dense traffic otherwise moderate traffic or low traffic will be displayed and for the process of detection of the number plates whenever the vehicle is stopped at the red signal. This process uses two cameras, one to capture the top view of the road and the one to capture the number plate of the vehicle will be attached to the parallel of the road through which a vehicle passes during a red signal camera will get on to capture the number plate. Thereby, the history of vehicle was also kept track.

Another way is using AI for smart traffic management. Several models are proposed by different researchers as presented in Figure 9.5 and use AI-based cameras which detect the vehicles moving on the road using a programming-based approach (python) which involves the Haar cascade files that have cascade classifiers to detect and classify the vehicles. Then for each detected vehicle, the speed of the moving vehicle on the road will be checked and if the speed of the vehicle is more than the particular threshold limit, then a challan will be generated for that particular vehicle. For detecting the speed of the vehicle, first mark two points on the frame and using frames per second, count the number of frames that have occurred from the first center point to the second center point. From this, we get to know that at how much time the vehicle passes from the first marked point to second marked point. The AI-based camera will be fitted manually so it can manually decide the distance of the road and then can convert it to the distance of our own frame accordingly. From this, the information related to the distance as well as the time can be monitored and can be used to calculate the speed of the car by using distance and time parameters as speed = distance/time. If the speed of the vehicle is more than the particular threshold, then the license plate of the prescribed vehicle is captured and by using python programming, detection of the license plate of the vehicle can be done. The information of this license plate can be used to extract the database of the car (car owner, etc.) from the RTO office which can be used to send a challan to the owner by means of message or mail from the extracted information and thus make the traffic management smarter and real time.

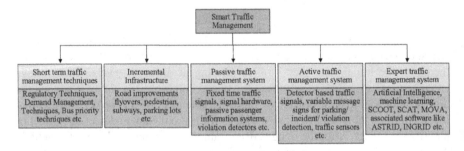

**FIGURE 9.5**   Classification of smart traffic management components.

Technologies used for smart traffic management can be divided into five groups as follows:

1. Short-term traffic management techniques
2. Incremental infrastructure
3. Passive traffic management system
4. Active traffic management system
5. Expert traffic management system

These five groups will cover nearly all aspects of smart traffic management system.

**Short-term traffic management techniques** includes regulatory techniques, demand management techniques, bus priority techniques, etc. These techniques are used to enforce constraints on the commuters to restrict with guidelines laid by the authorities. Techniques such as demand management and bus priority are used to enforce public transport based on real-time demand of the users. This can be based on past data collected from the traffic plan across the city or state.

**Incremental infrastructure** includes work such as road improvements, flyovers, pedestrian, subways, parking lots, etc. These technologies focus on maintaining the infrastructure layout of the area in order to ensure for secure and smarter traffic management by means of developing the infrastructure as per the demand and need of the area. This can be decided by means of the data collected and analyzed on previous basis.

**Passive traffic management system** includes techniques such as fixed time traffic signals, signal hardware, passive passenger information systems, violation detectors, etc. These are passive components of traffic management which help in laying down the traffic rules which help in managing traffic in a better manner.

**Active traffic management system** includes components such as detector-based traffic signals, variable message signs for parking/incident/violation detection, traffic sensors, etc. This includes those components which help in collecting data on real-time basis for ensuring smarter traffic management over an area. Mostly, these components include sensor-based technology which collects data in real-time basis to process and respond accordingly.

**Expert traffic management system** includes components such as AI, machine learning, SCOOT, SCAT, MOVA, and associated software such as ASTRID, INGRID, etc. which are used for real-time traffic data analysis and incident detection. These components are used for real-time traffic detection as well as taking action according to the coding and expert opinion by the automated system includes using the above components.

## REFERENCES

Ali, M., Kurokawa, S., and Shafie, A.A. (2013). Autonomous road surveillance system: A proposed model for vehicle detection and traffic signal control. *Procedia Computer Science* 19. 10.1016/j.procs.2013.06.134.

Bhaskar, P. and Yong, S. (2014). *Image processing based vehicle detection and tracking method.* 1–5. 10.1109/ICCOINS.2014.6868357.

Biswas, S., Roy, P., Mukherjee, A., and Dey, N. (2015). *Intelligent Traffic Monitoring System.* 380. 10.1007/978-81-322-2523-2_52.

Breed, D.S., Duvall, W.E., and Johnson, W.C.. *Vehicular monitoring systems using image processing*. U.S. Patent 6,856,873. Feb. 15, 2005.

Pukale, D.D., Chauhan, P., Satish, A.S., Nawal, P., and Kumari, N. (2016). Density based traffic control system using video processing (hardware and software implementation). *Imperial Journal of Interdisciplinary Research* 2(6).

Danti, A., Kulkarni, J., and Hiremath, P. (2012). An image processing approach to detect lanes, pot holes and recognize road signs in Indian roads. *International Journal of Modeling and Optimization* 2, 658–662. 10.7763/IJMO.2012.V2.204.

Gaikwad, O.R., Vishwasrao, A., Pujari, K., and Talathi, T. (2014). Image processing based traffic light control. *International Journal of Science and Technology Research (IJSETR)* 3, 4.

Hamsaveni, V.G. (2013). Application of image processing in real time traffic light control by traffic jam detection, *International Journal of Advance Research in Computer Science and Management Studies* 1(7), 81–86.

Hongal, R., Badiger, A., Shapur, C., Betageri, S., and Kumar, N. (2016), *SysteMatic and automatic road traffic junction.* 10.1109/ICEEOT.2016.7755322.

Hooda, Waris, Yadav, P., Bhole, A., and Chaudhari, D. (2016). *An image processing approach to intelligent traffic management system.* 1–5. 10.1145/2905055.2905091.

Hu, W., Xiao, X., Xie, D., Tan, T., and Maybank, S. (2004). Traffic accident prediction using 3-D model-based vehicle tracking. *Vehicular Technology, IEEE Transactions on* 53, 677–694. 10.1109/TVT.2004.825772.

Jain, Vipin, Sharma, A., and Subramanian, L. (2012). *Road traffic congestion in the developing world.* 10.1145/2160601.2160616.

Kanungo, A., Sharma, A., and Singla, C.. (2014). *Smart traffic lights switching and traffic density calculation using video processing.* 1–6. 10.1109/RAECS.2014.6799542.

Krishna, B., Kumar, K., Reddy, A., Gopal, N., Chowdary, K., and Madhav, B. (2014). Priority based traffic light controller with IR sensor interface using FPGA. *International Journal of Applied Engineering Research* 9, 7791–7800.

Swathy M., Nirmala, P., and Geethu, P. (2017). Survey on vehicle detection and tracking techniques in video surveillance. *International Journal of Computer Applications* 160, 22–25. 10.5120/ijca2017913086.

Maheshwari, P., Suneja, D., Singh, P., and Mutneja, Y. (2015). *Smart traffic optimization using image processing.* 1–4. 10.1109/MITE.2015.7375276.

Nagaraj, U., Rathod, J., Patil, P.P., Thakur, S.V., Sharma, U., and Nagaraj, P. (2013). Traffic jam detection using image processing. *International Journal of Engineering Research and Applications* 3(2), 1087–1091.

Oh, S.-Y., Lee, J.-H., and Doo Hyun, C. (2000). A new reinforcement learning vehicle control architecture for vision-based road following. *Vehicular Technology, IEEE Transactions on* 49, 997–1005. 10.1109/25.845116.

Ozawa, S. (1999). Image processing for intelligent transport systems. *IEICE Transactions on Information and Systems* 82(3), 629–636.

Pena-Gonzalez, R. and Nuno, M. (2014). Computer vision based real-time vehicle tracking and classification system. *Midwest Symposium on Circuits and Systems* 679–682. 10.1109/MWSCAS.2014.6908506.

Rajagopal, B. (2020). Intelligent traffic analysis system for Indian road conditions. *International Journal of Information Technology* 10.1007/s41870-020-00447-3.

Rosenbaum, D., Leitloff, J., Kurz, F., Meynberg, O., and Reize, T. (2010). Real-time image processing for road traffic data extraction from aarial images. *Proceedings of ISPRS Technical Commission VII Symposium: 100years ISPRS*, July 5-7, 2010, Vienna, XXXVII, 469–474.

Rotake, D. and Karmore, S. (2012). *A design approach for traffic volume monitoring and intelligent signal control system.*

Slavin, H. et al. (2018). *Lane-level vehicle navigation for vehicle routing and traffic management*, U.S Patent 9964, 414, May 8, 2018.

Teknomo, K. (2016). *Microscopic pedestrian flow characteristics: development of an image processing data collection and simulation model.*

Xie, W. and Wu, Y. (2015). License plate automatic recognition system based on MATLAB-GUI. *The Open Automation and Control Systems Journal* 6, 497–502. 10.2174/1874444301406010497.

Zhang, X. and Forshaw, M.R.B. (1997). A parallel algorithm to extract information about the motion of road traffic using image analysis. *Transportation Research Part C: Emerging Technologies* 5(2), 141–152, 10.1016/S0968-090X(97)00007-7.

# 10 Application of Image Processing and Data Science in Advancing Education Innovation

## 10.1 INTRODUCTION

Education is a light that shows humanity the right path to surge. The reason for education is not just a sensible proficiency; however, it includes logic, proficiency, and a way of independence. When there is potential for change, there is promise for progress in any field. In the case that education neglects to induce self-control and understanding to achieve duty about students, this is not their fault. The invention can be constructed, and technological development benefits both students and teachers. We need to turn education into a game and instill enthusiasm to understand the learning process, and they need to stay away from it to run back from the education field. Education should be fun and running rather than burden, boredom, and exhaustion. It is an essential part of their development, and this makes them productive members of the society.

Education is working as a base engine for the development and progress of any society. It accepts information, interests, and incites values, but, on the other hand, is responsible for the creation of human capital that determines race, drive, and technical advancement and financial development. At the present time, data and information are isolated as an important and basic contribution to development and endurance. Rather than looking at education simply as a method for accomplishing social uplift-ment, the society is additionally an engine of progress in the data period anchored by the wheels of improvement in information and research additional leading to development.

The technological innovation that has changed industry and business overall depends on progress in arithmetic and science. In any case, technological education has institutionally been kept particular from its constituent subjects. The exact reason behind this is historical records. Technological education has become a professional division, which tends to the necessities of understudies planning to enter the work environment legitimately, while arithmetic and science are a piece of the academic sector, traditionally used for preparing learners for advanced education in the academic education.

Digital image processing for creative teaching and education gives an amazing medium to energize understudies about science and arithmetic, programming, and coding particularly kids from minority gatherings and others whose requirements have not been met by customary "coded" methods of teaching these subjects. Utilizing proficient quality software on microcomputers, learners explore a variety of logical informational indexes, including biomedical imaging, Earth remote detection and meteorology information, and planetary investigation images. Learners additionally find out about the numerous numerical ideas that underlie image exploration, for example, coordinate system, slope and intercept, pixels, and binary arithmetic's, alongside numerous others. By learning management system-developed educational curriculum materials in all areas of arithmetic and science for the upper elementary and auxiliary levels, this learning tool was permitted to be utilized over an assortment of evaluation levels and understudy premiums. Primer signs demonstrate image preparing to be a successful and fun approach to contemplate the use of science and arithmetic to "real world" applications, as represented by advanced symbolism data. The utilization of image processing that emerged with data science is likewise a viable technique with which to draw in understudies in inquiry and revelation learning.

Education strategies need to reflect the fact that the most recent innovations, for example, computers and the Internet, are progressively omnipresent in regular daily existences. This chapter considers about the potential and real effect of image-based computerized information and communication technology on education and learning. It shows that from 2003 till date education through technology has upgraded continuously, and learners over the world have more prominent access to computers at school, despite the fact that the force and assortment of utilization shift across countries. It inspects the factors which urge educators to utilize ICT rise with image and data science in the classroom and takes at educator's problem-solving skills to their peers outside education. Finally, it considers about whether as an investment in innovation or learners' utilization of computerized technology and the Internet are identified with improved educational outcomes.

## 10.2 ROLE OF IMAGE PROCESSING IN EDUCATION

A human brain is a fast visual learner. The typical field of perspective on the human eye contains around 100 million bits of data that we amend and reanalyze a few times each second. Conversely, the composed or spoken words that an individual can assimilate in a small amount of a second would rise to just a couple hundred bits of data. Formally, an image is worth around a million words.

Image processing for education application explores the probability that computerized image processing may assume a significant role in science and mathematics education. The theory was that, because we as a whole are visual learners, image manipulation may give a more appealing entrée into science and mathematics than conventional language-based strategies. This probability is particularly huge for understudies from differing social foundations who are not aware of the phonetic code utilized in conventional directions. Moreover, we presumed that learning through image processing would praise and upgrade other learning procedures being used.

Image processing consolidates high innovation such as data science, information hypothesis, and intellectual issues. As needs be, it is a characteristic innovation for educating and learning. Additionally, the areas wherein image processing is being applied in the realms of science and innovation (for instance, space investigation and human physiology) are energizing to understudies and lengthen all subjects of school educational plans.

Image processing was developed to encourage investigation and revelation in the examination network. Accordingly, it is an intrinsically "constructivist" medium when utilized by understudies. Its successful use in a homeroom requires the deserting of "behaviorist" methods of utilizing innovation for educating. Image processing for training offers access to the broad unique imaging information that still cannot seem to be completely investigated by established researchers. This makes way for true logical revelation as understudies control the educational information.

## 10.3 INTEGRATING IMAGE PROCESSING IN TEACHING AND LEARNING IN SCHOOLS

Computer systems and the Internet are progressively part of the environment in which youthful grown-ups develop and learn. Schools, instruction, and education frameworks, in this manner, need to receive the instructive rewards of image processing–based data and communication technology. Coordinated image processing strategies are normal at the school, area, or national level. They help schools and educators to stay up to date with the consistent progression of a technology oddity and to deal with the change and disturbance that new devices may present. There are a few reasons for creating training strategies that intend to implant image handling all the more profoundly into schools and educators' practices. Initially, as a device, information- and communication-based image processing technological devices and the Internet hold the guarantee of improving the (conventional) learning encounters of kids and youths and maybe of going about as an impetus for more extensive change, where such change is wanted. Second, the broad nearness of image processing–based information and communication technology in the society, utilized for regular work and leisure activities, and the expanding number of merchandise and ventures whose creation depends on image-based innovation, attract interest in computerized capabilities, which are, seemingly, best learned in the context. Third, while learning with and about advanced image processing and data science may well happen outside of school, initial education can assume a key role in guaranteeing that everybody can utilize these advances and gain from them, spanning the separation among rich and poor learners. Finally, school can use image-based information and communication technology arrangements that might be founded on the longing to decrease authoritative and different expenses. Where educator deficiencies exist or can be expected, image processing–based computerized technology approaches may serve as an alternative to the different activities taken to pull in and hold instructors in the calling. Image processing–based computerized technology can support and upgrade the learning sector. With access to computers and the Internet, understudies can look for data and gain information past what is accessible through educators and course readings. Image processing technology likewise gives understudies better approaches to rehearse their abilities, for example, keeping up an individual website page or online distribution, programming computers, talking and tuning in to local speakers when learning a subsequent language, as well as setting up a mixed media introduction, regardless of whether alone or as a feature of a remotely associated group. Image processing–based computerized gadgets unite generally isolated instruction media (books, composing, sound accounts, video chronicles, databases, games, and so forth), accordingly broadening or incorporating the scope of time and places where learning can occur (Livingstone, 2011). The far-reaching nearness of image preparing-based data and correspondence innovation in regular day-to-day existences additionally makes a requirement for explicit abilities. At any rate, education can bring issues to light in youngsters and their families about the dangers that they face on the web. As a dynamic and continuously upgrading technology that requires its users to refresh their insight and abilities every now and again, image processing–based technology likewise invites the training segment to re-examine the substance and strategies for educating and learning. Users of image processing-based technology (as we all are active today) regularly need to acclimate to another device or programming or to new elements of their current device and applications. Therefore, image processing-based technology users must learn, and unlearn, at a fast pace. Just the individuals, who can coordinate this procedure of learning themselves, tackling new issues as they emerge, will completely receive the rewards of an innovation rich world.

All the more explicitly, education can get ready youngsters for work in divisions where new jobs and roles are expected to be made in the coming years. Today, image processing-based computerized technology is utilized over all areas of the economy, and a considerable lot of the parts with significant levels of picture-based information science use, for example, money related administrations and well-being are additionally those that have expanded a lot of work in the course of recent decades. Different segments of the economy that were protected from global rivalry, for example, retail exchange or news dispersal, have been changed by the ascent of the comparison on the web administrations. Whatever their ideal occupations are, the point at which the present understudies leave school or college will in all likelihood scan and go after positions on the web. As an outcome, an elevated level of recognition with image processing–based and data science–based computerized technology among the workforce can be an upper hand for nations in the new help economy. This section explores how the education system and schools are coordinating image–based technology into understudies' learning experiences. The utilization of information and communication technology unmistakably relies upon the accessibility of the sufficient foundation, equipping schools with more and better image based computerized technology resources but at the same time is identified with the more extensive setting molded by the instructor and curricular arrangements.

## 10.4  ROLE OF IMAGE-BASED COMPUTERIZED LEARNING IN EDUCATION

In this innovative world, computers play a fundamental role in each field. They help technology procedures; they discover applications in medication; they are the core of the product business; and they assume an essential job in the education sector. The employments of computers in education are complex. In this section, we are discussing about the significant features of the role of an image-based modernized learning framework in the education sector. At the point when we ask educators about for what reason we ought to have computerized technology in education, we continually hear that computer technology can help in spreading of education. The possibility that the computer ought to consistently make simple originates from an overview of the way that the computer entered our lives to help. The computer made money machines potential; computers are inside robotized gadgets, for example, microwaves, video recorders, vehicles, and so forth. These are models in which the life of the computer made something a lot simpler or made something accessible that was already inconceivable. Accordingly, something very similar ought to happen to training. The computerized technology ought to encourage training, making it a lot simpler for the understudy to learn, for the educator to instruct, and to arrange the managerial part of education.

The computerized innovation technology deeply affects education. Computer education structures a piece of the school and college educational program, as today is significant for each person, to have the fundamental information on computers. The benefits of computerized technology in education incorporate a productive stockpiling and execution of data, brisk data preparing, and significantly the sparing of paper. Find out about the significance of computerized education. Computerized education is playing a key role in present-day frameworks of the education sector. Understudies think that it is simpler to allude to the Internet than scanning for data in fat reference books. The way toward taking in has gone past gaining from recommended course books. Today, aspirers can fulfill their hunger for information by methods for the Internet. It is simpler to store data on computer than keeping up transcribed notes. To find out about the subject, read about course readings versus computerized educating.

Computerized technology-based online education has changed the education industry. Computerized technology has made the fantasy of separation learning a reality. Instructions are not any more constrained to study halls. They have reached far and wide, gratitude to computer technology. Genuinely inaccessible areas have approached each other just because of computer organizing. Computerized technology encourages proficient capacity and viable introduction of data. Introduction programming such as PowerPoint and activity programming like Flash and others can be of extraordinary assistance to the educators while conveying data. Computerized technology can end up being a splendid guide in educating. Computerized technology encourages various media portrayals of data, in this manner making way for learning intuitive and intriguing. Computerized technology helped showing adds a pleasant component to education.

The Internet can assume a significant role in education. As it is a colossal database, it can be harnessed for the recovery of data on a wide assortment of subjects. The Internet can be utilized to allude to data on different subjects to be educated to the understudies. In addition, computerized technology helps an electronic organization for the capacity of data, accordingly sparing paper. Schoolwork and test assignments were submitted as delicate duplicates spare paper. Electronically erasable memory gadgets can be utilized over and over. They offer vigorous stockpiling of information and dependable information recovery. The computerized technology along these lines facilitates the way toward learning. An existence without computerized technology would appear to be practically unbelievable for some.

The significance of computers is apparent today, and having the ideal skill of computers can just push one's profession the correct way. Today, computerized technology is a piece of pretty much every industry. They are not any more restricted to the product business. They are broadly utilized in system administration, data get to, information stockpiling, and the preparation of data.

They assume that purchasing a computer for their kid is sufficient to cause the person in question to transfer and participate in some educative projects, surf useful locales, and assets. However, they are harshly baffled when their kids invest the majority of the energy reveling into some idiotic shooter, tearing their adversaries to wicked pieces or visit similar clatter brained peers in some neighboring region talking about football or MTV. It was very obvious from the earliest starting point that a youngster or even an adolescent needs a direction to enter the Internet world, someone who might encourage them to act at various gatherings and online conversations the same number of them just as more seasoned people share a similar figment of absence of limitation which is by all accounts the Internet primary element. Yet, at some point or another, every one of them arrives at a type of resolution that computer aptitudes are basic for youngsters not to fall behind the time and be serious at the present training and workforce showcase. Computerized technology in education can be helpful in a few different ways. They can build the efficiency of understudies by making undertakings, for example, making papers and research simpler. They can make it simpler for educators to gather papers, grade them, and send them back to understudies. Computerized technology can likewise decrease the measure of paper fundamental for instruction since materials can be sent and seen carefully. One of the essential jobs of computerized technology in instruction is to encourage correspondence between understudies, educators, managers, and guardians. Email can permit educators to contact understudies rapidly without booking face-to-face meeting time. Assignments can likewise be conveyed by means of email, and completed work can be submitted in a computerized structure as an email connection instead of turning in a paper duplicate. Understudies might be required to browse their email routinely for class updates and assignments.

## 10.5 IMPORTANT ROLES OF IMAGE PROCESSING IN EDUCATION

Image processing-based computerized technology is the science and innovation of machines that see, where found for this situation implies that the machine can extricate data from a picture that is important to understand some assignment. As a logical order, image processing computerized technology is worried about the hypothesis behind artificial frameworks that extricate data from images. The image data can take numerous structures, for example, video successions see from various cameras or multi-dimensional information from a student and teachers also (Figure 10.1).

- Controlling Process: The control procedure includes cautiously gathering the data about a student and instructor individual or gathering of individuals so as to settle on important choices about each, for example, ordering databases of images and image sequencing.
- Detecting event: Event recognition is the way toward distinguishing that an occasion was produced in the use of image processing. Regularly, connectors

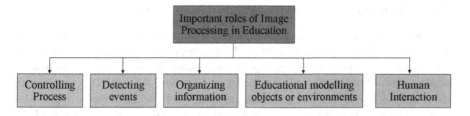

**FIGURE 10.1**    Important roles of image processing with data science in education.

use database triggers to distinguish an occasion. For example, visual surveillance or individuals checking.

- Organizing information: Organizing data is a major piece of perusing and composing achievement. So as to plainly understand what a student is perusing, you should have the option to assemble and compose the data being introduced. For example, ordering of databases of image and image groupings.
- Educational displaying items or situations: A model of educating is a portrayal of a learning domain, including our conduct as instructors when that model is utilized. Eggen (1979) characterized that models are prescriptive showing systems that help to acknowledge explicit instructional objectives, for example, modern review, clinical picture investigation, or land demonstrating.
- Human Interaction: Human interaction manages discussions and conversations among students and teachers. A facilitator conveying a talk to a gathering of understudies in a study hall where feelings, contact, and charge are present. We regularly accept that innovation is taking a front seat in instruction, for example, as the contribution to a device for computers human collaboration.

## 10.6 ASSESSING CREATIVITY AND MOTIVATION IN IMAGE-BASED LEARNING SYSTEMS

As clarified before, we accept that the state motivates learners through assessing issues. It is essential to build up a fruitful computerized learning the hang of learning condition, yet to do this isn't simple. Consequently, most research in the field of image-based modernized learning frameworks can be effectively handled by computerized learning frameworks. Up to now, the imaginative learning and inspiration in learning have been seen advanced as an issue of plan. As it were, legitimate instructional plan and fitting learning exercises will include all learners. While structuring a propelling learning condition is significant, getting understudies inspired for the whole learning time frame is probably the greatest test. Be that as it may, while in customary up close and personal learning and coordinated electronic learning, instructors have direct contact with learners, in order to break down the general conduct of students and along these lines have the option to find their inspirational conditions. Be that as it may, with regard to location of offbeat learning inspiration (for example, WBEL) is an all the more education process. Data about understudy persuasive conditions will empower content alteration and improve the inspiration of learners.

### 10.6.1 Building Character through Interactive Media

It is the capacity to think basically, imaginatively, inventively, interest, science, and innovation situated and intelligent will be astounding character improvement. Intelligent media intended to assemble basic reasoning abilities and innovative understudies. Furthermore, intuitive media ought to have the option to comply with the principles' governors who asked the guidelines and intelligent media ought to be custom fitted to the necessities of clients and can likewise be utilized as one of the holders to make a decent social atmosphere so understudies can take care of issues both independently and in gatherings so that can be assembled collaboration through the media.

### 10.6.2 Image Processing

Image processing is a type of advanced sign handling where the information utilized is an image, can be a photograph or video (Figure 10.2). The yield of image processing is a lot of highlights removed from the picture to additionally improve its quality. Most image processing strategies include taking care of images as two-dimensional signals and applying standard sign handling methods to it. The reason for image processing is expected to furnish a huge yield as per the particular needs.

#### 10.6.2.1 Image Acquisition

Image acquisition is the creation of a digitally encoded representation of the visual characteristics of an object, such as a physical scene of a learner or educator.

#### 10.6.2.2 Image Enhancement

Image enhancement is the process of adjusting digital images so that the results are more suitable for display or further image analysis. For example, you can remove noise, sharpen, or brighten an image, making it easier to identify key features.

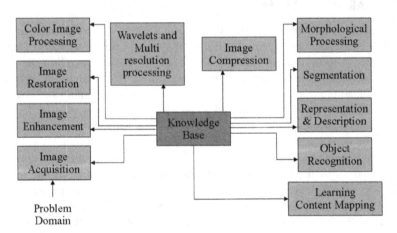

**FIGURE 10.2**  Fundamental steps of the image processing–based computerized education system.

### 10.6.2.3 Image Restoration

Image restoration is the process of recovering an image from a degraded version—usually a blurred and noisy image.

### 10.6.2.4 Color Image Processing

Computer vision technology based on color image processing and analysis is a useful tool for the evaluation of learner and educator behavior and activities.

### 10.6.2.5 Wavelets and Multiresolution Processing

Wavelet transforms are based on small waves, called wavelets, of limited duration. Wavelet transform provides time-frequency information. Wavelets lead to a multi-resolution analysis of signals. Multiresolution analysis: representation of a signal (e.g., an image) in more than one resolution/scale.

### 10.6.2.6 Image Compression

Image Compression is a technique used for representing the image using the image data, which are repeated in the image several times (data redundancy).

### 10.6.2.7 Morphological Processing

Morphology is a broad set of image processing operations that process images based on shapes. Morphological operations apply a structuring element to an input image, creating an output image of the same size.

### 10.6.2.8 Segmentation

Image segmentation is a process in which regions or features sharing similar characteristics are identified and grouped together.

### 10.6.2.9 Representation and Description

Representation is based on the boundary or textural features, while description is based on length, orientation, the number of concavities in the boundary, and statistical measures of region.

### 10.6.2.10 Object Recognition

Object recognition is a computer vision technique for identifying objects in images or videos. Object recognition is a key output of deep learning and machine learning algorithms.

### 10.6.2.11 Learning Content Mapping

Computerized education, for example, online learning content refers to the content of a learning program. According to Barker, the design of online image-based learning should be of a similar class format in terms of course description, objectives, learning content, objectives, scope, and evaluation. Multimedia without content is powerless. It emphasized that a message should be adjusted to the delivery method. Some media are better suited for conveying specific information. Furthermore, it suggested that the interaction and communication of instructor-to-student and vice versa should be carefully considered in designing and developing learning content. In the Indonesian context, Soekartawi found that problems in designing, developing, and managing an online learning program still exist. Empirical studies by Hussein et al. show it. The design and layout of the learning management system are very influential on students' ability. Thus the well-designed e-learning content can make easier to learn online and increase the motivation in order to use learning tool.

## 10.7 LEARNERS AND EDUCATORS ON THE IMAGE-BASED COMPUTERIZED ENVIRONMENT

### 10.7.1 TEACHING PRACTICES

The educating or teaching practices conveyed by instructors can assume a critical job in how much understudies learn. Innovation alone won't upgrade learning; however, utilizing it as a major aspect of good encouraging practice can open new ways to students and educators. It is striking that in spite of the fact that innovation is common in our day by day lives; most of the educators in numerous nations don't every now and again use picture-based modernized innovation in their teaching practices. In certain schools, this might be because of the absence of arrangement; however, instructors' expert turn of events and their convictions about work are keys to opening innovation's potential for educating and learning.

### 10.7.2 RAISING LEARNERS ATTAINMENT

There is a significant collection of research that has analyzed the effect of computerized devices and assets on kids' accomplishments in the scope of areas. Higgins et al. (2012) gave an outline of research discoveries from concentrates with exploratory and semi-test structures, which have been consolidated in meta-examinations to survey the effect of advanced learning in schools. Their inquiry recognized 48 examinations that integrated exact research on the effect of computerized devices and assets on the achievement of young students (5–18-year-olds). They discovered a reliable yet little positive relationship between advanced learning and instructive results. For instance, Harrison et al. (2004) recognized measurably critical discoveries, emphatically partner more significant levels of data and correspondence innovation use with school accomplishment at each Key Stage in England, and in English, mathematics, science, present-day unknown dialects, and plan innovation. Somekh et al. (2007) recognized a connection between elevated levels of picture-based data and correspondence innovation use and improved school execution. They found that the pace of progress in tests in English toward the finish of essential instruction was quicker in data and correspondence innovation Test Bed training experts in England than in identical comparator territories. By and large, schools with higher than normal degrees of data and correspondence innovation arrangement additionally have students who perform somewhat higher than normal, the facts may confirm that high performing schools are bound to be better prepared or increasingly arranged to put resources into innovation or progressively persuaded to realize improvement.

Higgins et al. reported that when all is said in done examinations of the effect of computerized innovation on learning, the run of the mill by and large impact size is somewhere in the range of 0.3 and 0.4—only marginally underneath the general norm for looked into mediations in training (Sipe and Curlette, 1997; Hattie, 2008) and no more noteworthy than other inquired about changes to educating to raise accomplishments, for example, peer mentoring or progressively engaged criticism to students. The scope of impact sizes is additionally exceptionally wide (−0.03 to 1.05), which recommends that it is basic to consider the contrasts among advances and how they are utilized.

Increasingly, subjective investigations have distinguished how enhancements in accomplishment are accomplished. From a wide investigation of essential and auxiliary schools in England that were early adopters in utilizing computerized learning and instructing, Jewitt et al. (2011) reasoned that:

- Using digital resources provided learners with more time for active learning in the classroom;
- Digital tools and resources provided more opportunity for active learning outside the classroom, as well as providing self-directed spaces, such as blogs and forums, and access to games with a learning benefit;
- Digital resources provided learners with opportunities to choose the learning resources;
- The resources provided safer spaces for formative assessment and feedback.

### 10.7.3 Inequalities Reduction among Learners

The learners groups for whom the writing furnishes proof from concentrates with relative groups or potentially testing learners when advanced learning can be extensively separated between those where the computerized learning gives help to close gaps in achievement, and the individuals who have extra help needs where computerized learning gives help to defeat learning issues.

Clas et al. (2009) found that advanced apparatus could assist optional with tutoring learners who had moderately lower education, a significant number of whom were learning the language of guidance. Trial of information and comprehension (in social examinations) when the utilization of an online thesaurus and online dictionary demonstrated that both improved their subject information and their comprehension and that the online word reference had a greater effect, most likely on the grounds that it was simpler to utilize.

Reed et al. (2013) found that advanced assets could help students beyond 8 (i.e., 6–8 years old) years old behind their age bunch in their perusing age to get up to speed. The phonics program which was followed in class helped most students to improve both their perusing and spelling in standard tests. Murphy and Graham (2012) found from a more extensive audit of studies that word handling commonly positively affected the composing abilities of more fragile authors. This was identified with assisting with amendment and spelling before the appraisal.

Zheng et al. (2014) found that giving a PC to get to advanced assets, so as to improve hindered lower secondary learners science learning, was successful in lessening the hole in information and comprehension, just as expanding their enthusiasm for science subjects. They ascribed this to the more individualized discovery that was conceivable. Jewitt and Parashar (2011) found that giving a PC and web association with low-salary families in two nearby power regions in England expanded the finish/nature of schoolwork, the time spent on it, and the degree of free learning.

## 10.8 DISCUSSION

The use of image processing and data science-based digital technologies in schools has on learning and teaching, followed by a consideration of the factors which are essential for implementing successful use of digital technologies for learning and teaching in schools. These advanced digital technologies can support educational attainment in general and improvements in numeracy/mathematics and science learning. These digital technologies can support educational attainment in literacy and closing the gap in attainment between groups of learners.

## REFERENCES

Mouza et al. (2008). Implementation and outcomes of a laptop initiative in career and technical high school education. *Journal of Educational Computing Research.*
Liao Y.-K.C., Chang, H-W., Chen, Y.-W., 2008. Effects of computer applications on elementary school students' achievement: A meta-analysis of students in Taiwan. *Computers in the Schools (Sic).*
Johannesen, M. (2013, March). The role of virtual learning environments in a primary school context: An analysis of inscription of assessment practices. *British Journal of Educational Technology.*
Huang, Y.-M., Huang, S.-H., Wu, T.-T. (2014). Embedding diagnostic mechanisms in a digital game for learning mathematics. *Educational Technology Research and Development,* April.
Formby, S. (2014). *Parents' perspectives: Children's use of technology in the Early Years.* London: National Literacy Trust.
Harris, S. (2009). Lessons from e-learning: Transforming teaching. *Proceedings of the International Conference on e-Learning.*
Smith, R.L., Flamez, B., Vela, J.C., Schomaker, S.A., Fernandez, M.A., and Armstrong, S.N. (2015). An exploratory investigation of levels of learning and learning efficiency between online and face-to-face instruction. *Counseling Outcome Research and Evaluation* 6, 47–57.
Tseng, F.-C. and Kuo, F.-Y. (2014). A study of social participation and knowledge sharing in the teachers' online professional community of practice. *Computers & Education* 72, 37–47.
Foray, D. and Raffo, J. (forthcoming), An Analysis of Business-driven innovation through educational patents. In Vincent-Lancrin, S. (Ed.), *Business-Driven Innovation in the Education Sector.* OECD Publishing, Paris.
European Schoolnet (2013). *Survey of schools: ICT in education: Benchmarking access, use and attitudes to technology in Europe's schools,* European Commission, Brussels.
Kärkkäinen, K. and Vincent-Lancrin, S. (2013). *Sparking innovation in STEM education with technology and collaboration: A case study of the HP Catalyst Initiative,* OECD Education Working Papers, No. 91, OECD Publishing, Paris, http://dx.doi.org/10.1787/5k480sj9k442-en.

# 11 Application of Image Processing and Data Science in Advancing Agricultural Design

## 11.1 INTRODUCTION

Image processing has been evidenced to be a powerful instrument for investigation in different fields and applications. In agriculture, different variables such as covering, yield, and the product quality or nature are the parameters that affect horticulture and are the significant measures from the farmer's perspective. Commonly, master counsel may not be moderate; predominately, the accessibility of specialists and their administrations may expend time. Image processing alongside the accessibility of communication systems and data science can change the circumstance of getting the master exhortation well inside time and at a reasonable expense because image preparation is a powerful instrument for the examination of parameters.

In development toward a sustainable agribusiness framework, obviously significant commitments can be made by utilizing rising innovations. Accuracy agriculture was new and creating innovation which prompts join the propelled strategies to upgrade farm yield and furthermore enhance the homestead contributions to a productive and earth reasonable way. With these procedures/devices, it is currently conceivable to decrease blunders and expenses to accomplish biological and monetarily supportable farming. Farmer inputs are significant parameters to be controlled, and if not regulated, then these will bring about antagonistic impacts such as causing a decrease in yield, breaking down plant wellbeing, and so on. Water pressure or irrigation system, fertilizers, pesticides, and the nature of yield were the central point of concern in agribusiness. More often, skill was required to break down the issues, which might be a tedious and costlier issue in creating nations. Image processing was one of the techniques which can be applied to gauge the parameters identified with agronomy with exactness and economy. Use of image processing in farming can be extensively characterized into two classes: the first relies on the imaging methods and the second depends on applications. This study basically centers on the use of image processing in different spaces of agribusiness.

Image processing uses sources of radiation such as gamma ray imaging, X-ray imaging, imaging in the ultraviolet (UV) band, and imaging in UV, infrared (IR), microwave, and radio bands for processing the image. Remote sensing is widely used in agriculture. Remote sensing is used for identifying the features of the earth surface. It can also be used for estimation of geo-biophysical properties of earth by making use of electromagnetic radiations. Different remote sensing sensors that are used for these applications are LANDSAT, TM, SPOI, MODIS, ASTER, etc.

With advancement in technology, the applications of image processing have also increased, and agriculture is one of the fields where it has been used. In agriculture, various factors such as canopy, quality, and yield of product are the parameters which impact agriculture. Image processing in integration with a communication network proved to be a milestone for farmers in the field of agriculture. This chapter deals with the application of image processing in the field of agriculture. The knowledge provided by image processing techniques can be useful for decision making with regard to measurement of vegetation, irrigation, sorting of fruits, etc.

Image processing in agriculture is used for precision in agriculture which is a fast process compared to the manual process and can be used to increase the productivity of the farm. The precision in agriculture leads researchers to focus on advanced techniques in order to enrich the inputs of the farm in a profitable and environmentally sustainable manner. These advanced techniques can be used to reduce errors in farming and also reduce the cost of achieving ecological and economical sustainable agriculture. In order to achieve these goals, the input parameters from the farms are controlled in a specified manner.

Some of the image processing techniques such as thermal imaging, fluorescence imaging, hyperspectral imaging, and photometric (RBG) feature-based imaging can be used in agriculture in areas such as crop management, detection of nutrient deficiencies, detection of weeds, and grading of fruits.

Computer vision, machine vision, and image processing are different techniques which can be used for the development of automated systems in order to serve different purposes in the field of agriculture. Major image processing modules can be divided into major four parts as follows:

1. Image acquisition
2. Image enhancement
3. Image segmentation
4. Object recognition and image representation and description

All these techniques have been covered in previous chapters in detail, but an overview of these techniques in the field of agriculture is given below.

**Image acquisition:** This is the initial phase which captures the object of interest by different image acquiring devices such as cameras, sensors, hyperspectral imaging, IR imaging, etc. and stores this image in a system for analysis and interpretation.

**Image enhancement:** This technique is used for removing constraints such as noises, dullness, and brightness which can disturb the quality of the image and thus improve the quality of the image. This is carried out by using various filtering techniques based on various parameters. It also uses various smoothing and sharping techniques for enhancing the quality of the image.

**Image segmentation:** This technique is used to divide images into segments and extract the segment of interest from the background. This segregation is performed by identifying the rapid change in pixel value or by region- or boundary-based methods.

**Object recognition and image representation and description:** This technique can be performed by using different approaches. Object recognition extracted the region of interest from previous modules and converted the same into useful information that can be interpreted and used for decision making. Recently, machine-learning approaches are widely being used for this method. Image processing with a decision support system proves to be a major change and way of approach toward development in agriculture. The type of approach used depends on the type of application where we need to recognize the object and represent or describe the image.

## 11.2 IMAGE PROCESSING TECHNIQUES IN AGRICULTURE

Image processing in agriculture is performed by capturing images by means of remote sensing, using aircraft and drones, or data of satellites. These data can be processed and analyzed to process useful results as per the requirements and need of the hour. Day-by-day invention of newer technologies in the field of image processing helps to improve the yield of agriculture by different means and medians. Various image-processing techniques for agriculture, as shown in Figure 11.1, are discussed below.

### 11.2.1 THERMAL IMAGING

Thermal imaging is a strategy to change over the imperceptible radiation example of an item into obvious pictures, and this strategy includes extraction and examination. Thermal imaging is a remote detection method that was created by the military and now has been received by the business organizations to advertise for business use. IR thermal imaging was first created for military purposes; however, later there was an increase in its application in different fields, for example, aviation, horticulture, structural building, medication, and veterinary. IR thermal imaging innovation can be applied in all fields where temperature contrasts could be utilized to aid the assessment, finding, or investigation of a procedure or item. Potential utilization of thermal imaging in farming and food industries incorporates foreseeing water worry in crops, arranging water system planning, malady and pathogen recognition in plants, anticipating organic product yield, assessing the development of natural products, wound location in leafy foods, the discovery of outside bodies in food materials, and temperature dissemination during cooking. With respect to an on-going premise, this strategy gathers thermal imaging information on the speed of light from different

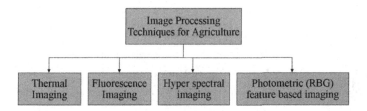

**FIGURE 11.1**   Some of the image-processing techniques for agriculture.

platforms such as land-, water-, or air-based vehicles. This method can be utilized in day time or evening time.

We talk about the history of thermal imaging which comes around 1950s for the military purpose. At that time, these cameras are very heavy, expensive, bulky, and large in size and require liquid nitrogen for their cooling purpose. With advancement of time, the cameras are modified with new detector elements, array fabrication techniques, coolers, optics, electronics, software, and packaging for improving the performance of these cameras.

Thermal imaging is a process of converting IR radiation (heat radiation) into visible images in order to depict the spatial distribution of temperature differences in a scene which can be viewed using a thermal camera. In thermal imaging, thermal cameras, which are equipped with IR detectors in the focal plane array of pixel, are used. Based on the material comprising the array and camera's intended use, the detector array can be kept cooled or uncooled.

In this process, the lens system focuses scene radiation onto a detector array, and appropriate processing electronics display the imagery. IR radiation was attenuated by the atmosphere where the degree of attenuation depends on local atmospheric conditions at the time of collection of imagery. The response of the detector is matched with two atmospheric windows as a midwave IR band (MWIR) or long wavelength IR band (LWIR). Most of the survey work in thermal imaging is related to the temperature differences between objects in the scene.

### Components of Thermal Imaging

A thermal imaging camera consists of five components: an optical system, detector, amplifier, image processing, and display (Figure 11.2).

**An optical system:** The optical system in the thermal imaging system is used for collecting the maximum amount of radiated energy from a scene containing the target and project image of the scene onto the system detector array. The IR optical system is the most important subsystem of a thermal camera, because it plays a key role in defining some of the overall system parameters such as system resolution and system field of view. IR optical systems offer long ranges and better see-through capability; for this reason, they are a preferred choice over image intensifier tubes for civil services and military forces.

**Detectors:** This component is used to capture the IR radiation produced by all objects above complete zero temperature. The temperature differences of the captured section are denoted as a hectogram.

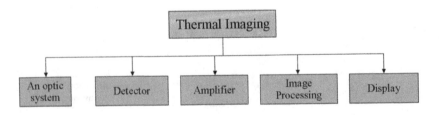

**FIGURE 11.2**  Components of thermal imaging.

**Amplifier:** The amplifier that is used to amplify the output signal from a detector will itself introduce noise. How significant this noise is will depend on the level of the signal from the detector and on how well the output of one is electrically matched to the input of the other.

**Image sensor:** One of the most widely utilized image-based sensor frameworks is the night-vision device (NVD)) or image intensifier. An image intensifier has restrictions because of the normal marvels or qualities of light proliferation through the climate. The NVD intensifies light photons under low-light conditions through a progression of electron–photon change.

1. **Thermal imager:** The thermal imager is correlative to the picture intensifier. In contrast to the image intensifier, the history of the improvement of the thermal imager is not as energizing, halfway because of the fact that the thermal imaging had delicate military applications and was costly when it originally began. The advancement of the thermal imager is focused for the most part on the methods of identifying thermal radiation from nature utilizing diverse rising materials and locator plans. The primary locator method utilized in the improvement of the thermal imagers examines a solitary component finder to deliver line pictures. The following significant advancement was the smaller scale bolometer with its patent granted in 1994. Ensuing advancements concentrated predominantly on consolidating the gadget into hardware frameworks, for example, the drivers' watcher for heavily clad vehicles, weapons sights, and hand compactness. Some different upgrades concentrated on the improvement of enormous scope central plane array.

2. **Thermography:** Thermography or thermal imaging is a type of thermal imaging that recognizes electromagnetic radiation in the thermal IR area, normally between the wavelengths of 3 and 15 μm. Other recognizable terms to characterize the locales might be near IR (NIR—0.7 to 1 μm), short-wave IR (SWIR—1 to 3 μm), mid-wave IR (MWIR—3 to 5 μm), and long-wave IR (LWIR—8 to 12 μm). These terms are characterized to be dependent on the environmental transmittance, which influences the capacity for the radiation to spread through the air and be noticeable. Other IR locales are significantly constricted or consumed by the climate with the end goal that the investigation on these districts does not yield any advantages. As thermal imaging depends on thermal radiation discharging from focuses out of sight, it is subsequently essential to see how this thermal radiation is created and how it might be received by locators.

**Display:** This part cooperates to render IR radiation, for example the radiations emitted by thermal items or flares, into a noticeable light portrayal continuously. The camera shows IR yield differentials, so two articles with a similar temperature will have all the earmarks of being the equivalent "shading."

## 11.2.2 FLUORESCENCE IMAGING

Fluorescence imaging is an imaging procedure that is utilized or images natural procedures in a living life form. Fluorescence itself is a type of glow that comes from a substance transmitting light of a specific frequency subsequent to retaining electro-magnetic radiation. Particles that reproduce endless supply of light are called fluoro-phores. It depends on the idea that any atom retains light and the vitality of the particle rises to a higher energized state. At the point when this atom comes back to the ground state, it discharges vitality by discharging glaring light which can be dis-tinguished and estimated (Figure 11.3).

The main components involved in fluorescence imaging are as follows:

- **Excitation source:** This is a device that produces broad wavelength sources such as UV light or narrow wavelength sources such as lasers.
- **Detection, amplification, and visualization:** It makes use of a photomulti-plier (PMT) or charge-coupled device (CCD) for detecting and quantifying emitted protons.
- **Light display optics:** It is the mechanism where light illuminates the sample which is done through direct illumination of the sample.
- **Filtration of emitted light:** It makes use of an optical filter which removes reflected and scattered light from fluorescence. The emission filter can be of three types, namely, long-pass filter, short-pass filter, and band-pass filter.
- **Light assortment optics:** It consists of lens, mirrors, and filters where the light is collected by itself.

For fluorescence, light energy is a fundamental part. In this, light sources fall into two general classifications—wide-region, broad frequency sources, for example, UV and xenon bend lights, and line sources with discrete frequencies, for example, lasers. Expansive frequency excitation sources are utilized in fluorescence spectrom-eters and camera imaging frameworks. Despite the fact that the otherworldly yield of light is expansive, it very well may be tuned to a limited band of excitation light with the utilization of gratings or channels. Conversely, lasers convey a limited light emis-sion that is transcendently monochromatic.

For identification and evaluation of the produced light, the system utilizes either a PMT or a CCD device. In both cases, photon energy from discharged bright light is changed over into electrical energy, in this way delivering a quantifiable sign that is relative to the number of photons recognized.

After the discharged light is recognized and intensified, the simple sign from a PMT or CCD indicator is changed over to a digital signal. The procedure of

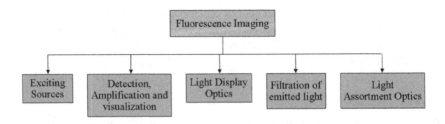

**FIGURE 11.3**  Components of fluorescence imaging.

digitization transforms a deliberate constant simple sign into discrete numbers by presenting force levels. The quantity of force levels depends on the advanced upset of the instrument, which is normally given as various bits, or examples of 2. 8-piece, 12-piece, and 16-piece computerized records compared to the number of power levels distributed inside that picture document (256, 4096, and 65 536, individually). Advanced goals characterize the capacity to determine two signs with comparable powers.

### 11.2.3 HYPERSPECTRAL IMAGING

Hyperspectral imaging is a spectral imaging technique which employs each pixel of image for acquiring set of images with certain spectral bands. This technique combines the advantages of optical spectroscopy as an analytical tool with two-dimensional (2-D) object visualization obtained by optical imaging. Thus, the sensor samples the hyperspectral cube in four different ways as spatial scanning, snapshot imaging, spectral scanning, and spatio-spectral scanning.

In hyperspectral imaging, each hyperspectral sensor collects information as set of images where each image representing a narrow wavelength range of electromagnetic spectrum is termed as the spectral band. These different images are combined to form a three-dimensional $(x, y, \lambda)$ data cube which is used for processing and analysis purposes. In this three-dimensional data, cube $x$ and $y$ represent two spatial dimensions of the scene, whereas $\lambda$ represents the spectral dimension which comprises wavelength. These three-dimensional datasets $(x, y, \lambda)$ of data cube can be obtained through four basic techniques, namely, spatial scanning, spectral scanning, non-scanning, and spatio-spectral scanning. The type of technique to be chosen depends upon the type of specific application.

**Spatial scanning:** In this scanning, the 2-D sensors represent the output in a form of slit spectrum with $(x, \lambda)$ by means of projecting a strip of scene onto a slit and then using prism or grating for dispersing the slit image.

**Spectral scanning:** In this type of sensing, the 2-D sensors represent monochromatic$(x, y)$, which is a single-colored spatial map of the scene. The hyperspectral imaging device used for this scanning is based on tuned or fixed optical band-pass filters. The scenes are scanned spectrally by means of exchanging one filter after another while keeping the platform stationary.

**Non-scanning:** In this scanning, the 2-D sensor provides three-dimensional $(x, y, \lambda)$ data as spatial $(x, y)$ and spectral $(\lambda)$ combinedly. In this scanning, the HIS device yields a full datacube at once without scanning. In this approach, the three-dimensional structure is reconstructed by perspective projection of the datacube through a single snapshot. This scanning provides a higher light throughput and a shorter acquisition time.

**Spatio-spectral scanning:** In this scanning, the 2-D sensor represents the output as the wavelength coded (rainbow colored $(\lambda = \lambda\,(y))$, spatial $(x, y)$ map of the scene. Thus, this scanning combines the advantages of spatial and spectral scanning, thereby removing certain disadvantages of these techniques.

## 11.2.4 PHOTOMETRIC (RGB) FEATURE-BASED IMAGING

The photometric component or RGB-based imaging merits referencing due to its reliance on the shading variety of various organic examples. In recent years, significant advancement in the uses of RGB-based imaging has been seen in the different fields of horticulture and plant science. It has supplanted the human vision framework to survey the nature of various food articles, acknowledgment of weeds and ailments in huge agrarian fields, and assurance of the supplement status of plants. In particular, RGB-based picture examination has been applied in horticulture for weed recognizable proof (Hemming and Rath, 2000), weed, and yield mapping (Tillet et al., 2001), weed and harvest segregation (Aitkenhead et al., 2003), measurement of turf grass shading (Karcher and Rechardson, 2003), quantitative investigation of a particular factor physiological procedure over a leaf surface (Aldea et al., 2006), weed acknowledgment (Ahmad et al., 2006), seed shading test for distinguishing proof of business seed qualities (Dana and Ivo, 2008), and non-obtrusive estimation of nitrogen (Mercado-Luna, 2010). In plant tissue culture, RGB-based picture investigation has been carried out for distinguishing proof and estimation of shoot length (Honda et al., 1997), optional metabolite assurance in furry root societies (Berzin et al., 1999), bunching of recovered plants into gatherings (Mahendra et al., 2004; Prasad and Dutta Gupta, 2008), and estimation of chlorophyll content in miniaturized scale spread plants (Yadav et al., 2010; Dutta Gupta et al., 2013). The fundamental concepts of the RGB color model and its application for the determination of nitrogen status in plants have been detailed in Chapter 4 of this book. In this survey, we portray quickly the utilizations of RGB imaging in different fields of farming and delineate its potential in plant tissue culture frameworks.

## 11.3 APPLICATION OF DIGITAL IMAGE PROCESSING WITH DATA SCIENCE IN AGRICULTURE

Digital image processing (DIP) is one of the potential technologies used in precision agriculture to gather information such as seed emergence, plant health, and phenology from the digital images. The number of applications using DIP and data science techniques in the agricultural sector is increasing rapidly. These applications include land/aerial remote sensing of crops, detection and recognition of pathological stress conditions, and shape and color characterization of fruits, among many other topics. In fact, quantification of the visual properties of horticultural products and plants can play an important role in improving and automating agricultural management tasks. Some of the major applications of DIP in the sector of agriculture as shown in Figure 11.4 are discussed below.

### 11.3.1 MANAGEMENT OF CROP

Management of crop is needed to improve the growth, development, and yield of crops. Crop management includes activities such as management of pest, irrigation, and detection of weeds. There are many techniques involved for management of crop which will be discussed in this section.

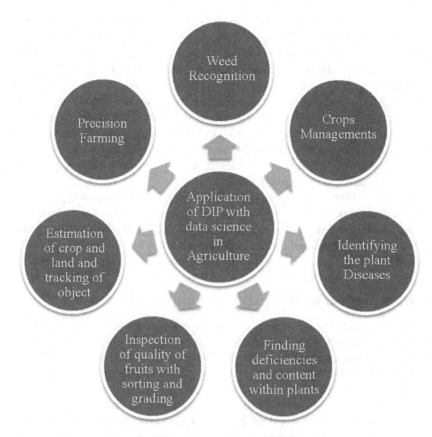

**FIGURE 11.4** Different applications of DIP in agriculture.

There are many researchers who have proposed image processing for management of crops. Piyush et al. (2012) used the image-processing technique and proposed an algorithm for spotting the disease segmentation in a leaf of a plant. In this paper, they used median filters for smoothing of images. In this approach, the authors used the Otsu method to calculate the final threshold on color components for detecting the spot of disease within a plant. The proposed algorithm was free from background noise, the type of plant and disease spot color was developed, and experiments were carried out on different—"Monocot" and—"Dicot" family plant leaves with both noise free (white) and noisy background.

Kamal et al. (2012) used the image-processing techniques for detection of weeds. In his approach, he used a set of 16, including eleven shapes and five texture-based, parameters coupled with predictive discriminating analysis for identification of weeds. In this approach, the geometrical features were indexed successfully to eliminate the effect of object orientation. This paper used linear discriminating analysis for classification of weeds which provides 69–80% of accuracy.

Yunseop Kim (year) proposed real-time in-field sensing and control of a site-specific precision linear move irrigation system. This includes design and instrumentation of devices using a wireless sensor network and software-based approach. This approach is for a specific area where six in-field sensors are deployed based on the soil property map in order to monitor the condition of field, and the sensed data are periodically sampled and transmitted to the base station. A program logic controller is used to electronically control the irrigation machine such that it updates the georeferenced location of sprinklers from a differential Global Positioning System (GPS) using WSN technology the information communication to the base station for further processing. Interfacing of the communication signal from the sensor network and irrigation controller to the base station is performed using low-cost bluetooth wireless radio communication. This paper proposes a software-based graphical user interface for providing real-time user friendly data of the field for proper monitoring on real-time basis and maintaining the field.

Phadikar (2012) focused on rice plants and proposed a software prototype for detection of diseases in rice plants based on images of infected rice plants. This technique uses a digital camera for capturing the images of infected rice plants which is then processed by means of image enhancement and image segmentation for detection of infected rice plants. This infected part of leaf is used for classification using a neural network.

### 11.3.2 Identifying the Deficiencies of Nutrition in Plants

Natural factors such as nutrients, water, environmental conditions, etc. are some of the important factors, which are responsible for quality of cultivated crops. Various image-processing techniques are used for finding the nutrients within plants, which can be used for taking future decisions for increasing the cultivation of crops.

Sunagar (2014) proposed software termed as "Nitrate app" which is used to find the amount of nitrate within maize leaves. It makes use of image processing which processes using software-based application. In this approach, the image of maize leaves is captured which is then pre-processed to remove the noise of the source image and then extract the color and texture characteristics of maize leaves. The color characteristics are extracted using RGB and HSV models. Thus, this approach makes a relationship between extracted features and nitrogen content in order to find the amount of nitrogen within maize leaves.

Ali (2012) developed an algorithm for determining the amount of the chlorophyll content within a plant. This value is non-linearly mapped with a normalized value of Green color (G), with respect to Red (R) and Blue (B) by making use of Logarithmic sigmoid transfer functions as given below.

$$CHOL = logsig\left[\frac{\left[G-\left(\frac{R}{3}\right)-\left(\frac{B}{3}\right)\right]}{255}\right]$$

where *CHOL* represents the chlorophyll estimation by Opt leaf, *G* represents green color, *R* represents red color, and *B* represents blue color.

Abrahão et al. (2013) developed an approach to determine the level of leaf nitrogen and chlorophyll using original, segmented, and reflectance images. This approach developed a classifier for determining the level of nitrogen and chlorophyll based on different combinations of spectral bands and vegetation indices. This approach makes use of remote sensing application which consists of a helium balloon and two small format digital cameras.

### 11.3.3 INSPECTION OF QUALITY OF FRUITS ALONG WITH THEIR SORTING AND GRADING

This approach is used for finding the quality of fruits of a tree in order to sort and grade them accordingly. Various authors have proposed different approaches in this regard some of which are discussed below.

Liming Xu (2010) used a K-mean clustering approach for grading strawberries into different categories. This grading was done based on the shape, size, and color of strawberries. They make use of devices consisting of a camera and a photo sensor with a small chip microcontroller. This device captures image which is converted to G-R to separate the background after threshold. Then it makes use of the R-G channel and segmentation in order to grade the shapes of strawberries as long-taper, taper, rotundity, and square. Thus, this approach is useful in finding contour which is used for finding the major axis of direction and horizontal lines with threshold for identifying size. Similarly, the strawberry color feature was extracted by the dominant color method on a* channel in La*b* color space. Thus, the proposed system was meant for multifeature gradation systems which provides 88.8% of success rate for color detection and 94% for overall grading.

Rocha et al. (2010) used an approach for classification of fruits and vegetables using feature and classifier using fusion. This approach collects the images as data from a supermarket over the period. It classifies the 8-bit color image on statistical, structural, and spectral basis. For describing the image, various techniques such as global color histogram, Unser's descriptors, color coherence vector, border/interior, appearance descriptor, and supervised learning are used. Background is subtracted using the K-mean approach. Various machine learning approaches are used such as support vector machine (SVM), linear discriminate analysis (LDA), classification trees, K-nearest neighbors (K-NN), and ensembles of trees and LDA and fusion for classification of images. For custom-tailored solutions, a multiclass classification approach is used for the problems which give better results. Thus, the proposed model was helpful in classifying the species of produce and variety.

Blasco (2009) used real-time-based inspection and sorting using morphological process-based image analysis. This approach captures the images in RGB format which are illuminated with a constant source. These images were segmented in background and objects of interest. The morphological process used in this approach is used for identifying the objects in complete and broken format. Then the analysis of image is performed using perimeter and area calculation. Thus once we obtained the contour, then the determination of size is performed using FFT which discriminates low and high frequency details. After this, the classification is performed using Standard Bayesian discriminate analysis. Sorting speed is limited using a mechanical system. Thus, this model provides a real-time classification with high accuracy.

## 11.3.4 ESTIMATION OF CROP AND LAND AND TRACKING OF OBJECT

Jiang (2014) introduced a particle filter which is used for a data assimilation strategy using the Crop Environment Resource Synthesis—Wheat model. This approach is used to improve the performance of crop models for regional crop yield estimates. Two experiments involving winter wheat yield estimations were conducted at a field plot and on a regional scale to test the feasibility of the PF-based data assimilation strategy and to analyze the effects of the PF parameters and spatiotemporal scales of assimilating observations on the performance of the crop model data assimilation. The significant improvements in the yield estimation suggest that PF-based crop model data assimilation is feasible. Winter wheat yields from the field plots were forecasted with a determination coefficient ( ) of 0.87, a root-mean-square error (RMSE) of 251 kg/ha, and a relative error (RE) of 2.95%. An acceptable yield at the county scale was estimated with a determination coefficient ($R^2$) of 0.998, a root-mean-square error (RMSE) of 9734 t, and a relative error (RE) of 4.29%.

Svotwa (2013) focused his research on tobacco crop in Zimbabwe. In his approach, the author uses a remote sensing approach for timely information on crop spectral characteristics which is used for estimation of yield of crop. Various satellite platforms have been used for identifying the land size of tobacco crop followed by spectral resolution for segregating the tobacco crop from the adjacent non-crop or crop vegetative area.

## 11.3.5 IDENTIFICATION OF DISEASES IN PLANTS

Diseases in plants is one of the major issues with the current world as the number and types of diseases in plants are increasing day by day, and identifying and classifying these diseases manually is a time-consuming and labor-intensive task with a high rate of error. Image processing has played a significant role in identifying and classifying the diseases in plants with different approaches. This section discusses the types of approaches used from traditional to recent years.

Tan et al. (2004) focused on diseases in soybean leaves by establishing a multilayer BP neural network model. This is done by finding and calculating the chromatic value of the leaves. Tian et al. (2007) in his research found the disease in grapes by extracting the color and texture characteristics of grape leaves. He uses a SVM recognition method which provides better results than the neural network. Similarly, Wang et al. (2014) focused his research to identify the lesion in cucumber by using a discriminant analysis method. He performed his research by extracting the features such as color, shape, and texture of lesions from the leaf of cucumber. Zhang et al. (2015) used the method of extraction of color, shape, and texture of lesions after lesion segmentation for identifying types of corn leaves, which can be categorized into five different types using the K nearest neighbor (KNN) classifier.

In a similar manner, the application of machine learning and artificial learning in agriculture is developed and proposed by Ron et al. (2017), who proposed a robotic spray which can detect targets of infected in the plants and automatically perform the spraying task in the field. In their study, they proved that the proposed method yields 30–35% better results in terms of losses in crops. David et al. (2017) developed a spraying pesticide which can automatically select the infected area and accordingly spray pesticide in the infected area. This approach consists of an auto-driving robot which detects plants in the area of crop and then injects to the selective area only. The authors used spectroscopy and image processing for detection of disease in the plants. Xie et al. (2018) used a multilevel and imaging technique for automatic classifiers of field crop pest. Sindhuja et al. (2010) developed a ground-based sensor system for monitoring of health and status of plants and diseases in the field crop. Li et al. (2019) used a convolutional neural network (CNN) of ZF (Zeiler and Fergus model) and a region proposal network with Non-Maximum Suppression for automatic localization and counting of agriculture crop pest. Yang et al. (2017) performed his research using deep convolutional neural networks for finding diseases in rice plants. His research focused on 10 common rice diseases and tested a dataset containing 500 natural images of diseased and healthy rice leaves and stem captured from rice field. Less than a 10-fold cross-validation strategy, the proposed CNN model proves an accuracy of 95.48%.

### 11.3.6 Precision Farming

Image processing with different tools and technologies can be used for precision farming. Precision farming is information and technology-based farming, where farm is managed by means of identifying, analyzing, and managing variable parameters within fields in order to provide optimization. This technology can be used to assist the farmers for a better decision-making process in order to yield maximum profitability. Thus, using this technology, farmers have pre-acquired knowledge of technology and their working. There can be various technology tools that can be used for precision farming such as information management, crop scouting, variable rate fertilizer application, remote sensing, yield monitoring and mapping, geographical information system (GIS), gird soil sampling, and GPS. The purpose of precision farming is to try and mechanize in agriculture in order to prevent the crop losses because of natural climatic uncertainty such as sudden climate change, pest, soil borne diseases, etc. Many research studies suggest different techniques for adoption of precision agriculture in order to increase the farming output for the farmer.

Baudoin et al. (2013) suggested that artificial methods such as growing plants like greenhouse, factory farm, etc. are one of the fundamental types of precision agriculture. Precision agriculture will enable growth of plants around the year by controlling and adjusting the surrounding environmental parameters such as humidity, $CO_2$ (carbon dioxide), temperature, light intensity, nutrient, air flow, etc. which are controlled artificially. Savvas and team present soilless plant cultivation as one of the most disruptive inventions ever presented in the field of artificial plant growing system. This technique provides artificial solid material or water nutrient solution as growing medium instead of soil.

### 11.3.7 Weed Detection

Spraying of chemical herbicide manually is wasting of herbicides as well as labor and also leads to environmental pollution as well as lower quality of food, which are some of the issues that make researchers find an alternative for the above-said problem. Thus, there is a need for accurate finding of weeds and precisely spraying of herbicides promoting agriculture sustainability.

There are many researchers who had contributed to weed detection who proposed many new approaches for the same. Li (2014) used ground imaging and spectrometer data for finding distinguishing features of field crop and then used combined multiple features for weed detection through the SVM algorithm. The proposed algorithm gives a high precision in finding the weed. Yang and Le (2014) used a BP neural network for detection of weeds. This research provides higher precision for the identification process. The precision of the identification is affected by the selection of training samples. Gebardth and Khbauch (2007) used a morphological method for obtaining leaf images and a segmentation process whereas using color and texture feature for identification of weeds. It was found that leaf identification provides 90% accuracy, but the proposed algorithm suffers with the problem of complex calculation and a slow rate of identification as well as poor real-time capability. Amruta (2016) detected and managed the weed using a five-texture-based approach. In their research, they adopted five features, namely, as energy, entropy, inertia, local homogeneity, and contrast for detection of crops. Morphological size-based features are used for detection of crop and weeds. Image segmentation with image processing is used for taking out cells from image, whereas the decision-making approach is used for determining the cells need to be sprayed. A Cartesian robot manipulator is used for locating the position of weeds by calculating the coordinates to selectively spray the herbicides. Batriz Nathlia et al. (2016) used computer vision for detection of unwanted weeds from one area of crop field with extra agriculture impact. The infected area is captured by means of image processing which is processed by means of a neural network to find the weeds from the infected area.

## 11.4 NEWER TECHNIQUES IN THE AGRICULTURE SUPPORT SYSTEM

There are some newer techniques and approaches that have been proposed by several researchers for efficient agriculture. These techniques can also be used and applied with image processing techniques proposed above for more fruitful results.

### 11.4.1 AEROPONIC SYSTEM

This is a soilless system where plants grow in air by means of assistance through the artificial support system. This is an air–water plant growing technique where roots of plants are hanged inside the growth chamber in complete darkness under controlled conditions. The upper portion of plants such as crown, leaves, fruits, etc. is extended outside the growth chamber. The entire plant is divided into two parts as roots and leaves by means of artificial support systems such as plastic, thermoform, etc. which provide the support and are used for dividing the plant into two halves.

In this approach, the plant root which is in free air is irrigated with small droplets of water nutrient at a regular time period through atomization nozzles with or without high air pressure. This is a better and advanced approach as it eliminates the need for large-scale land use and can be set up at any place without having to consider the external environmental factors and weather conditions. This approach also improves and promotes agroecosystem, health, and biodiversity. This approach also increases the cultivation yield and quality of plants and also provides an opportunity to increase the rural environment.

There are many research studies in this direction where research is conducted on roots of plants to make them responsive to drought, root microorganism, arbuscular mycorrhizal fungi production, legume-rhizobia interaction, effects of different oxygen concentrations on plant root development, etc.

## 11.4.2 ARTIFICIAL INTELLIGENCE IN AGRICULTURE

Many artificial techniques can be used with image processing to obtain better results in agriculture; but for research purposes, additional artificial intelligence techniques have been provided in this section for better understanding of its application in agriculture.

The word artificial intelligence was developed in 1956 as "the science and engineering of making intelligent machine" whose main purpose is the creation of intelligent techniques for finding an optimum solution to complex problems and to work, react, and respond like humans. In recent years, the use of artificial intelligence in agriculture is increasing in a tremendous manner which is used for increasing the efficiency of agriculture by various means like using robots and drones, crop health monitoring protocols, automated irrigation system, driverless tractors, etc. Popa (2011) in his research revealed that some of the developed applications for agriculture are expert systems and software is the planning process such as strategic or operational. Ali et al. (2016) in their research revealed about a humidity and temperature controller which can be used inside a greenhouse using a fuzzy logic concept. This study opens up the approach in this area and later on many researchers reveal the use of neural network, fuzzy logic controller, adaptive predictive control, PID, and non-linear adaptive PID control in the greenhouse. Zhu et al. (2010) proposed a remote wireless system for monitoring water quality online in an intensive aquaculture environment using an artificial neural network. The proposed system reveals a high precision result. Mahajan et al. (2015) proposed the use of computer vision application in agriculture which helps in reducing equipment costs, increased computational power, and increasing interest in non-destructive food assessment methods. Thus, the principle of artificial intelligence in agriculture is one where a machine can perceive its environment and, through a certain capacity of flexible rationality, can act to address a specified goal related to that environment.

## REFERENCES

Abrahão, S.A., Pinto, F.D.A.D.C., Queiroz, D.M.D., Santos, N.T., and Carneiro, J.E.D.S. (2013). Determination of nitrogen and chlorophyll levels in bean-plant leaves by using spectral vegetation bands and indices. *Revista Ciência Agronômica* 44(3), 464–473.
Agrawal, K.N., Singh, K., Bora, G.C., and Lin, D. (2012). Weed recognition using image-processing technique based on leaf parameters. *Journal of Agricultural Science and Technology. B* 2(8B), 899.

Ali, M.M., Al-Ani, A., Eamus, D., and Tan, D.K. (2012). A new image processing based technique to determine chlorophyll in plants. *American-Eurasian Journal of Agricultural and Environmental Sciences* 12(10), 1323–1328.

Ali, R.B., Aridhi, E., Abbes, M., and Mami, A. (2016, March). Fuzzy logic controller of temperature and humidity inside an agricultural greenhouse. In *2016 7th International Renewable Energy Congress (IREC)*, pp. 1–6. IEEE.

Aware, A.A. and Joshi, K. (2016). Crop and weed detection based on texture and size features and automatic spraying of herbicides. *Int J Adv Res Comput Sci Softw Eng.* 6(1).

Baudoin, W., Nono-Womdim, R., Lutaladio, N., Hodder, A., Castilla, N., Leonardi, C., ... Duffy, R. (2013). Good agricultural practices for greenhouse vegetable crops: Principles for Mediterranean climate areas. *FAO plant production and protection paper (FAO)*.

Berenstein, R. and Edan, Y. (2017). Human-robot collaborative site-specific sprayer. *Journal of Field Robotics* 34(8), 1519–1530.

Blasco, J., Aleixos, N., Cubero, S., Gómez-Sanchís, J., and Moltó, E. (2009). Automatic sorting of satsuma (*Citrus unshiu*) segments using computer vision and morphological features. *Computers and Electronics in Agriculture* 66(1), 1–8.

Chaudhary, P., Chaudhari, A.K., Cheeran, A.N., and Godara, S. (2012). Color transform based approach for disease spot detection on plant leaf. *International Journal of Computer Science and Telecommunications* 3(6), 65–70.

Feng, T. and Xiaodan, M. (2009). The method of recognition of damage by disease and insect based on laminae. *Journal of Agricultural Mechanization Research* 6, 441–443.

Gebhardt, S. and Kühbauch, W. (2007). A new algorithm for automatic Rumex obtusifolius detection in digital images using colour and texture features and the influence of image resolution. *Precision Agriculture* 8(1–2), 1–13.

Jiang, Z., Chen, Z., Chen, J., Liu, J., Ren, J., Li, Z., ... Li, H. (2014). Application of crop model data assimilation with a particle filter for estimating regional winter wheat yields. *IEEE Journal of Selected Topics in Applied Earth Observations and Remote Sensing* 7(11), 4422–4431.

Kim, Y., Evans, R.G., and Iversen, W.M. (2008). Remote sensing and control of an irrigation system using a distributed wireless sensor network. *IEEE Transactions on Instrumentation and Measurement* 57(7), 1379–1387.

Li, W., Chen, P., Wang, B., and Xie, C. (2019). Automatic localization and count of agricultural crop pests based on an improved deep learning pipeline. *Scientific Reports* 9(1), 1–11.

Liming, X. and Yanchao, Z. (2010). Automated strawberry grading system based on image processing. *Computers and Electronics in Agriculture* 71, S32–S39.

Lu, Y., Yi, S., Zeng, N., Liu, Y., and Zhang, Y. (2017). Identification of rice diseases using deep convolutional neural networks. *Neurocomputing* 267, 378–384.

Mahajan, S., Das, A., and Sardana, H.K. (2015). Image acquisition techniques for assessment of legume quality. *Trends in Food Science & Technology* 42(2), 116–133.

Panqueba, B.N.S. and Medina, C.A.C. A computer vision application to detect unwanted weed in early stage crops.

Phadikar, S. and Sil, J. (2008, December). Rice disease identification using pattern recognition techniques. In *2008 11th International Conference on Computer and Information Technology*, pp. 420–423. IEEE.

Popa, C. (2011). Adoption of artificial intelligence in agriculture. *Bulletin of University of Agricultural Sciences and Veterinary Medicine Cluj-Napoca. Agriculture* 68(1).

Reiser, D., Martín-López, J.M., Memic, E., Vázquez-Arellano, M., Brandner, S., and Griepentrog, H.W. (2017). 3D imaging with a sonar sensor and an automated 3-axes frame for selective spraying in controlled conditions. *Journal of Imaging* 3(1), 9.

Rocha, A., Hauagge, D.C., Wainer, J., and Goldenstein, S. (2010). Automatic fruit and vegetable classification from images. *Computers and Electronics in Agriculture* 70(1), 96–104.

Sankaran, S., Mishra, A., Ehsani, R., and Davis, C. (2010). A review of advanced techniques for detecting plant diseases. *Computers and Electronics in Agriculture* 72(1), 1–13.

Sunagar, V.B., Kattimani, P.A., Padasali, V.A., and Hiremath, N.V. (2014). Estimation of nitrogen content in leaves using image processing. In *Proceedings of International Conference on Advances in Engineering & Technology.*

Svotwa, E., Masuka, A.J., Maasdorp, B., Murwira, A., and Shamudzarira, M. (2013). Remote sensing applications in tobacco yield estimation and the recommended research in Zimbabwe. *ISRN Agronomy, 2013.*

Tang, J.L., Chen, X.Q., Miao, R.H., and Wang, D. (2016). Weed detection using image processing under different illumination for site-specific areas spraying. *Computers and Electronics in Agriculture* 122, 103–111.

Wang, X., Zhang, S., Wang, Z., and Zhang, Q. (2014). Recognition of cucumber diseases based on leaf image and environmental information. *Transactions of the Chinese Society of Agricultural Engineering* 30(14), 148–153.

Xie, C., Wang, R., Zhang, J., Chen, P., Dong, W., Li, R., … Chen, H. (2018). Multi-level learning features for automatic classification of field crop pests. *Computers and Electronics in Agriculture* 152, 233–241.

Youwen, T., Tianlai, L., Chenghua, L., Zailin, P., Guokai, S., and Bin, W. (2007). Method for recognition of grape disease based on support vector machine. *Transactions of the Chinese Society of Agricultural Engineering* 2007(6).

Zhang, S.W., Shang, Y.J., and Wang, L. (2015). Plant disease recognition based on plant leaf image. *Journal of Animal and Plant Sciences* 25(3), 42–45.

Zhu, X., Li, D., He, D., Wang, J., Ma, D., and Li, F. (2010). A remote wireless system for water quality online monitoring in intensive fish culture. *Computers and Electronics in Agriculture* 71, S3–S9.

# Index

Printed in the United States
By Bookmasters